Thirty-Three & Single

My young adult heart in search of
love, captured instead by His
Unfailing Love, Jesus, who was
Thirty-Three & Single!

TINA M. BROWN

WESTBOW
PRESS®
A DIVISION OF THOMAS NELSON
& ZONDERVAN

WestBow Press books may be ordered through booksellers or by contacting:

WestBow Press
A Division of Thomas Nelson & Zondervan
1663 Liberty Drive
Bloomington, IN 47403
www.westbowpress.com
844-714-3454

ISBN: 979-8-3850-1661-7 (sc)
ISBN: 979-8-3850-1662-4 (e)

Library of Congress Control Number: 2024900728

Print information available on the last page.

WestBow Press rev. date: 08/23/2024

But those who hope in the LORD will renew their strength. They will soar on wings like eagles; they will run and not grow weary, they will walk and not be faint.

—Isaiah 40:31 (NIV)

It's not our goal to be more amazing for Jesus. It's our goal to be more amazed *by* Jesus.

—Ray Ortlund Jr.

I want to dedicate this book with love,
gratitude, and appreciation to

My precious Lord and Savior, Jesus Christ, who loved me, pursued me, and called me His own. He saved me and made me new. His infinite love, through His sovereignty and grace, overwhelms me every day. I am forever grateful!

All the amazing young adults who have allowed me to walk with them in their faith journeys, even when things were hard. They entrusted me with their stories and allowed me into the private spaces of their hearts. To know them, do life with them, and watch them reach their life's pursuits, to know and trust Jesus more, has been one of the most precious blessings ever. *Thank you, Lord, for these beautiful lives and all the other young adults out there who are in pursuit of walking with You. Guide them in Your truth all the days of their lives. Amen.*

Keli Rutledge and Justin Linkletter, two young adults in our ministry whose lives were taken too soon from car accidents, two years apart. Keli was eighteen, and Justin was twenty. They were incredible young adults, on fire for Jesus in refreshing and relentless ways, showcasing Christ in all they did. They inspired me to live boldly. They are missed deeply and thought of continuously by all who knew them. Their legacy of faith lives on. Without a shadow of a doubt, we will see them again because of Jesus' resurrected life. Because He died and rose again, they live!

Special Thanks

To my family, who always believed in my passion to serve young adults. Their help behind the scenes on countless occasions to run a young-adult ministry was priceless. I couldn't have done it without them. *Thank you, Rob, Libby, Tatum, and Dylan. I love you so much.*

To my mom, who inspires me to love others well and chase after my dreams. She is an awesome prayer warrior to everyone in her life. She's been a solid rock of faith to all who know her. I'm honored to call her Mom. *Thank you, Mom, for your godly influence in my life. I am eternally grateful.*

To my niece Sarah—producer, actor, and creator of Havoc Girls (a program that invests in teenage girls through the arts, helping them navigate through difficult situations). She has always encouraged me to love young adults in this life stage. *Thanks, Sarah.* She and her husband, Malcom, reside in London. Their marriage and faith are resilient, as even a pandemic and global lockdown didn't deter them from getting married over Zoom.

To my friend Ellen Marrs, who came to speak to our young-adult group with her book, *Lessons from the Finish Line.* She challenged our group to tell their stories. "God has given each of you a story. Share it! You never know who might need your story, so don't keep it to yourself." *Thank you, Ellen.* Ellen's words that day and a promise I made to the Lord, decades ago, is why I wrote my story.

To Lead Pastor Josh Watt from Redemption North Mountain. He helped me recognize God's purpose in all that I was doing with young adults and believed in me sharing my story. He said, "Sometimes God puts someone or something in our paths to slow down the 'life train' so we can get off and take up another path." *Thanks, Josh, for all your encouragement and for writing the foreword to this book.*

To others who contributed to the ministry and encouraged me to write, their names and influence in my life are mentioned at the end. Their help and encouragement have been priceless.

Contents

Foreword

I have spent my whole life working with the next generation—teens up through the young-adult years. There are so many milestones, so many changes, so many learning opportunities, and so many chances to see God work through it all. If I could sum it all up, here is the one question I think this stage of life boils down to: "What voices will I let influence me?"

As kids, you are forced to listen to your parents and other adults in your lives. As you move into the teen years, however, especially into college and beyond, you get to choose who will influence you. You now get to make your own decisions and, more importantly, you get to pick the people who you will listen to, to make those decisions.

In your current stage of life, what voices will you allow to be the loudest in your life?

Tina Brown is a voice that needs to be heard. She is an authentic voice in a world filled with fabricated social media personas. Tina has walked the same road with struggles we all face in those formative years. She has been broken in getting to the top of what she thought would bring her life joy, only to see it all crumble around her.

Tina, however, doesn't just walk us through the pain; she shows us hope. She points us to answers, and most importantly, she points us to *the* answer. She shows us that Jesus is always working. Whether you are thirty-three and single and hating it, or your life is just not what you hoped it would be, Jesus is there. Jesus is in it with you. And Jesus is taking you somewhere. You are not alone on this journey. You are loved. And you have a God who wants to walk with you whether you are thirteen, thirty-three, or ninety-three. He wants to walk through life with you.

This book will help you see that God is with you in the details. My prayer is that Tina's story will encourage us all that God is writing a magnificent story in all our lives. His story might not match up completely with how we would have written it, but if we will trust Him and listen to the right voices, we can enjoy the story He is writing for us in this very moment.

—Joshua Watt
Lead Pastor, Redemption North Mountain, Phoenix, Arizona

Introduction

For starters, a disclaimer. This is *not* a book telling you to stay single *or* to get married. Instead, it is the story of how God taught me to trust Him with matters of the heart. Through personal defeat and heartache, God got my attention in a most peculiar way—a way only He could've orchestrated—to tell me of His love story of being thirty-three and single. This is His story lived out in my life. Where is God in the middle of your dreams and life goals? Where is He in your relationship status, single or not? Too often, God is set aside in our life's pursuits, but then we wonder where He is when something goes wrong or when things don't go our way—like when a relationship we thought was meant to be doesn't pan out.

That's where I was, and this is my story.

You might be asking, "How does a Gen X-er, born in '65, have anything of value to say to me? How could she even begin to understand anything I am going through in my personal life or comprehend the pressures of my generation consumed with social media, let alone with all the pain in our world, wars breaking out, even most recently in the Middle East of biblical proportions, with hatred spewing at every turn? How could she get any of what I'm feeling?" Good questions. It is true. Times are different and darker than ever before, but God wants you to know He is the same today as He was yesterday and will be tomorrow. What happened then happens now. We may live in different times, but hurt, fear, confusion, fitting in or being and/or feeling purposeful, especially in unpredicted chaos and unprecedented times, can be hard to handle no matter your age.

God brings clarity to life by mending our brokenness, comforting our loneliness, and giving us hope in place of fear as we look to the future. "I have told you these things, so that in Me you may have peace. In this world you will have trouble. But take heart! I have overcome the world" (John 16:33 NIV). When we start to grasp God's bigger picture for our lives, His love story shines through us and is as relevant today as was the day it was written.

> The word of God ... is at work in you who believe.
> (1 Thessalonians 2:13b ISV)

Throughout my story, you'll find teaching points from sermon notes, podcasts, book references, poems, and lyrics to songs that all point to God's love through His Word. The beauty of the Bible is that it is not out of touch, nor is it irrelevant or dated.

> For the word of God is alive and active. Sharper than any double-edged sword, it penetrates even to dividing soul and spirit, joints and marrow; it judges the thoughts and attitudes of the heart.
> (Hebrews 4:12 NIV)

A quote below from an excellent book by Paul Miller called *Love Walked among Us: Learning to Love like Jesus* takes the reader into the years of Christ's ministry, where He serves others selflessly and with great purpose and passion, even unto death.

> Most of us have lacked good models for love. We don't even know what's normal anymore. Let me suggest this: The person of Jesus is a plumb line to which we may align our lives. He satisfies our hunger for a hero—someone who is both good and strong—to change the world.[1]

In one of his other books, *J Curve: Dying and Rising with Jesus in Everyday Life*, he uses the letter J to represent Jesus' name. The downward motion of the curve illustrates dying to self and being buried, and the vertical line of the J represents Christ rising up into new life. To this point, an excerpt from his book says this:

> Life's inconveniences, disappointments, and trials can leave us confused, cynical, and eventually bitter. But the J-Curve plots the ups and downs of our lives onto the story of Jesus. It grounds our journeys not in some abstract idea but in union with Christ and his work of love. Understanding our life in light of the J-curve roots our hope, centers our love, and tethers our faith to Christ.[2]

We're invited to step into new life with Christ! How amazing is that? Not only do we rejoice in what God has done for us through Jesus, but we delight in what's ahead by serving as Christ served, loving as Christ loved, and joining Him where He is at work. Like Jesus, we can live, love, and serve others with passion.

The remarkable trait about Jesus is that everything about Him is unequivocally *passion-filled*. Everything! He desires us to be passion-filled as well, first and foremost for the things that matter most to Him.

It never dawned on me until I started putting my thoughts together for this book that God had been weaving a tapestry of my life that spanned over forty years. (Ironically, the time frame of forty years appears in the Bible on several occasions, such as when Moses was wandering in the wilderness with the Israelites in pursuit of the promised land for forty years. Exodus 15–40 tells this story.) I indeed have lived in the desert, literally as a native Arizonan and figuratively, at times, wandering, lost, confused, and alone in a vast and weary land. God created His story in me. He's weaving your story into a beautiful tapestry as well, all for His good and glorious plan. We may never know what God is up to, but we can always, without a shadow of a doubt, trust Him! His ways and plans are perfect and far better than any plans of our own.

In moments like these, God impresses upon us to pause and take account of all He has done. He shapes and molds us to show us His blessings in our lives. It is only then that we begin to appreciate His pursuing love for us so intently. It's only when we recognize He chose His life's ministry as a single man to serve perfectly and love completely—even unto death, giving His own life on a cruel cross at age thirty-three—that we even begin to grasp the vastness of it all. Jesus is the lover of our souls, the only one to satisfy our deepest longings, to walk through our darkest valleys, and to fulfill our every need. His love is *so* amazing!

Thank you in advance for reading my story and the ABC verses with reflection questions at the end. It is my prayer that something in my life's journey will resonate with you. Even when life gets raw and messy, His steadfast love, faithfulness, kindness, and forgiveness are always constant. God's goodness never leaves us. He was always there for me and is there for you too. If your pursuit in life is to love and to be loved, great news—it's right in front of you. His name is Jesus! He's been there all along. Run to Him. His loving arms are open wide.

I'd love to hear from you if something encourages you from my story and add your story to those yet untold of His amazing grace. Or if I can pray for you, please don't hesitate to reach out.

tinabrown.az33@gmail.com, or
Instagram messaging @tinabrown_az

Bible References

All Bible translations used throughout these pages are noted at the back of the book in alphabetical order, by abbreviation first and then by the full name of the translation. To find the full context of a verse or passage, go to sites such as BibleGateway.com or Bible.com[1], which also provide helpful commentary.

Be sure to read chapter 10's sections, "Why Is the Bible So Important?" and "Why So Many Translations?" I chose to use different translations throughout my story to best fit my point and make it easier to understand. My hope is that people from all walks of life who read my story will see that at its core is God's love, which is refreshing to any soul.

I'd encourage you to pull up the Bible app[2] on your phone or grab a Bible to read through the entire passage as you find verses throughout this book. See how the verse is used in the context of the passage to get a full picture of the historical account. The Bible is God's love story to us. No matter its translation, the meaning remains the same.

CHAPTER 1

Time to Start Writing

t had come time for me to sit down and write what the Lord had given me, decades earlier, to share.

God prompted my heart one night, a night etched in my mind forever, to commit to telling people what He had shared with me by writing my story in a book. He also impressed upon me that the title would be *Thirty-Three and Single*. Decades passed, and though I had thought about writing time and again over the years, it never felt like the right time.

For months leading up to what would be my last lunch event with our young-adult group, I had been meeting with our NextGen pastor to brainstorm and establish the next steps for our young-adult ministry, with all the growth coming to our community. Our original church plant of fifty, which we'd been with since its inception, had now grown into a megachurch within a decade, permanently rooting us in the community in our new church home and campus. With change came a fresh new vision for our young-adult ministry.

Pastor Josh was hopeful I'd take a well-deserved break when all was said and done to refresh and reset after running our church's young-adult ministry as a volunteer for years. I remember telling him in our last meeting that I didn't want my involvement to end. I also knew, though, that this was a moment when God was calling me to lean into a life principle that He had taught me a very long time ago: "Hold anything that is precious and that matters to you [in this case, this young-adult ministry] very loosely with open hands because you never know when that special something or someone may be gone, or circumstances are such that what was once yours no longer is." God was once again calling me to follow His lead, even though every ounce of me wanted to resist. At that moment, an old hymn filled my heart:

> You are the potter, I am the clay,
> Mold me and make me,
> This, Lord, I pray.

> Like clay in the hand of the potter, so are you in
> my hand (Jeremiah 18:6b NIV).

The lesson for my heart rang clear. One day, I may be shaped like a pot to pour out that which is in me; another day, a cup to hold within me that which fills me. Or maybe I'll be a plate to put on display all He has done for me. The point is to learn to be flexible in whatever season the Lord chooses to have you in. No matter the season ahead, though all may be hard and difficult to understand, God is in control!

I knew in my heart of hearts this young-adult ministry was His, had always been His, and would always be His, so to claim it as my own would be my agenda over God's. "Not my will, Lord, but Your will be done" was on repeat in my heart. Pastor Josh encouraged me in our final meeting, which gave me the right mindset to let go. "There will always be needs," he said. "Even Jesus walked away and rested."

I hated to hear those words, but I knew they were true, and

I needed to trust God in that moment. My mothering heart was being challenged for sure.

Additionally, my own mother's words were encouraging to me when she learned of our last event approaching. She said, "You always know God is up to something when He chooses to set us aside, even though we may not understand. In those moments, He allows others to step in and carry the load to be a blessing." Her words were spot on and were so very, very true! God was setting me aside so others could step in and be a blessing to this ministry. When situations happen in life, He allows us to see His glory, drawing us ever so closely to Him in these moments that can sometimes be really hard. God is in all the details of our lives. Amen.

Even when it was hard for me to let go of something I loved so deeply, I had to trust God's plan over my own. He gives hope to the new chapters in life that will surely come in due time. In this case, God allowed me to see all He had done and would continue to do. What a joy it was to walk and do life with so many amazing young adults during this season of ministry. He continues to do a good work in and through their lives as they now make their impact on the next generation.

I was ready to support whatever decision would be made, knowing the ministry would carry on in the loving care of everyone who believed in its mission. And so it was; His plans unfurled.

Last Young-Adult Lunch

I was told by our incoming young-adult leaders that the last lunch would be an opportunity for them to share their vision of the new and upcoming young-adult ministry. Unbeknownst to me, it was quite the contrary. As I stood near the kitchen door, busily preparing a salad and sides to go with the pizzas that were just delivered, a stream of faces from over the years continued walking through the doors of our room where we met on campus. My thought at that moment was how neat it was for them to come and hear about the upcoming ministry opportunities to get involved in. I was so excited for our new leaders to share! *How wonderful of these friends to attend, showing their support,* I thought.

But instead, they were there for *me*. What?

I wasn't expecting any of what was coming. They shared how God had used this ministry to bring them friendships and how they had been encouraged by me and others who had loved them in this life stage.

It was completely beautiful and a tearful time to rejoice in all God had done. I remember saying at one point, "All my favorite people on planet earth are all in the same room together, truly a slice of heaven before me!" I was completely overwhelmed with their love toward me and the ministry it had become. My heart was full and humbled, knowing they were blessed by this ministry that existed for them in their life stage to challenge them, walk with them, and point them to Jesus.

And though it is true that God gives and God takes away, He never leaves us without recounting the beautiful season it was and how much richer our lives are because of the opportunities He gives us in this journey called life. He was in it all along, and I'm so thankful to have been a part of it.

Later that evening, while processing through all that had happened that day and reading through cards that had been given to me, a common theme rang through their sentiments, which affirmed to me that no matter the generation, each person, when they're *single* and feeling alone, processes similar emotions. I remember such emotions with questions stirring in me when I was single.

"Does God really care about me in my loneliness?"
"Does He care enough to bring someone into my life?"
"Doesn't He want me to be happy?"
"Why won't He give me someone to love who will love me back?"
"Does He really have a plan for me?"
"What is His purpose for my life?"
"Where are You, God?"

Questions of this nature don't necessarily represent all singles, but in my experience, working with singles in a variety of seasons, more people have these thoughts than one would think. When one has a longing heart with questions such as these, it gives space for people to walk alongside them to help them work through these difficult life questions, care for them, love them, and point them to the truth. Oftentimes, their hearts are tender, which allows Christ to step in to give hope and provide direction and purpose. It's a beautiful thing to watch a heart blossom and grow deeper in love with Jesus! Where fear and doubt once existed, now hope and joy reside instead.

Young Adult Ministry Is Like Family

When I was a young adult, the ministry I was a part of was like family. I desired to start something similar, to pour into young adults' hearts and assure them that God cares deeply for them, loves them, and is there for them. I wanted them to know His acceptance far outweighs the pressures for approval in this life stage. Jesus' unconditional love is better than anything this world has to offer. His approval affirms us and frees us from the pressures and expectations this world will put on us to fit in, to be noticed, to be accepted, to be loved. Instead, we can be strong and courageous, even when it's tough. The best news to share with anybody, young or old alike, is that God has a purpose and a plan for their lives. It's the good news of this book; it's the good news of Jesus! He loves you *so* much.

As I said my final goodbyes to shepherding this group, I knew God was giving me time to write my story. In it, there is authentic pain from deep loss in my young-adult years. Sometimes we create our own pain—those times we invite unwelcomed drama into our lives by doing things our own way. I know I did. In doing so, we ultimately cause great conflict in our own lives and relationships with others.

As for the layout of my story, God gave me two significant wake-up calls. The first wake-up call mentioned was when I turned thirty, and the second time mentioned happened earlier back in my twenties. I tell it in this order because this is how the story starts—where God meets me in a particular moment in time, backtracking as He walks with me through everything He was showing me since childhood, significantly in my twenties. He brought me to a place of hearing Him through the storms of life—a literal storm in this case. This is my entire life story with lots of teaching points along the way as topics are covered. I share what God has taught me and shown me over the decades throughout my life's journey.

During the seasons and rhythms of life, God reminds us at every turn of His unfailing grace and affirms His loving presence amid each episode in our lives as they unfold. He loves and treasures the young-adult heart more than anyone can ever imagine. I know so because He did so for me. And so it is, God whispered, it is time to write your story.

May something shared within these pages encourage you in your faith walk as you carry on in His good and loving care.

CHAPTER 2

Looking Back at the Word Single

The young-adult group I was a part of decades ago was called Single Vision. (Surely not a name you'd call a young-adult group today, or so my then-twenty-two-year-old niece, Sarah, told me.) When telling her about a group I started called Redemption Single Life (RSL), she told me the group could *not* have the word *single* in it at all!

"The word *single*," she continued, "is *so* dated, so '80s, and labels a person so quickly in a bad way."

To her point, she spoke truth for this generation, so I greatly appreciated her input on the matter. From it, the name changed to Redemption Life (RL) but later became Redemption Young Adults (RYA), representing our church's name, Redemption, and speaking to who the group was—young adults.

As for the name Single Vision back in the day, I was a part of a brainstorming team with other young adults to come up with a new name for our ministry. Our current ministry was called College and Career, which explained exactly who we were and what we were—many were in college, especially since we were close to a major university, and many more were now in their careers, like me. So, it suited us. But we desired something that would be more marketable for our church to promote. We landed on Single Vision, with a logo and all, that had double meaning, capturing the essence of who and what we were—a singles ministry in the same age and stage of life. Our ministry "vision" was to be focused on Jesus and Him alone, so we landed on Single Vision. Thinking back, I thought it was very cool. No? To Sarah's point, wrong in every way. She also pointed out that the word single carried a lot of negative connotations.

"No one wants to admit they're single," said my then–high school daughter, while visiting with her on the topic of Valentine's Day. She explained to me when someone doesn't have a significant other, the holiday is referred to as "Single Awareness Day" or SAD. (The mindset of feeling sad, if single.) For that reason alone, I wanted our young-adult ministry to emphasize God's love for singles because those feelings of singleness, especially on days like Valentine's Day, are real and legitimate.

Thinking back, I didn't like Valentine's Day very much either. I experienced all those same emotions. They were emotions that were hard to wrestle with and difficult to manage at times, especially with a big milestone birthday lurking in my midst. I was going to be turning thirty years old, and I was *still* single. Everything shouted at me in my head, *"You're thirty and single. What a loser you are!"* I was close to wanting to crawl in a hole. There, I would be safe from judgment from others and myself!

CHAPTER 3

My Thirtieth Birthday

t was the evening of my thirtieth birthday. I was going to meet up with a few friends at the Spaghetti Company. Little did I know there was a surprise party with more friends waiting for me at the restaurant. I was completely surprised and overwhelmed by their kindness. (When our young-adult group, mentioned in chapter 1, planned that unexpected going-away party for me, memories flooded back to this evening, a night that changed everything.)

The evening ensued with these loving friends showering me with birthday wishes and gifts for my big 3–0. As much as I appreciated everything they had done for me, in the quietness of my longing heart, I found myself asking, "How is it I'm turning thirty years old, and I am still single?" I was physically present at this party, but my mind was elsewhere, as my thoughts drifted to plans I had later that evening to see an exclusive friend, a guy I was getting to know in our group, who I had a big crush on. Maybe this night all those doubts would change, and my future would start to make sense.

Here I was with these amazing friends, most of whom were younger than me by a few years. Nevertheless, we were a family going through the same life stages together. Why would my mind drift off to anything beyond this special moment? God was so good to me through these friends' thoughtfulness. Why would I long for more? I figured God wouldn't bring me to my thirtieth birthday without opening a door to my future. I knew there must be more in store; maybe tonight that door would open a crack. No one knew exactly how I felt about this guy, as I kept everything very low-key. Only God knew how I really felt, and my journal where I poured out everything—the good and the bad. This evening would no doubt be a wonderful journal entry.

Our church was near a major university, making our ministry one of the largest in the area. Some Sundays, our ministry had up to three hundred attending. Outside of having a full-time career, our young-adult ministry was my life. The ages spanned from early to late twenties to a few here and there who were thirty or early thirties. My joining those ranks was an unwelcome feeling for me, but it was what it was. Now, as an older single in the group, I had taken on a very active role on the leadership team. I was leading the worship team and was a discipleship leader to younger gals in our group. If I wasn't at work, I was active with ministry with all the different things we always had going on.

We were a busy ministry with volleyball nights, Saturday worship practices for Sunday gatherings with worship sets, Sunday lunch outings, midweek Bible studies, preparing meals and providing worship music at homeless shelters once a month, and on and on. My life was filled with full-time ministry coupled with a full-time job. I had lots of plates spinning. I remember telling a friend once, "I love ministry so much, I wish I could make it my profession so I could devote more time and energy to it than I already am." But the bills had to be paid, so I juggled both. In that incredibly busy season of life, I was truly thankful for the family of friends the Lord had blessed me with to take away the pangs of being single. Maybe all of that would change this evening, and God would surprise me with a special someone.

My pastor told me once that I made guys feel intimidated. That felt odd to hear, but was it true? Was it because I was seen as a leader in our group? Or was the title on my business card my identity, and they didn't know who the real me was? I learned a great life lesson in that comment. It's an incredible blessing to have a career, but if it becomes what defines you, try asking yourself, as my pastor asked me, "Who is your identity in? Is it in what you do or in who you serve? Titles, or what you do, shouldn't define you. Don't let those things become your idol. If you find yourself talking more about what you do over the passion you have, let it be a self-check." It was a great piece of advice, one I learned was oh so true. Jobs and titles will come and go, but my identity in Christ—that lasts forever, a lifetime and beyond.

As for this guy, though he was five years younger than I was, he didn't seem to shy away from me. He was well-respected in our group, with high hopes of being a pastor someday—he had great charisma. I just knew the Lord had great things in store for him. He was mature in his faith, carried himself well, had set goals for himself, and had admiral qualities that were attractive in his leadership abilities in our group. Plus, he was super cute. Our age difference was a nonissue for me. I was getting to an age where I knew I needed to consider all the options out there, so if I found someone younger than me, I was OK with that. Plus, in my mind, we were a perfect fit. He wanted to be a pastor someday, and I wanted to be a worship leader. We would make a great team together. I completely saw where the Lord was going with this.

Leading up to that evening, he told me he wanted to give me a birthday present and asked if I could come over. I was over-the-moon excited, knowing I had something even more wonderful to look forward to—a special evening awaited me. Now, I just needed to politely excuse myself from this most unexpected evening of kindness shown to me. God certainly had more in store for me on this milestone thirtieth birthday year; I could feel it in my bones. Good things were surely coming my way.

The plan was to meet at his house, where he lived with a few of the guys from our group. We had been hanging out in our group, and I sensed there was a connection between us. Whenever there was a group outing, I always had butterflies in my stomach if he showed up. To say I was smitten was an understatement; I was crazy about him. And to think he wanted to give me a gift that night—I was absolutely elated. Since we were established as good friends, I figured he'd ask me if I'd like to date him, making us an official couple in our group. I just knew this was where things were headed. I couldn't contain my excitement!

When I arrived at his house, he met me at his front door. He heard about the surprise party thrown for me (to which I found odd he wasn't there, but didn't think anything more about it), and then, very matter-of-factly, he gave me his unwrapped gift—a sleeping bag from REI. I felt so excited! REI was the trendsetting store for all things outdoorsy; it was located near the university campus, where all the super-cool young adults hung out and shopped. It affirmed to me that he was including me in his world with a thoughtful gift that meant a lot to him. It certainly was expensive, as he pointed out that it was the top of the line in sleeping bags. He was an outdoorsy kind of guy, into hiking and camping, so this all made sense. I had gone on a few hiking trips with the group in the past before he was around, but now that he was leading the trips, maybe he was going to invite me to go on the next camping trip he was planning. And how wonderful—I could bring my new sleeping bag. I remembered he'd asked me if I had one, which I did not, so this was a perfect gift. I could see where this was going.

I never expected what I'd hear next. He proceeded to tell me that as great of a gal as I was, he didn't have mutual feelings toward me that he sensed I had for him. He was sorry it couldn't go any further and that I needed to move on.

What was I hearing? How could this be? I was completely crushed but couldn't show it. I didn't know what to say. It was an awkward goodbye, with his final words being, "See you around at group."

I sheepishly got in my car with my new sleeping bag, wondering if I should keep it or give it back. I kept it but always hated it at the same time.

In those moments, it's difficult to see beyond the disappointment, the hurt, and the confusion. But in hindsight, he was a complete gentleman toward me always, and I clearly misread him. It was evident I had some major, deep soul-searching to do.

(As for that guy, he went on to marry a wonderful gal from our group who was a perfect match for him. God was indeed in their story; He just needed me to get out of the way. Guess a good, loving shove from the good Lord above worked. God knows what it takes to get a hold of our stubborn hearts—or is that just me? Wink, wink!)

CHAPTER 4

The Night That Changed Everything

That weekend, I was housesitting at my uncle Dave, aunt Michelle, and cousins Monica and Mark's house. They were a second family to me, as I'd lived with them when I was student teaching. I was so thankful to have their home to go to instead of my lonely apartment to think through all that had happened that night. Their sweet dog, Shatzie, would certainly distract me with all her tail wags and puppy kisses.

I felt numb as I drove to their house after that harsh (or so it felt), unexpected ending. I had been in this place before. I knew it so well, and I hated it. I didn't want to be in this pain again. This was turning out to be the worst birthday ever. I couldn't even recollect the goodness God had shown me earlier in the evening from the sweet friends He had blessed me with. How selfish of me! All I could see in front of me was my brokenness. I was in a pit of despair.

I was sleeping in my cousin Monica's room, surrounded by her stuffed animals and dolls. I was sobbing so deeply that the pillowcase was flooded with my tears. I was screaming out to God,

"Why, Lord, why? Why is it that when I meet someone fantastic, it just never works out?" The flood of emotions overwhelmed me, taking me back to my first love that also ended in a major heartbreak. Not only did I give my whole heart away, but I gave my entire self away. It had taken everything in me to regain trust again. My pain was so deep that I hurt and cried inconsolably. Nothing had changed; it was all the same. *God, You must not care about me*, were my thoughts. I concluded there must not be anyone out there who would ever love me. I cried out to God, "What is wrong with me?"

All the memories from my past came flooding back. I was so exhausted from it all that I eventually cried myself to sleep well after midnight. God would choose to answer my longing heart by reaching deep into my aching soul. For now, sleep was my only refuge.

When the Clock Read 3:33 a.m.

I woke up from a deep sleep, as if something had nudged me. I thought it was Shatzie, but she was fast asleep on the carpeted floor next to the bed. Shining bright were the red numbers on the digital clock in my cousin's room. The time glaring at me was 3:33 a.m. In that moment, God appeared so loudly in my heart, it was as if He was standing right there in the room, as now the room didn't appear so dark. Was I dreaming? I very matter-of-factly asked out loud, "Lord, are You here?" I was scared. "Please calm my anxious heart!"

My stirring woke Shatzie. She jumped up on the bed and licked me with kisses. A calmness came over me. God had my attention. I was awake. My beating heart gradually slowed down. I resumed my breathing, only now a bit frightened. As I gathered myself, I sat up in bed, hugging Shatzie, and prayed, asking God,

"What is happening?" I was shocked at what God was impressing upon me. My heart heard,

*"Child, lift up your weary head. I am here! I have always been here. I want you to stop trying to figure things out. I've got this relationship thing all taken care of. You just need to stop worrying about things and trust Me. My Son was thirty years old when His ministry started. Jesus came to serve and save; He identifies with you, and He was **single**. My Son came to serve, to heal, to care for and teach the lost, all while doing the will of Me, His Father. He came to die and raise up in new life for **you**. He even cried out, 'Father, Father, why have You forsaken me?' But He knew it was My will for Him to go to the cross, to save you. He said, 'Take this cup from Me, yet not My will, but Yours be done.' His purpose was complete in Me, to go to the cross to save you! Through my Son, Jesus, I've saved you from your doubt, your worry, and your sin of not trusting Me. I want you to stop second-guessing Me and trust that I have your best interest at heart. I am working all things together for your good. Trust me, child! Trust me."*

God was speaking to my heart, big time! How selfish I was to have made this whole thing about me. Shatzie was fast asleep again, so I got down on my hands and knees and cried out to God, "Oh God, forgive me!" It was apparent God was using the number thirty-three as a message to get to my doubting heart, as if time stood still at 3:33 a.m. He had my full attention, and He had much more to convey to my weary soul.

"Child, you are thirty years old now. That was the age My Son was when He started His ministry. All His years prior were preparing Him for such a time as this. His time was focused on doing ministry as a single person without interruptions of having someone in His life, a spouse, or a family, and He did it joyfully in union and in harmony

with Me, never questioning Me. Do as Jesus did. Serve and love others. He came to serve, not to be served. Do not be self-serving. Serve with your whole heart. Serve with everything you have, wrapped in love. Be complete in Me. My love is sufficient for you. You need NO other person to complete you but ME! I am more than enough. Have a relationship with Me that is complete. I am here."

He made it clear to me that I needed to stop worrying about this topic in my life, stop having a pity party for myself, and learn to trust Him completely. He affirmed to me that I was loved unconditionally and that I could be content in Him and Him alone. He impressed upon my heart the most important message of all—His love story to me, the gospel message. Christ was thirty years old when He started His ministry. He died at thirty-three, and every day until then He filled His time fulfilling His mission and His purpose, never complaining, never off task, focused and set on what God called Him to do—to love us even when we turned from Him. He died in our place for our sins and was raised again so we could have new life in Him. It was a wake-up call in my life for sure!

Was I filling my time with His mission, His purpose in my life, or was I wallowing in my pain when no one else was looking? I was wallowing. I wanted to have my heart mended from my past hurt, and with this newfound interest who had trampled on my heart yet again (or so it felt), I knew I couldn't be overwhelmed by it. Not this time. I couldn't fall into despair; I just couldn't. I knew the road it led to, and I couldn't go there again! God was calling me to trust Him completely.

Peace flooded over me. I was bathed in God's loving arms. Jesus chose to identify with me. He knew what loneliness felt like. He knew what hurt felt like. It was everything He had to experience, leading up to His final act of service, His life paid for me on a cruel cross. He was in the prime of His life, not wasting time and energy on what-ifs or why-nots. He was alive, active, healthy, and good to all who knew Him. He was my age. He was where I was. He knows me! He understands me! He loves me! His Spirit within me comforted me as He spoke to my broken heart.

With tears of repentance, I asked God, "How could I have ever doubted You? All these years, I've doubted You in this area of my life. Why would I question You about a relationship when You placed the desire of a relationship in my life in the first place? Who am I to question Your plan for my life? You know me far better than I know myself. You know my needs and the matters of my heart far more than I could ever know. Please help me to trust You in all areas of my life."

It was apparent I had held back from God in this area. Surely God had no idea what I wanted in a relationship—or did He? Had I made God small and me big? Who was I to think I knew what I needed in my life? Maybe it wasn't a relationship at all; it was bigger than that. He tugged on my heartstrings.

> *"Daughter, I want a deeper walk with you. I want a relationship with you that only I can satisfy. I am your Father, your protector, and I created love. I am love!"*

As for matters of the heart, was I ready to trust Him completely without holding back? After this God-ordained moment that rattled my untrusting heart all these years, I unequivocally could say, "Yes, Lord, I am ready to trust You with my whole heart! Do with me as you will."

Quietly, He spoke to my heart. *"Do not question me, child. For I am good, and I work all things out for your good and for My glory."*

I surrendered my all to God in those early morning hours. I

turned over every ounce of my being to the Lord in prayer. No holding back—not ever again! My life was, now and forevermore, completely His.

It was evident at that moment that God had truly given me the best birthday present I had ever received. I was redeemed in His blood. His love and grace washed over me. I would no longer wallow in my doubt and despair, but instead, I would lift up my eyes to the Lord. Yes, I was ready and willing to trust and surrender all of me, every part of me to God, my precious Lord and Savior, Jesus Christ. No holding back. I was completely His.

New Mercies Every Morning

I woke up hours later feeling refreshed, with a new sense of hope in my heart. Shatzie was such a sweet gift the Lord had given me that night. He never left out a single detail for my untrusting heart but loved me completely as I encountered a new, affirmed relationship in Him. He assured me of my worth and His promise to walk with me in this newness with Him.

It was true; all my past relationships seemed to have had me traveling down dead-end roads many times over. Something needed to change. This pattern—meeting someone, dating for a while, ending in a breakup, then resulting in a heartbreak, depression, and surmising a wrong pattern of thinking that God had no one for me—all needed to change. I needed to change! I used to jokingly tell my friends, "I should change my name to Paulette, a female version of Paul. Maybe being single was my ministry and the calling on my life and not a relationship." Maybe God wanted me to be single for the rest of my life. Questions lingered in my mind. Was I OK if that was His plan? Was He more important to me than a relationship? Was I putting my worth in a person or in Jesus? Was I mature enough in my faith to trust Him with my whole heart? Had I really healed from my past, which brought me to this point of never fully healing and trusting God with my whole heart completely?

He was patiently waiting to take me to a newfound hope if I was ready to trust Him completely with my whole heart. God was going to mend my heart—not a man, but God!

He is my comfort, my strength, my God, my Father. He is the lover of my soul. He is who I was looking for and longing for all these years. I can trust Him. He is who I can run to. He is who I can cry out to. He is there, always was there, and always will be there.

He was restoring all that was broken in me. He was holding me that night as I cried out to Him. He then whispered, *"I am here, child. I am here! Run to me."* And so, I did.

In moments like these, awesome promises from God's Word of His unfailing love and kindness wash over us like living water.

> Come to me, all you who are weary and burdened, and I will give you rest. Take My yoke upon you and learn from me, for I am gentle and humble in heart, and you will find rest for your souls. (Matthew 11:28–29 NIV)

> Why, my soul, are you downcast? Why so disturbed within me? Put your hope in God, for I will yet praise Him, my Savior and my God. (Psalm 43:5 NIV)

> You are my hiding place; You will protect me from trouble and surround me with songs of deliverance. (Psalm 32:7 NIV)

The name of the Lord is a strong tower; the righteous run to it and are safe. (Proverbs 18:10 NKJV)

The Lord is good to those whose hope is in Him, to the one who seeks Him. (Lamentations 3:25 NIV)

Now may the God of hope fill you with all joy and peace in believing, that you may abound in hope by the power of the Holy Spirit. (Romans 15:13 NKJV)

He will give you a new life. He will sing and be joyful over you. (Zephaniah 3:17 GNT)

After my encounter with God that night, I was eager to revisit the story of Job and Jesus. Their personal stories and experiences of deep pain, rejection, and loss were both met with God's mercy upon them; their stories would surely be affirming to my renewed heart. As well, I wanted to read through a list of promises I had that reminded me of who God says I am and a letter a friend had given me called "A Letter from God" that spoke of relationships from God's perspective. I knew, this time, I was ready to receive what it had to say.

Job and Jesus

Job experienced incredible loss, and when he questioned God, God responded to him in his brokenness and asked, "Where were you when I laid the earth's foundation?" (Job 38:4a NIV). God was surely in my night's episode of wallowing, silencing me to stop complaining and start trusting. God showed me, through Job's story, that even when I don't understand my situation, I can still hold on to hope because God is in the middle of my circumstance.

A Tim Keller Instagram post said it well: "Job never saw why he suffered, but he saw God and that was enough." (For the full story of Job and all he went through and how God restored him after, read the entire book of Job.)

In Mark 15, Jesus goes to the cross. He died for me and for you! He was beaten and bruised, mocked and shamed, naked and betrayed, though He never acquitted Himself. He was on a mission to complete His Father's will—to die a cruel death in my place. How could I ever doubt Him? God assured me He was present then, now, and in the future. It was all true. I didn't need to question Him, even though my past flinch was to doubt. God had my life in His loving care.

I needed to lay everything at the foot of the cross and start thinking and processing everything, from that moment forward, in light of the work Christ did for me at Calvary, to acknowledge He is worthy of my complete trust and utmost praise. He paid it all! There was nothing I could do or needed to do to work for His approval, to gain His acceptance, or to strive for in life to gain accolades. I just needed to breathe and trust Him with my whole heart—my life—completely. His love is sufficient for me.

> But He said to me, "My grace is sufficient for you, for my power is made perfect in weakness." Therefore, I must boast all the more gladly about my weaknesses, so that Christ's power may rest on me. (2 Corinthians 12:9 NIV)

I was freed from my old way of thinking, and I was set on a new path, with God as my guide. I was ready to trust Him completely. He was thirty-three and single, and He loved me! The chains of my old self that were holding me back from trusting God fully were now gone. Nothing was holding me back from running to Him.

The following promises and some lyrics to the song "You Say" are what God says about you, along with a letter (given to me when I was a young adult), will encourage you to embrace God's heart when it comes to relationships. He knows. Amen.

What God Says About You

God says you are beautiful (Psalm 45:11), unique (Psalm 139:13), loved (Jeremiah 31:3), special (Ephesians 2:10), created for purpose (Jeremiah 29:11), cared for (Ephesians 3:17–19), lovely (Daniel 12:3), precious (1 Corinthians 6:20), strong (Psalm 18:35), forgiven (Psalm 103:12), a new creation (2 Corinthians 5:17), protected (Psalm 121:3), chosen (John 15:16), "You are Mine" (Isaiah 43:1).

The awesome song "You Say" by Lauren Daigle speaks to what God says about you over the voices in your head. In talking about her song in an interview[1] she encouraged listeners to have victory over their struggles by putting their trust in the right hands. Here are some of her lyrics:

> I keep fighting voices ...
> I'm not enough ...
> I will never measure up
> You say I am loved
> You say I am held ...
> You say I am Yours ...
> And I believe

A Letter from God

Everyone longs to give themselves to someone, to have a deep soul relationship with another, to be loved thoroughly and exclusively.

God says, "No. Not until you are satisfied and fulfilled and content with living with Me alone. I love you, My child, and until you discover that your satisfaction is found only in Me, you will not be capable of the perfect human relationship that I have planned for you.

You will never be united with another until you are united with Me, exclusive of anyone or anything else, exclusive of any other desires or longings. I want you to stop planning and stop wishing and allow Me to give you the most thrilling plan in existence—one that you cannot imagine. I want you to have the very best.

Please allow Me to bring it to you. Just keep your eyes on Me, expecting the greatest things. Keep experiencing that satisfaction, knowing that I Am!

Keep learning and listening to the things I tell you. You must be patient and wait. Don't be anxious. Don't worry. Don't look around at the things others have or the things I have given to them. Don't look at the thing you think you want. Just keep looking at Me, or you will miss what I want to give you.

And then, when you are ready, I will surprise you with a love far more wonderful than you could ever dream of. You see, until you are ready, and until the one I have for you is ready, I am working, even at this moment, to have you both ready at the same time.

Until you're both satisfied exclusively with Me and the life I have prepared for you, you won't be able to experience the love that exemplifies your relationship with Me and this perfect love.

And dear one, I want you to have this most wonderful love. I want you to see in the flesh a picture of your relationship with Me and to enjoy, materially and concretely, the everlasting union of beauty and perfection. I am God Almighty. Believe and be satisfied! (anonymous)

A Pause before High School Years

Chapter 5 starts in high school, then dips back into my childhood years, covering stories of my upbringing and how Jesus invaded my young heart; then it heads into life lived now. My journey stops along the way to cover some hot topics, as well as what God taught me about His purpose in the workplace through different jobs and careers I had. God's been in the wilderness, on mountaintops, and in the valleys with me, where life is lived daily while breathing and trusting Him in all things.

Woven within these chapters, you'll find life lessons that God used over the decades to teach me about His love and His ways over my own, which is the essence and premise of this book. It closes with reflection questions at the end for you to ponder, as well as a friend's raw and authentic relationship story that will encourage you, showing how Jesus captured her heart as a young adult, and she followed Him, even through her pain.

I want to share the prayer I wrote to God on January 2, 1998, a year before I turned thirty-three. It was written a month before I went on a ski trip (mentioned later in the book). Finding this letter, decades later, was a miracle in and of itself, as I thought I'd never find it; then, it just appeared on a shelf one day. I was in awe! The prayer written (since typed) is why you're holding this book.

Before that letter, I wanted to share a song that has spoken to my heart over the years by Tenth Avenue North called "By Your Side."[2] It asks these questions: Why do we strive so hard to find love when it's right in front us? Why do we seek approval from people for their love and attention when it is God who wants to extend grace and love to us? Here are a few of their lyrics to encourage you to seek God instead:

> Why are you looking for love? …
> Searching as if I'm not enough?
> I'll be by your side, My hands are holding you!

January 2, 1998
Dear Lord,

This may be one of the most important prayer requests I have ever asked You. Every part of it comes from a sincere and pure place. I give You my all in this prayer!

It's a new year, the second day of 1998. I'm thirty-two years old. Next year at this time, come spring, I will be the age You were when You hung on a cross for me. You bore all the sins of the world. Wow, thank you, precious Savior! After that profound night two years ago on my thirtieth birthday, with the flashing clock reading 3:33 a.m., and all You impressed upon my heart then, You also prompted me to share what happened. I wasn't sure what it all meant at the time, but as I get closer to what You went through when You were thirty-three, I think it's becoming more clear.

I am single and complete! I don't know who I'm to tell this feeling exists, but all I know is You are tugging on my heartstrings to tell people to experience Your life at thirty-three that gives so much to a hurting world. No matter their age or relational status, they can give a hug, give an encouraging word to someone, be a voice of truth, help determine right from wrong, smile at someone who is sad, give a helping hand of hope, and on and on and on. Jesus, Your only Son, was single! He stayed focused on His calling. He gave all those things, and He gave Himself completely. He fulfilled Your ultimate plan of freedom and deliverance from sin. The world needs Jesus!

He died alone at age thirty-three. What did He experience, emotionally, spiritually, physically, during His last year here on earth? God, You became man. Were You alone? Afraid? Eager? Disappointed? Sad? Burdened? Jesus knew His last hour, but the weight of that moment must have been so heavy. We don't know our last hour, but does our heart hurt for the lost, as Yours does?

Lord Jesus, give me clarity of what is in my heart. Am I hearing You clearly? Am I to write a book? What is it to be about? Thirty-three and single? That was Your story! Your face, Your cross You bore for me. Is that to be included somehow? All those pieces? All I know is I am the same age You were a year before You died. Your time invested to love and serve others while on earth inspires me. You accomplished so much at such a young age. You changed the world through love!

Who said one must be older and wiser in years or that they are only complete in marriage to affect God's kingdom for good? That is not true at all! Christ proved that.

What can I offer in a book, Lord? I would want to tell readers their lives are complete in You. I would want to encourage them, no matter what age they are, no matter male or female, their marital status, financial status, ethnicity, no matter what the world labels them as—in Your eyes, none of that matters. They are Your children! You love them, just like You love me. You want them just as they are. May I be Your vessel? Let me tell them how much You love them.

God, please direct me and guide me as to what I should do with this nudging. Give me discernment. I want to glorify You with my absolute best. Without You, I am nothing. Whatever "this" is, Lord, may it glorify Your name completely.

God, guide my heart and my mind. Show me what I need to learn and need to do to make such a project come to life. Provide me with the right resources. Please put in front of me the specific people to give me clear direction on how to start this "God-sized assignment."

God, this is completely Yours. I have no idea what I'm to do. I just know I'm to be obedient, I'm to be faithful, I'm to flee from sin in my life. I'm to pray often, be in fellowship with You through church community, study Your Word, and give back, as it is all Yours anyway. I am to reject Satan any time he would want to interfere.

I am Your vessel. Pour through me, Lord, if You choose. May You find me faithful in completing this task, Your task. Help me, Holy Spirit. Thank you for Your sovereign will. I am excited to watch Your plan unfold. Until then, keep me still, never going ahead of You. Instead, help me to grow in You, watching and waiting for Your timing, if this is Your will, and that I will trust You in the process.

Thank you, loving Father.
Your daughter,
Tina

CHAPTER 5

Looking Back at High School

We were all chatty at our friend's birthday-party sleepover, eating midnight munchies and talking about our dreams and futures. When it came time for me to share, my future was predictable because I knew exactly what God was doing. I'd be married after college by age twenty-three and have three children with the man of my dreams.

I was dating that Prince Charming I met in student council when I was a sophomore, and he was a junior. Our adviser and the entire student council knew we liked each other, but since we were both a bit shy around each other, they creatively put us in a role-playing ad-lib piece together. I was the damsel in distress, and he was the town's hero who would defeat the evil villain. As the script read, the town's hero saves the damsel, dipping her down into a dance-style move, and gives her a big kiss—my first kiss ever! My face was beet red when I was kissed in front of all our friends by the boy I would fall madly in love with very fast.

He played varsity football and basketball, so I went to all his games, cheering him on, as I was a cheerleader. He was smart and handsome and wrote me poems and gave me cards all the time. We dreamed together that someday, after college, we would get married and have three children. I was so set on our future; nothing could have been more perfect! I just knew we were meant to be together.

Shortly before he graduated, I gave in to his desires of me. All the temptation build-up after a year and a half—everything I tried so hard to resist—I fell short and caved, but because he loved me so much, it all seemed OK. I was scared but trusted him and loved him as I had never loved anyone before.

Somehow, even as a believer, I justified my sin as OK and was certain God understood. God was obviously looking out for me, for us, as it was our private business and no one else's. We weren't hurting anybody. We were good students, never troublemakers. We worked hard in school and were involved in lots of things. All seemed so right. Someday, we would be married. He loved me, and I loved him. What could be wrong with any of it?

In looking back now, how was any of this OK? What voices were in my head, telling me any of this was OK to cross boundaries I had set up for myself and promised God I would never cross? Isn't it interesting what we'll do when we are powerless, or so we think, under the guise of love?

My boyfriend was not a Christian, so it became apparent to me that I needed to save him so we would be equally yoked, like the Bible speaks of, to be one in mind and spirit. I just knew I could save him.

(Note to self: you cannot save anyone, only God can.)

> For by grace you have been saved through faith. And this is not your own doing; it is the gift of God, not a result of works, so that no one may boast. (Ephesians 2:8–9 ESV)

God may allow us to be a part of His work, using us to draw others to Him by a conversation we have or by simply living our lives out in front of them, but salvation in Jesus is definitely all God's doing. Being present with people you care about and are praying for with a sincere heart is a great place to start. Had I done more of that, praying God's will and not my own, perhaps I would have been a bit more focused on my relationship with God and less on my relationship and need for love from a boy. Our hearts are so fickle!

Thankfully, God set me aside in his faith story and had a plan for his life and did save him. When he wanted to be baptized as a new believer, it was evident his parents were upset when they came to his baptism but even more so that we had become an item. This new Christian faith experience wasn't sitting well with them, which drew us even closer. Since he was now a new follower in Christ, he wanted to grow his faith away from his family. God was doing a beautiful work in his life, and I was certain it would always include me. We were inseparable.

(The following section came about after I went through a similar situation with a teenage couple who got tangled up in their own mess of immature love. They crossed their own boundaries on many fronts. As I told them all that I'd learned from my own experience, it became apparent to me that I needed to include such a piece in this book.)

What I'd Tell a Younger Me

(So, you're tempted to cross boundaries? Let's talk! *No matter your age—teenager, young adult, or older—don't have regrets later on in life. Follow God's plan over your own. He knows what's best for your life. Trust Him in the process.)*

Oh, to go back and talk to my sixteen-year-old and young-adult self. No one talked to me about this kind of stuff, or if they did, I obviously tuned them out. Let me be that person for you now. It might feel like I'm a bit blunt, but that's OK. I'm a mom of teenagers and am around teenagers a lot, so pull up a chair and let's talk.

I recently learned of an app used to track and describe people who have "friends with benefits," telling what they've done with a person or how many they've been with, and so on. Really? It's come to this? I shouldn't be surprised. When a person is desensitized by pornography, which is so readily available to them by a swipe on their phone, it becomes easier to buy into the impulsiveness of dehumanizing a person to get what they want. Perhaps it wasn't an app back in the day, but people are people, and the lures then are the same lures now. No matter if you're a stat on a phone app (and if that is you, I am so sorry. I want to reach through this book and give you a big hug. You can be freed from this—I promise!) or if you're in a serious relationship with someone you really care about, ask yourself what your boundaries are when everything in you seems to be out of control. Where do you start? How do you get self-control?

You have impulses larger than life living inside your body. Those raging hormones can be stroked by everything to which you're exposed to in our overly sexualized world. If you don't have a game plan going in, you will fail! You can't escape the world around you by living in a bubble, but you can make good choices of what you're going to allow into your life to influence you. Even when you're exposed to things, *you* decide, not the culture, what's right and what is clearly wrong or inappropriate for you.

If you don't have a plan in place for how to process the overflux of everything that vies for your attention at every turn, your brain will become numb to it all, to where you can't undo, unwind, or unprocess all that you're exposed to. It's everywhere in our culture, from movies with suggestive sexual overtones to Netflix binges that are laced with messages of casual hookups and scenes that make you uncomfortable until you want more, and music videos, some that are close to being soft porn. In addition, there is social media, where your eyes glaze over as you scroll through your phone, not putting any filters in place in your brain by choosing to unfollow things you know aren't right for your mind to process. Then there is PDA (public display of affection) right in front of you in hallways at your school or out in public places. You find yourself wanting and craving this kind of attention for yourself, someone who is yours exclusively because, well, it seems like everybody else is in a relationship. You say you don't (you won't) go past certain points because you've set up boundaries for yourself, but let's pause a moment—what are your boundaries?

Is your bar so low that you'll do anything except go all the way so you can justify to yourself that you are saving yourself till marriage? Are these your standards? Don't allow your impulses to overtake how you treat another person. If you're lusting over someone, you're surely not loving that person but are selfishly fulfilling your own sinful cravings and desires. Even justifying such thoughts through a phone conversation, Snapchat, or other apps with another person is not what God has for your life—or theirs. You need to step back and reevaluate what you're doing, as this is not what God wants for you. He wants you to respect that person in your life, and respect yourself. Learn self-control.

Let's reel this in! Boundaries—what does God want for you? This? No. Not this. If you're in this deep, you must get help to dial it down and get accountability. I didn't, and it's the reason you're holding this book in your hands. Learn from my mistakes. You have crossed the threshold that is no longer honoring to God in your dating relationship. You are out seeking personal gratification. You do not have willpower. You are not in love—you are in lust! You have developed a sexual appetite, and you must get that under control. If you don't get this need satisfied, you will keep vying for more each time you're together. Start by changing your mindset, your purpose in a relationship, your respect for yourself and the other person, and your activity. For example, don't be alone in a room with the other person, especially in the dark. Be around other people, and if you can't handle it, you can't handle a relationship. You are too young and too immature!

How about holding hands? Giving a respectful kiss? A good place to start, but if you don't discuss your level of hand-holding (touching) and kissing, these too will become distracters, and each time you say goodbye, it will turn into a make-out session where the lines are blurred, and you'll keep vying for a little bit more each time. So, set your bar high, and don't make out in the first place. Just kiss him or her, even on the cheek, and say good night with a goodbye wave or a simple, quick, friendly side hug. The longing to see that person again with a simple smile is romantic and respectful enough. To turn your episode into a dramatic love scene isn't reality! It's a false sense of truth that will leave you empty and lusting for more.

You Must Have a Plan

The bigger thing, no matter your age, is that you *must* have a plan to help you stay on track, long before a relationship comes into your life by setting relationship goals. Seek help from a parent; a trusted, mature, faith friend (mentor); a young-adult leader; or a youth pastor to help you stay focused. Write your goals in a journal so you can revisit them often to help you maintain healthy and appropriate boundaries. Once a relationship wanders into your life, you know going in that you have support, accountability, and prayer, so you aren't faced with a point of no return. Your discussion shouldn't be, "Do you have a condom on you?" Or "Oops, we went too far. I guess go out and get a morning-after pill." No, it should be, "I am saving myself for marriage. I don't want to put myself or you in any compromising situation that hinders the boundaries I've set for myself before God that would disrespect Him, myself, or you."

If you struggle in this area, get help! If not addressed, it can be very destructive in your future marriage. God created and reserved the intimacy of sex for marriage between a man and woman, as He designed it. God speaks a lot about sexual sin in the Bible. Even with all the nuances of sexuality described today, nothing is foreign to God. Things get confusing when lines are blurred. Love becomes distorted through a foggy lens, causing a lack of clarity of what is right and true.

Ask God for self-control. People fall too quickly and give in too easily to their fleshly desires. Get a deep understanding of what God says about your purity. Have integrity and respect for yourself and others. You were bought with a price. Don't waste the commitment you made to the Lord and to yourself on a one-night stand or a relationship that is built on sexual pleasures. Those feelings will lie to you! They are like vapors that vanish in thin air.

There was a time I embraced the cultural mindset that said, "I'm my own person. I can do what I want. It's my body anyway." Those thoughts stemmed from my being hurt and feeling rejected and not feeling loved. It wasn't until God got a hold of my heart to reshape my thinking and change patterns within me. Being grounded in truth will deliver you when you're chased in your weakness. Run to Jesus. He'll rescue you!

Sweet friend, reading these words right now, understand that there will be a time and place in your life for this level of intimacy, if the Lord chooses, but it is not now! Respect yourself as a child of God by not ruining or jeopardizing God's plan for your life in any way. It may feel all too old-fashioned for you, and you think it makes you sound holier-than-thou (which you are not; you're a sinner saved by grace), but you have an enemy on your back, and if you don't fight him off with everything you have, you will fail! Vow not to fail, because God is bigger than your impulses or your desires to be enticed by some cute guy (or gal) who is distracting you by his handsome (or her beautiful) ways. You must stay the course because, in Christ, you can do all things through Him who strengthens you (Philippians 4:13). If a person says he or she likes you—or, for that matter, loves you—or you have those feelings toward a person, come together on a plan for purity. As a dating couple, get the help you need from people who love you both and will help you stay accountable, so you won't slip up with regrets later. You don't know if this is the person you will marry someday, but you do know you want to honor God in all your ways and save yourself for your future husband or wife in every way he or she deserves. You don't want to mess that up by any selfish ways or lack of self-control, or worse yet, mess up things for your future spouse because of your immature fleshly impulses. Trust God to give you strength and pray the same for the person in your life. Pray as well for those things you're challenged with by asking God for help. Had I prayed about my relationship, I believe God would have helped me in my struggle. He's there to help you too. Cry out to Him, saying something along these lines:

"God, help me! I can't do this alone. I want to honor You in my actions and activities with my boyfriend (or girlfriend). If I'm not strong enough to honor You in this request, then please help me be strong enough to walk away. It's not worth it to him (her), me, and my future spouse. I need Your strength! I am weak and You are strong. I trust You over myself, and I surrender all of this to You. Be my ever-present help in times of trouble. Help me trust You completely! Thank you, Lord. In Jesus' name, amen."

To you high school student or young adult who struggles with your boundaries, you *can't* do this alone. You just can't! You *must* have accountability. This is a Mack truck that is bigger than you are. If you try to stand in its way on your own, you will lose. You will be run over; you will be demolished; you will not come out ahead! You do *not* have the strength on your own. You need a new set of standards for yourself, and it starts at the foot of the cross. He will guide you.

Here are some helpful verses so you can better understand how much God detests sexual sin, as well as His desire to help you. When Christ was faced with temptation, He fought and defeated the enemy with scripture. Do the same! Bathe yourself in God's Word. You must desire to do everything to honor Him, especially with your thoughts. If your thoughts are unchecked and are put into action, those actions can hurt you or somebody else. Don't follow those impulses you feel. Walk away—in fact, run!

If you have already crossed your boundaries, start anew. God is the way-maker, making all things new. Don't lose hope. He is there and will see you through. If your actions resulted in a pregnancy, keep that precious life! God has a plan for you and for your baby. If an abortion ensued, He forgives you. Run to Him so He can hold you and give you hope and a future wrapped in His loving grace.

Most importantly, don't get discouraged. God loves you and wants to help you. He has a plan for your life. Don't rush things.

Go at His pace. And if you've messed up or mess up (I know I did), God forgives you. Go to Him and confess your sins to Him. He is there to carry you to a new place, a new hope. His ways are *far* better than your own. Don't try to grow up so fast. Being an adult is *hard*. No need to complicate things with poor choices that you'll regret later on. I promise you—it's not worth it.

Helpful Verses of God's Plan over Sexual Sin

+ Don't allow love to turn into lust, setting off a downhill slide into sexual promiscuity, filthy practices, or bullying greed. (Ephesians 5:3 MSG)
+ But when you follow your own wrong inclinations, your lives will produce these evil results: impure thoughts, eagerness for lustful pleasure. (Galatians 5:19 TLB)
+ But I say, anyone who even looks at a woman with lust has already committed adultery with her in his heart. (Matthew 5:28 NLT)
+ Run from sexual sin! No other sin so clearly affects the body as this one does. For sexual immorality is a sin against your own body. (1 Corinthians 6:18 NLT)
+ If we tell Him our sins, He is faithful, and we can depend on Him to forgive us of our sins. He will make our lives clean from all sin. (1 John 1:9 NLV)
+ For God wants you to be holy and pure and to keep clear of all sexual sin so that each of you will marry in holiness and honor. (1 Thessalonians 4:3–4 TLB)
+ That is why a man leaves his father and mother and is united with his wife, and they become one. (Genesis 2:24 GNT)
+ Whatever is true ... noble ... right ... pure ... lovely, whatever is admirable—if anything is excellent or

praiseworthy—think about such things. (Philippians 4:8b NIV)

+ Do not throw away your trust, for your reward will be great. You must be willing to wait without giving up. After you have done what God wants you to do, God will give you what He promised you. (Hebrews 10:35–36 NLV)

Lord, enlighten what's dark in me, strengthen what's weak in me, mend what's broken in me, bind what's bruised in me, heal what's sick in me, and lastly, revive whatever peace and love has died in me. Amen. (anonymous)

When Jesus becomes our focus, we will be in the center of God's will for us! (iBelieve.com)

A woman's heart should be so close to God that a man should have to chase Him to find her. (anonymous)

It can go both ways— A man's heart should be so close to God that a woman should have to chase God to find him.

CHAPTER 6

Off to College

I followed my boyfriend off to college to pursue a degree in elementary education with a minor in music. We were about two hours away from our family homes. We were both involved in the Greek system, which became our way of life in our college experiences.

Prior to college, I had no idea what a sorority was. One of my endearing high school teachers, Ms. Hall, encouraged me to get involved in a chapter. She was a part of the Greek system and benefited from the positive outcome it had on her life. She wrote a letter of recommendation for me that opened doors throughout the process. Plus, her suggestion to get involved in some level of leadership proved successful in my college years and was seen favorably on my future résumé.

Although Greek life is typically known for its parties, in my experience there was so much more. I became the song leader and led our sorority in carol singing at dinners and special occasions. But the best part for me was meeting fantastic girls along the way who made it a beautiful experience. I'm still friends with some of those ladies today.

During the Greek system's recruiting week, I ended up pledging to the house where the very first girl I met was a Christian named Libby. She was the first Libby I had ever met. Her name matched her contagious, joyful personality—a name I'd be very fond of later in life. Our house president, Shari Davies, had graduated from my high school and was another amazing gal of faith. After graduating, she married a pastor and joined his ministry life in Texas, where they've raised their beautiful family. She took me through pledge initiation and prayed for me in my upcoming college years—a moment I'll always remember. Her brothers, John and Greg, also friends from high school, were kitchen hashers who helped with meal preps at the house. They were a wonderful faith family. God was all around me at every turn—even my roommate, Julie, was a Christian.

A Bible study started shortly thereafter with all these amazing ladies. We met once a week in our house mom and dad's onsite apartment suite. We affectionately called them Mom and Dad Vest. They were the sweetest couple. Dad Vest would dress as Santa every Christmas, and Mom Vest was a dynamic woman of faith with a gentle spirit who made herself available to us any time. Once, she very privately pulled me aside to ask me more about my dating relationship with my boyfriend, as if she knew. How did she know? She was the first person to ever question me. He and I worked very hard to keep our ongoing physical relationship very private, not letting anyone know the boundaries we had crossed, especially since we were seen as a Christian couple.

I heard her words as motherly advice, but I knew who we were as a couple and that we were meant for each other. Nothing could stand in our way. She just wanted me to know how much God loved me, regardless of the nice boy he was. She never condemned me but just loved me. I appreciated her well-meaning thoughts on the matter but assured her we were in God's good care.

We were seen as a couple who took our faith seriously and

were exclusive, though he never escaped the pressure from different guys in his fraternity house to date other girls. He was working part-time, modeling campus clothing that was featured in our university magazine, and he was around a lot of pretty girls. His mom and sister modeled. They were stunning women! I always felt intimidated around them because of how pretty they were. He, too, was very handsome, so modeling was a perfect fit for him. I often didn't feel pretty enough for him. Plus, the pressure from his mom wore on him all the time—she told him I was an average, American-looking girl who wasn't anything exceptional and not the right match for his long, lean frame because I was too chubby, in her eyes. (More on this topic at the end of this chapter.)

Even with all the mounting pressures around him, his devotion to us went as far as his pinning me with his fraternity pin at a surprise pinning ceremony one night at a house dinner. It was a beautiful moment I wasn't expecting—truly a big deal, considered almost as a pre-engagement, in front of my entire sorority house and his brothers, who all came to serenade me. He promised himself to me in front of all those people, a big step for any guy. It confirmed to me, even with all the pressure he was under, that he did have hopes for us heading in the direction of the future we had dreamed about together ever since high school.

Hectic College Schedule

During college, I was a babysitter/nanny for two adorable boys whose family owned a Greek restaurant in town; they even took me on family ski trips. I also worked at Dillard's Department Store at the mall for twenty-plus hours a week and overtime hours during holidays. Having two jobs to cover college and living expenses, going to school full time, being active in my sorority, having a boyfriend, and serving in the high school ministry at the church I attended, I was super-busy but always sensed God in the midst of my crazy schedule. Though, hands down, my boyfriend was always there to encourage me and lift me up.

He was perfect in every way and was there to help me at every turn, even tutoring me in math and science. He'd hold my hand while we studied in the engineering library, though he often was teased by his fraternity brothers who had classes with him. He made my world complete. God was there too but not in tangible ways, like my boyfriend was, helping me in the day-to-day, week-to-week, crazy, busy college life we were living. We made it work. God was in the picture and was there for us when we needed Him.

He'd graduate the year before me and would start his career as an aerospace engineer, having landed his dream job in Florida. It was a big deal and more confirmation that God was laying out all the pieces in front of us for the future we were planning together. We would make the long-distance relationship work because we were both committed to each other in every way, minus a wedding ring. We were mature adults making choices that worked best for us. Who could question that? We were in love!

Thoughts of Me That Started in High School

His mom's opinion of me and my appearance started when I was a high school cheerleader. She didn't think I was pretty enough or thin enough for her son. Her thoughts toward me spurred me on to focus more on my outward appearance, never realizing—more importantly—how much inner work I needed to do. Nevertheless, I was motivated to become the best me I could be.

I was your average-looking girl and was completely OK with that. I never obsessed over it or was jealous of other girls who were prettier or thinner than me, but her opinion of me motivated me to work out more and eat healthier—definitely not a bad thing. I had been on a summer swim team in junior high and was on the freshman swim team in high school, so I hit the university lap pool as often as I could. Also, I started running, which got me into 5K races along the way. Plus, I started going to the gym to get more fit and toned. The results of all my hard work started paying off, and better yet, I felt better and more confident in my own skin.

About that time, a professor in our music department encouraged me to participate in the city's talent/beauty pageant, which awarded scholarship money and would help promote the College of Music department by having one of their students participate in it. At first, I turned down the idea, but after thinking more about it, I figured I'd give it a shot, mostly because it would be good vocal practice for me. Plus, with the opportunity to earn scholarship money, what did I have to lose?

I trained in all areas for that pageant by working with a vocal coach, an interview coach, and an etiquette coach on how to walk in heels, in a gown, and in a one-piece swimsuit. My childhood girlfriend Tonya loaned me her gold-sequined fitted gown she'd once worn in a pageant. All the hard work paid off. I was able to fit into her beautiful dress and gained the confidence I needed to conquer my fear of wearing a bathing suit on stage. I placed third runner-up, but the most thrilling part was being awarded scholarship money that covered my tuition that semester.

Most eye-opening for me was seeing what some girls were willing to do to get to their ideal weight for that pageant. Some nearly starved themselves and had eating disorders, which I later learned was happening to a few girls in my sorority house. The intense pressure they put on themselves to be accepted by others told of a deeper pain they were suffering. There's a fine line between being healthy and being obsessive. Don't ever feel you need to cave to the voices that are lying to you about your looks. You're perfect just the way you are, the way the Lord made you, no matter your size.

I was invited to share my story and a recording of me singing a solo at church that aired on a local radio talk show; the host was a Christian and would become a lifelong faith friend and career mentor further along in my life. From that interview, some schools called to have me talk to their classes about my experience. I shared about positive body image. So many students, boys and girls alike, needed to hear that they are not defined by their outward appearances but that their *character* inside is what matters most. That message resonated with them. It's an important message for any of us to hear.

It gave me boldness to share privately with one of the girls in my sorority who struggled with anorexia. We could hear her vomiting in our sorority's small guest bathroom, but she told any of us who heard her that she was sick from dinner. I knew how much she was hurting. She really wanted to talk to someone but was afraid of being judged. Seeing someone get help is such a beautiful thing. A person may feel powerless to stop, thinking he or she doesn't have anyone to turn to for help. If you're reading this and you struggle with an eating disorder, please tell a friend who loves you what you're going through. Together, you can seek the help you need. Take care of yourself. You matter! Be healthy!

From that experience and from everything that brought me to that place of my own body-image insecurity, God taught me I am complete in Him as He made me. To be worried about the approval of others wasn't where I needed to put my energy. I can't control people's opinions about me, but I *can* control how I respond, inwardly and outwardly, by gaining my assurance through Christ, who heals all wounds. For in Him, I am satisfied, no matter if I am thin or curvy. It doesn't matter. I am not a mistake! God created me just the way I am.

Don't ever forget that you're beautiful the way God made you! Appreciate who you are in Christ, no matter your jean size or the number on the scale. And believe me, those numbers will fluctuate in your lifetime—they have for me. Don't let that define you. Don't ever let your size or your looks dictate your mood or your actions. Certainly, be healthy and make wise choices about your health, but be confident in who you are in Christ so God can use you in beautiful ways.

Even though I was confident and content in who I was, unbeknownst to me, God had a lot of work to do in me to change my inward appearance—*my heart*. He was about to do some major heart surgery in the coming season.

CHAPTER 7

My First Year of Teaching and Summer Break in Florida

A fter student teaching in Ms. Molstad's sixth-grade class, I was hired as a fifth-grade teacher in a new school. I was excited about my first teaching job but nervous nonetheless. It was hard to say goodbye after an incredible student-teaching semester. Leaving her classroom and guidance behind would be an adjustment for sure, but it was now time for me to embrace all that awaited me in my own classroom in a brand-new school in the same district.

My aunt Bonnie was my role model and inspiration in my wanting to become a teacher. I wanted to follow in her footsteps after visiting her classroom during high school and college breaks. She was an exceptional, well-respected, and seasoned teacher in the district, whose connections helped me land my student teaching assignment, as well as my first teaching job. I jumped in with eagerness, as we were a fast-growing district with high expectations to stay abreast of all the career-development requirements and district classes. I worked long hours after my students left, grading papers and writing lesson plans. I loved teaching and poured everything I had into making every day the best day for my students.

I was at the school so much that the running joke was, "Since you're the last one to leave the building, make sure you turn off the lights on your way out." They knew me too well! It did cross my mind a time or two to just sleep under my desk instead of going home, only to have to turn around to come back again the next morning—that would have made life so much easier. I was a devoted and diehard first-year teacher who usually felt a bit overwhelmed—but I gave it my all!

Might I just say that teachers are the most dedicated, hardworking people I have ever met. Teaching was the most rewarding yet exhausting job I've ever had. If you are a teacher or plan to become a teacher, know that you are appreciated immensely. For those who had to weather semester-long bouts of COVID shutdowns, navigating through remote learning, returning to your schools in masks, while wearing lots of different hats to cover the shortfall with many out sick, know you're a hero! You're a difference-maker in students' lives and for their families. Thank you.

Sick Days

I received a note from a parent, telling me their child was home sick with mild cold-like symptoms and a small rash from maybe a bug bite but would be back the next day—I found out later that he had a case of chicken pox. Throughout the day, I started feeling a bit fatigued, so I headed straight home after school to grab a quick nap and a hot bath to revive myself so I could head back to school—it was the Wednesday before the last week of school and so much needed to be done. When I got out of the bath, I had red bumps all over my body from head to toe.

This could not be happening! I called my mom immediately, asking her if I'd ever had chicken pox. She didn't recall that I had. With a tone of disbelief, I wondered why she had never exposed me to them when other kids on the block had them. My situation felt dismal. This was not good! I did not have time to be sick.

I was hit hard with the outbreak—fever, fatigue, and quarantined from my classroom, ugh. I would miss the entire last week and a half of my first year of teaching. This was awful! There was still the end-of-the-year testing, final projects, and our class party, as well as my needing to finish report cards that were to be passed out on the last day of school. How was I ever going to pull this off? Thankfully, my roommate, Angie, also a teacher at my school and lifelong friend to this day, brought home my students' papers and projects for me to grade, along with a batch of get-well cards they and the staff made to cheer me up. Angie was indeed my lifeline, keeping all the balls in the air while not only closing out her own classroom but mine as well, with the help of a substitute teacher. I was so thankful for these two women who carried my burden with such love and care.

When the students were dismissed on the last day of school and all the teachers were gone, I returned to my classroom to take down my bulletin boards and pack up my room, as was customary for cleaning purposes and to be ready to move if classroom assignments changed over the summer. It was a major chore when I wasn't feeling 100 percent and was still quite lethargic, but I was now boxed up and ready to go after a long and tiring day.

Summer Break in Florida

All I could think about now was the much-needed summer break I was looking forward to in Florida. It would be my first time ever to go to Florida and to spend it with my boyfriend; I was elated! It had been a long-distance relationship throughout this entire year, and we'd finally be together! I dipped into my savings to make the trip happen, while still paying toward my student loan and car payment, as well as paying my roommates for summer rent and utilities. Finances would be tight, but I figured I'd be fine for the summer. I did set some money aside for one special purchase that would be a treat to myself—a beach-cruiser bike I'd buy in Florida.

Since my boyfriend would be working a lot, it was the better plan that I'd have my own transportation so I could do some sightseeing and apply to some local districts, which were some different ideas we were throwing around. I would have to become a certified teacher in Florida but was open and prepared to do anything to move us in the direction we had always talked about. He would fly out to see his family and would then drive back to Florida with me in my car. Because I was still recovering from being sick and felt completely exhausted, he drove most of the way so I could sleep, and when I drove, he'd sleep. Blaring cassette tapes with all our favorite bands filled our time as we drove cross-country—something we loved to do, listen to music and drive. There was little conversation, but all was well. We were together, and that was all that mattered.

Once in Florida, he spent his days working excessively, leaving sometimes before I was awake and getting home late at night. I didn't press him on things, as I knew he was in a high-pressure job. I wanted to show my support by not bothering him too much. Since he didn't have a television and the internet and smartphones weren't a thing yet, my days were quiet and a bit lonely in a new town. So, I read a lot. I also bought that new beach-cruiser bike and explored every inch of that town.

I found a tiny neighborhood-community Bible church I fell in love with and started attending regularly. I was singing in their small choir, which led to singing solos occasionally in their worship services. Looking back, that season of worship was a precious gift God had given me to draw me closer to Him. The church's band had some incredibly talented musicians who were a part of a jazz band at a neighboring jazz club. They invited me to sing with them on a few different occasions, which allowed me to make some extra money to help cover some of my expenses. It was one of the most incredible musical experiences I've ever had. God was so sweet to provide in that manner.

I also joined a gym and signed up for scuba diving lessons at Ron Jon Surf Shop. I was studying for my scuba diving test and was excited to go out into the deep blue ocean waters for my first dive with my diving class. What a thrill! I had made a wonderful, busy life for myself and was always excited to tell my boyfriend all about my new adventures every day and the people I was meeting. All was going well in *my* little world, but everything with him felt as if our once-magical world of "us" was crumbling away.

I sensed he was growing apart from me, and I was quickly feeling unwelcome. We were merely roommates. I sensed we weren't the same couple we'd been in college in our protected little bubble and needed to understand why any of this was happening. I assumed with all our past years together, we'd be discussing our future, and maybe marriage would be part of that conversation, though he hadn't proposed yet. It still seemed like the logical next step. This new shift and change in him had me baffled. I was very taken aback. The man I had fallen in love with was treating me unkindly with his silence and distance, and he was very standoffish. What was happening? Everything had changed, but what? It was very apparent we needed to talk, and he agreed.

He had an open-air jeep, which we loved to take rides in. He carved out time for us to take a long ride on the beach. This time, it was another quiet ride with music filling the space, but we were at least in the same space together. He wanted to take me to a park on the beach. It was near sunset. The sky was majestic in its hues of red and orange. I figured this would be a turning point, a time to reconnect. All felt right.

There, at that little park, with no one else around, we sat on the park swings and talked for the first time in a long time about us. He then went to his jeep to put in a cassette tape of his favorite band, U2, and turned it up for me to hear a song he said had been playing in his head, over and over again, for a few weeks as he'd tried to figure things out. As I sat on the swing, swirling my feet in the sand, listening to a song I'd heard many times before, but something felt different hearing it this time, and the lyrics pierced my soul. What was he trying to tell me through this song? I was puzzled and confused about what he was trying to communicate to me with its song title, "I Still Haven't Found What I'm Looking For."

He went on to say he didn't think he found what he was looking for in me and had come to the decision that we weren't meant to be together anymore. He was breaking up with me. The song title said it all. He was having doubts about us and was calling it quits. Lastly, he told me he had met someone else. *What?* He proceeded to tell me about a girl he'd met in a local surf shop. He'd met her earlier that year when he was taking surfing lessons, prior to my coming out for the summer.

Was I hearing this right? Another girl was invading "us?" How? What just happened? Wait—was this really happening? Was this all a bad dream? I couldn't believe what I was hearing. I couldn't breathe. Everything I had hoped for and was dreaming about—our future, us—came crashing down in one single moment. My mind trailed off; I wondered if she was from the same surf shop where I had just been certified in scuba diving the week prior, having spent many hours there for my class. I was relieved to hear she was not.

This was all hitting too close to home. Why would he betray me like this? Who was this girl? What did she have that I didn't have? Insecure thoughts filled my mind. Did she look better in a bathing suit than me? Was she the prettier girl his mom always wanted for him? Was he really trading us in because his mom got in his head about me, and this girl fit the bill?

He tried to hug me, but all I could do was cry and push him away. I didn't want his condolences or his comfort. How could he throw us away after all we had been through together all these years? Even though there were a few stops and starts along the way, mainly due to our differing school schedules, we always knew we were meant to be together, ever since I was that dreamy-eyed, fifteen-year-old girl, head over heels in love with that sixteen-year-old boy. We always dreamed of a life together, married someday with a family of our own. How did he get to decide this was how things would be? How could he ruin everything? Why was my world falling apart? How could this be happening?

I felt so rejected, so alone, so hurt, so troubled, and so in pain that my heart was broken in two. And to think I'd given this man everything—all of me. I hated him for that! How could he? I felt so dirty, so ashamed. I wanted to run, but where? I was still in Florida.

It became apparent that my plans to stay the entire summer had fallen short. I was coming to the end of my money quickly, as I never thought I'd be paying for everything on my own—I'd expected shared groceries, outings, and so on. He wasn't interested in helping me; I just needed to leave.

Morning couldn't come soon enough. I hardly slept that night, wanting to just put this nightmare behind me. I packed my things that next morning when he was at work, loaded my beach cruiser bike on my little red car, and was on my way.

My plan was to drive to Texas, where I would meet up with my sweet roommate, Angie, who was home visiting her family for her summer break. From there, we would drive back to Arizona together. I was broken and didn't even weigh the heaviness of driving cross-country by myself as a twenty-three-year-old, the age I'd said back in high school that I'd be married. Where was God in all of this? I was alone and rejected. I was a complete wreck!

CHAPTER 8

The Long Road to Amarillo

God was on that trip with me, meeting my every need through random acts of kindness all around me—from a discounted hotel room to a stranger picking up my tab for a meal. I felt numb most of the time, never recognizing that those random acts of kindness were blessings from God. Instead, I just assumed they were coincidences as I went through the motions, crying all the while.

I finally arrived in Texas and planned on calling Angie's family to let them know I was in Dallas. From there, they would give me directions to their home. I needed a pay phone, as cell phones were nonexistent. We didn't think about phones like we do today, where you can easily make calls, send texts, or pull up directions on an app. Any call you ever had to make on the road was from a pay phone. I could hardly scrounge up enough coins to make the call; plus, I was hungry and needed to find a bathroom. I was now officially on a mission.

Oblivious to my surroundings, I drove aimlessly until I spotted something that looked promising. And like manna from heaven, a Burger King popped into view. I was thrilled! I suppose I stood out a bit with my Florida tan and sun-bleached blonde hair when

I pulled up in my red car with a bike cruiser on the back. I was in an older part of town, where some places might not be too keen on letting you use their restroom, let alone their phone, but I figured if I ordered something, they'd have favor on my situation. Keeping an eye on my spending, I glanced over the menu board mounted behind the counter and found a mini-biscuit-and-juice-box combo from the kid's menu. Perfect—filling and affordable.

The manager must've sensed I needed help when I asked if I could use their phone—it was hanging on the wall with a long cord that would stretch over the counter. Instead, he offered me the phone in his side office off the kitchen, as if he knew I needed a moment of privacy. He even handed me a pad of paper and a pencil, should I need to write something down. This kind man, as well as everyone else I met along the way since leaving Florida, was very friendly and willing to help me. It was as if God had placed all the right people in my path, which was exactly what my vulnerable state of mind needed. He carried my burden of traveling alone because it never crossed my mind how truly alone I was.

When I called Angie's family, her dad answered. His voice was such a welcoming comfort to my hurting heart. I told him I had made it to Texas and asked him how much farther it was to their home.

He said, "Darling, we live in Amarillo, the panhandle of Texas. You have another nine hours till you get here." He proceeded to give me directions as my shaky hand wrote them down. I was deflated! I was such a weary traveler already, and I was overwhelmed with the idea of having to go much further. I was so alone; I didn't think I could possibly make it. Then something deep inside of me took over, giving me a glimmer of hope, even though I felt so defeated. Something motivated me to press on. I could make it. I had to make it. I was almost out of money; I needed to make it to my next destination so I'd have a traveling companion for the last leg home to Arizona.

It was about 10 o'clock that morning. I figured if I made minimal stops, I could get to Amarillo by nightfall. The kind manager asked where I was headed. When I told him Amarillo, he said, "Sweet girl, storms are a-coming. You best be careful!" Those words put a drive in me like I never knew I had. I was now running on pure adrenaline and not focused on all the hurt that had been consuming my every thought. I thanked him and the other employees for their help and asked them, if they wouldn't mind, to keep me in their prayers. They said they would. I felt so encouraged and uplifted when they said they'd be praying for me. I was emboldened to carry on by their support. Now, it was just me against the mighty storm-filled skies. Even though I was scared, I knew God would protect me. Onward, I went!

The skies were ominous, and the clouds were massive! Lightning danced between the billowing, heavy, gray, black, and white towering cloud formations. The road was open for endless miles, as hour after hour I drove. I never experienced such peace, though at the same time, I was gripped in fear that God could swallow me up in that storm at any moment if those skies opened. I pleaded with God to keep me safe on that treacherous drive. It felt as if I was the only one on that road, and I think I was. It was just me and God! He had my undivided attention. While turning on the radio to find a signal, I stumbled onto a Christian station. Song lyrics broke through the sounds of my sobbing. Every word in every song washed over me like living water. I was so grateful God was giving me hope through music and was so thankful He kept the storm at bay. Even with thunder and lightning all around me, my little car was spared much rain—only drops seemed to fall here and there, escaping the storm's ultimate wrath. I drove as fast as that little car could take me. I was praying the entire time, begging

God to forgive me for walking into the path of my own making all these years. How could I have been so stupid? All I wanted was to be loved. Wherever did I go wrong?

I played back in my mind, over and over again, every detail and every word he said while we were sitting on those swings at the park. What I didn't recall until that moment was his saying I was too clingy. *Too clingy?* What did that mean? Did he think I was after his money and prestige of what our future would look like? Was I too clingy because I wrote letters to him in our year apart, expressing how much I loved him? What had happened? The person who knew me better than anyone else on planet earth was now throwing me out like garbage. Had I become like trash? Was I that? Clingy trash? How did this happen?

I had an aha moment on that long road to Amarillo. Why had I been so quick to give myself completely to another person, only to have my heart trampled on years later? I wanted to blame it on the fact that I didn't have a father in the picture as I was growing up, which would make perfect sense as to why I would gravitate so quickly to the first boy who told me he loved me and told me I was pretty. Isn't that what every girl dreams of hearing? Why didn't I have a daddy telling me these things? Why did I need to hear it from another male, only to follow along with his desires for me? Where was my dad? In that moment, I heard God speaking to my heart. *"I am right here, child. I have always been right here!"* His love started to break through to my broken heart.

On that long road, with a sky filled with threatening storm clouds, God met me through worship music, wiping away every tear and helping me breathe when I had no strength to keep my hands on the wheel. He met me right where I was, in my utter state of despair and brokenness. God always knows where to meet us and how to get our attention. He certainly had mine as He held me and cared for me, on that long and lonely road, with His loving compassion.

The long and seemingly never-ending hours of driving eventually passed, and I was finally there—I'd made it to Amarillo! Seeing Angie and her family was such a soothing balm to my weary soul. I fell into their loving arms as they embraced me with their big-hearted, Texas family hug. Being with Angie's family for those couple of days before we headed back to Arizona was such a healing remedy to my hurting heart. I observed what a healthy family looked like from love displayed between her mom and dad in their marriage and the kids they'd raised together. It was life done in the right order, all loving each other so beautifully. It was what I longed for. I was trying so hard to lead such a grown-up life, "adulting" all on my own, yet I was so young and so immature. I had so much growing up to do. If I continued in this manner, I was surely on a crash course to fail. I had created all my own current pain. I had chosen to leave God out of my relationship, and I knew something needed to change. I needed to change!

CHAPTER 9

When I Met Jesus as a Child

had loved the Lord for as long as I could remember. When I was nine and my sister was eleven, our love for God grew even stronger when a significant moment happened in our mom's life that would change her forever and would ultimately impact us as well.

It started out like any ordinary Saturday night. Mom, my sister, and I were watching TV as we sat around our living room coffee table, eating TV dinners. The best part of those TV dinners was the dessert compartments hidden under the peel-back foil. That night, it was peach cobbler to go along with the main dish, Salisbury steak, with a side of peas. I hated peas, so I fed those to our dog, who was on the floor next to me. I was her favorite human because I'd slip her table scraps all the time. She'd eat anything, even peas.

Remote controls weren't a thing then, so Mom sent me to the TV to turn the big dial to each of the five available channels: 3, 5, 8, 10, and 12. If a channel reception was fuzzy, I'd rearrange the wire clothes hanger on the back of the TV box affixed to the bulb to get a better signal. We usually watched the *Lawrence Welk Show* at this time, so I was a bit surprised when she had me stop at another channel that appeared to be another talent show of sorts, as someone was singing. Since the channel came in clear, we decided to watch it to hear the beautiful singing. We figured we'd stumbled onto a church program, as the song was about the Lord. As it went on, Mom kept listening more intently, as if the room stood still. We were watching a program we had never heard of before called, *The Billy Graham Crusade*. Mom felt as if he was talking directly to her. When it ended, Mom got on the floor and started crying. Out of nowhere, she started praying out loud to God, something we had never seen or heard her do before.

The Loving Influence of Grandmothers when Growing Up

Grandma Mary

We were raised in a family who had great reverence for the Lord. Grandma Mary was the matriarch of our family and our faith. (Grandma's middle name, Elizabeth, would become a future namesake.) She was a true hero to our extended family because she raised her four daughters all on her own—my mom and her three sisters. She prayed her rosary every day for everyone in her family—her four daughters, her eight grandchildren, and her nine siblings, who all grew up together on their family farm in South Dakota. She was a woman we all loved dearly.

My sister and I went to catechism classes and had our first Holy Communion, thanks to Grandma Mary, who took us to church every Sunday. Most people assumed we were twins, as she'd buy us pretty, matching, ruffled Sunday dresses to wear with matching shoes. After church, she'd take us to the local diner, where delicious doughnuts were on display in a glass cabinet. We loved to spin in circles on the tall stools at the counter while we each enjoyed our selected doughnut and a tall glass of cold milk while Grandma read the Sunday paper. She'd take us to midnight mass on Christmas Eve with extended family. Even though it was hard to stay awake, the peace I felt as we'd light candles and listen to the beautiful music is a fond memory.

Grandma Mary worked as the bookkeeper for decades at Karsh's Bakery, a popular, well-known and loved, family-owned Jewish bakery in town. The Karsh family loved us like their own and introduced us to their rich culture, traditions, and yummy pastries. Grandma Mary always smelled of delicious, freshly made, oven-baked bread and bagels. Even when food was scarce in our house, she'd always make sure we had fresh bread to eat. I'll always be thankful for her kind and caring ways.

Angie and I lived near Grandma Mary when we were teaching. (*Angie continued teaching and is still her students' favorite teacher. Her dedication to countless children over the decades is so commendable. She is a true difference-maker and was in my life as well.*)

Since Angie's family lived in Amarillo, Grandma Mary considered Angie like another granddaughter. She loved that Angie attended the local university parish and would come to Saturday campus mass whenever I'd sing occasionally with their worship team. Every Friday afternoon, Grandma Mary came to our classrooms and graded our students' math quizzes and spelling tests, as well as bring homemade cookies. They loved her visits.

Because we didn't have a washer or dryer in our apartment, I'd head over to Grandma's townhouse every other Friday after school to do my laundry. She'd always have a Marie Callender's chicken pot pie in the oven for me, and after I ate, we'd graze on jelly beans from a mason jar. I'd scout for red ones, and she looked for the purple and orange ones, as we watched *The Price Is Right* and *Jeopardy* while doing crossword puzzles or playing checkers. Grandma Mary was a best friend to me in my young-adult years. She was always there for me, as she was for all her grandchildren.

Grandma Helmi

Our other grandmother, Grandma Helmi, was riddled with rheumatoid arthritis throughout her tiny body. Her overall frailty, crippled little fingers, and pain-stricken hands never seemed to stop her from taking the time and energy to write me long letters when I was in college. She'd always tell me she loved me and was praying for me. She was as sharp as a tack and remembered every detail of her childhood days in Finland.

In her later years, she lived on Gimel floor at Kivel Care, a Jewish senior assisted-living home. With kosher meals provided, she'd have us purchase butter for her that was set aside in another refrigerator with her name on it. It was always known that Helmi enjoyed her butter with hot rolls.

She thoroughly enjoyed the rabbi's visits when he made his rounds through the halls. He was always so kind to me and would encourage me toward the things of God. He was one of the first people I told I'd be making a trip to Israel when I was teaching. He was so happy for me to get to experience all the history there. (It was indeed an amazing and life-changing trip! Plan to go someday, if you're able.)

> (With the current turmoil and unrest in the region, may we be vigilant to pray for peace and healing of innocent lives affected on all sides. Lord willing, peace will resume in the area, and the region will fully reopen without restrictions so generations to come can experience the Holy Land. Only the Lord knows what will come of these painful times.)

Grandma Helmi also had her minister from her Lutheran church visit once or twice a month to serve her communion. She always requested that I be there to sing hymns and join her during that time. Such precious memories.

Their Legacies Live On

Both grandmothers passed away when I was in my thirties. In their later years, our visits were filled with listening to music together, sometimes with me singing or playing music for them on a tape recorder. Per their requests, I sang at their memorial services, which was a true honor, though bittersweet, as I knew it'd be the last time I'd sing for them. Grandma Mary requested "Ave Maria" by Franz Schubert, her favorite, and "Danny Boy," her favorite Irish song, so fitting for the sweet Irish girl she was, sung by all the ladies in our family. Grandma Helmi requested "Amazing Grace" and the tune of "Edelweiss" from *The Sound of Music* with different lyrics fitting for her:

> May the Lord, mighty Lord
> Bless and keep you forever
> Grant you peace, perfect peace
> A peace that endureth forever
> Close your eyes and see His face
> Know His grace forever
> May the Lord, mighty Lord
> Bless and keep you forever

Both grandmothers' lives were marked with love for their families and the Lord. I'm so thankful for the impact they had on my life, leaving such a lasting imprint on my heart. Two praying grandmothers through all those years—what an incredible gift and blessing! Is it any wonder God was on the move, and prayers were being answered in my life?

A God-Shaped Hole in Every Heart

After that night in front of the TV, Mom later explained she always knew of God's love for her when she was growing up, as was taught to her by the sisters at her parochial school, but felt ashamed of being a single mom. She thought God didn't love her or forgive her from her past. She was broken and felt she heard, for the first time, a Savior who loved her and wasn't out to judge her, who wanted to meet her right where she was and give her hope.

It is said that every person has a God-shaped hole in their heart. Just like a puzzle with a missing piece, it isn't complete until the right piece is found. If it was through a TV program that mom experienced that Jesus loved her, then it was indeed a very special and significant moment. Heaven came down to meet Mom right where she was, broken and in need of a Savior to fill her God-shaped hole in her heart. Watching God's transforming love break through her pain and wash over her that night through her tears was something I'll never forget!

If this moment was drawing Mom back to the Lord, we were happy! He'd seemed absent from the picture for quite a long while. Whenever we brought up wanting to go to mass, she was either too busy or too tired because of her two jobs to take us. I remember feeling so bad for her, wishing I could get a job to help pay the bills to take some of her burdens away. She was always so tired at the end of the day. My sister and I took it upon ourselves to help with all the household chores so she could sleep. She worked so hard; it made me feel so sad for her. I just wanted to fix her from all her problems, but I didn't know how.

Food for Thought: Ways to Help a Single Parent

If you want to volunteer or start a ministry, consider supporting a single parent. No matter the reason why they're single, they need loving, nonjudgmental help to walk alongside them and help them with their kids by giving them a break so they can rest, recharge, and tend to the things they need to get done. They need to be seen for who they are and not what their status says about them so they can be their true selves without feeling bombarded with a lot of questions. They most likely won't ask for help as they are just trying to survive.

When a child sees his or her parent suffer and doesn't know where to turn for help, it would be hoped that a caring adult would step in and help out. You may be the very help they need at that moment. Sometimes, you just need to step in and help carry their burden.

There are lots of ways you can help. Observe the situation and step in where you see a need, such as doing yard work, repairing their car, delivering a meal, or taking their child (children) to the park and ice cream after. The ideas are endless, as the needs are endless. Lean into their situations and bless them with your time, talent, and treasures. You will help lift a burden that will be deeply appreciated.

Mom's Jobs and Praying Friends

One of Mom's jobs was as a waitress at Hobo Joe's Diner. Unbeknownst to her, two ladies she worked with were Christians and were praying for her. They invited her to visit their Baptist church. She refused, mostly because she didn't want to dishonor her family. She politely said, "Thank you, but no thank you. I won't ever go to another church. It's not how I was raised. I'm a Catholic." When time and again, she refused to go, they asked her if she'd at least consider allowing her girls to go to their kids' program. They would provide transportation to get us there if she couldn't. That was enough for her to decide to give their church a try, especially after her episode of praying on the floor in front of the TV. She was wary of going to another church but figured there wasn't any harm in a kids' program for her girls to learn more about God, so she agreed we'd visit their church.

> (About this same time, Mom was introduced to Mary Kay Cosmetics through her cousin Paula, my godmother. Mom loved the product and started selling it to earn extra income. Mary Kay Ash, the founder, was a Christian who based her business model on Christian principles and was a great role model for Mom. A few women in Mom's division were Christians and encouraged her to trust in Jesus in all aspects of her life. Mom's Mary Kay journey has been a beautiful blessing in her life all these years.)

Mom's two friends drove over that next Sunday to pick us up for church. My sister and I felt uncomfortable going because we didn't have proper dresses or shoes to wear like the fancy ones we used to wear when Grandma Mary took us to church. All we had were last summer's matching sundresses that we wore when we were on the *Wallace and Ladmo Show*, a local TV program. It was all the rage for area kids our age to be on their show if they picked the picture that you mailed in. They chose our picture of us wearing matching tutu ballet skirts and slippers our aunt gave us for Christmas. We were so nervous to be on TV but so excited to be given a large Ladmo Bag packed with all kinds of goodies.

(We ended up being the last group to receive a large bag as groups after us received smaller bags. We felt so special! Getting a Ladmo Bag was such a big deal that I even brought mine in for show-and-tell when school started!)

Now, wearing our outgrown sundresses that no longer covered our knees, and wearing the same ballet slippers that got us on the *Ladmo Show*, we went to mom's friends' church. I figured we must've looked ridiculous in our summer dresses too small for us as we stepped off the open-air shuttle that drove us to the front doors of the church parking lot. I was certain everyone would look at us, and we'd be completely embarrassed, but no one commented or even seemed to notice our dresses or our slippers. What were we so worried about?

As a wide-eyed little girl, the experience was all new to me. There was a full choir in the front, an orchestra, a lady playing a grand piano, and a man playing an organ, with the large organ pipes hovering over the choir. The music was lively and majestic. The sunlight beamed through the stained-glass windows in the balcony, making everything look so vibrant. Everyone we met was friendly and welcoming.

The man at the front of this church was not wearing a robe, like I was used to seeing, nor was he called a priest; he was called a pastor. It was the beginning of my observing that each church might have a different style and delivery about God's love, like different homilies or different singing and praying. This church didn't have kneelers, but if what we were hearing and experiencing lined up with the same God we knew, and it referenced the same Bible we had heard stories from growing up, it felt OK for a new person—us, *me*, a child in a new place. Since these pieces were central and present, we listened with open hearts. Perhaps our experience was different that day, but it was what God was using to open our eyes and ears to see and hear about Jesus in a whole new way. If a prayer of confession and inviting Jesus into my life would draw me closer to God, I was listening.

I must pause a moment to share what God used from my earlier childhood faith. (*Never miss those things God uses to teach you more about Him.*) God was weaving all my early faith memories together to bring me to this day, whetting my appetite to learn more about Him, and answering some unknown questions, all the while keeping my affection toward my early childhood upbringing.

Childhood Snapshots That Shaped My Young Faith

It was apparent this new approach to forgiveness and connecting with God sounded and looked much different than what I was used to hearing and seeing. My understanding of confession was going before a priest in the confessional box that, to me, looked a bit like a fancy telephone booth. My imagination surmised that the priest was like the telephone operator, who gave God a message. In return, he would get a message back from God to share with people on what they needed to do for their sins. It wasn't out of any disrespect that I thought about these things, as I had very high reverence and regard for all church clergy. It was just how it played out in my young mind.

I must've visited the confessional at least once before my First Communion, which probably had something to do with my needing to confess that I needed to be nicer to my sister. We did have our sibling moments. It was explained to us in our catechism class that our father, the priest, would guide us through our confession time and would end with saying comforting words over us, such as, "Your sins are forgiven. Now go in peace, child."

For my First Holy Communion at age eight, I wore a pretty white-lace dress, fancy white shoes with white ruffled socks, and a white veil. Family came for the special occasion. I was given my first rosary as a gift from Grandma Mary. During the reception, our priest, our parish's nuns, and the church laypeople who helped at the parish were acknowledged. Grandma Mary extended personal thanks of gratitude to them for their help over the years to our little family of three—Mom, my sister, and me.

At the start of mass every Sunday, Grandma Mary would always light candles for those she was praying for. With her assistance, she'd allow me to light some too. A hush of quiet filled the air, as the mood was always very reverent. Candles were placed around the sides of the church, in the back, and some around the statues of the Virgin Mary and the crucified Christ. I felt deep sadness when looking into Jesus' eyes, wondering why He was punished so harshly. I had a longing to connect with Jesus but didn't know how. As for Mary holding baby Jesus, she had a halo atop her head, perhaps the reason why they call her the Blessed Mother of God. One statue had a snake under Mary's feet. Perhaps she crushed it to protect baby Jesus. I never fully understood it all, but it was always very peaceful, especially when the choir's angelic voices sang in the balcony with their hallowed echoes surrounding the parish.

Appreciating My Faith Roots

Whenever I attend a mass for a wedding or funeral, it feels a bit like putting on an old sweater. There's something comfortable and familiar about it all. With my eyes closed, I go back in time and see Grandma Mary on a prayer kneeler, praying her rosary.

When Notre Dame Cathedral went up in flames right before Easter of 2019, it was heartbreaking to watch. People from all faiths around the world were deeply saddened by the raging fires brought upon the 850-year-old iconic architectural landmark in

Paris. Beauty from ashes was on display as the cross at the altar stood tall and unscathed by the flames. What an encouraging sight! As Archbishop Michel Aupetit of Paris said, "Here we move from the scandal of death to the mystery of the resurrection. Our hope will never disappoint us because it is based not on buildings of stone ... but on the Risen One who remains forever."[1]

A month later, more disheartening news—St Joseph's Catholic Church, a staple for decades in our metro area, went up in flames. Many of my high school friends' families attended this church. Seeing my friends share their memories on social media took me back to my early faith roots, for which I am thankful.

Meeting Jesus in a Whole New Light

Taking into consideration my faith journey thus far, going to God myself and asking for forgiveness was a new concept to me. I'm sure it was something I had yet to learn, but I certainly did not feel important enough, as I was just a child. How could this big God listen to me? It seemed too simple. There had to be more.

A verse I heard for the first time that day stayed with me:

> For God so loved the world that he gave His one
> and only Son, that whoever believes in Him shall
> not perish, but have eternal life. (John 3:16 NIV)

Was it true He loved me just the way I was—in my ballet slippers and that too-small-for-me sundress? Was He a loving Father who gave His very best to me? How could this be? It was something I had never experienced before. It might have resonated with me for obvious reasons—not having a father prominently in the picture at the time—but I loved that moment of realization. Every part of it.

I now understood what Mom prayed for in front of our TV that night. She prayed for Jesus to come into her life, to give her hope and a future. Something that resonated with her that night from Billy Graham's sermon was, "Faith points us beyond our problems to the hope we have in Christ."[2]

Turning from her *old* life of sin and pain and coming into a *new* life, free and forgiven in Christ, was what her heart desired. She did not hesitate then to walk down the aisle that Sunday morning when the pastor asked if anyone wanted to come forward for prayer and make a public profession of faith to follow Jesus. With eyes filled with tears, she made her way down to the front. Seeing how much joy Mom had after that moment, I walked the aisle the next week, saying a simple prayer from the heart, probably something like, "Lord, thank you for loving me. Thank you for Your Son, Jesus, who died for me and forgives me of my sins. Come live inside me. Change me and make me new. In Jesus' name I pray, amen." My sister walked the aisle to accept Jesus as her personal Lord and Savior the following Wednesday night.

Being Baptized

That next Sunday, we were all baptized together. That was a super-special moment! We had previously been baptized when we were christened as infants. When baptized as an infant, your given name—first, middle, or both—is to reflect that of a canonized saint's name. My given name, Christine Marie, fit the bill.

Before I was born, my mom thought for sure I'd be a boy, as ultrasounds weren't a thing then, but when I was a girl, and she needed to decide on a name, my mom's aunts liked the name Tina, who was a soap star at the time. The closest saint's name to Tina was Saint Christina, sometimes referred to as Christine, who tended to the poor and needy in the third century and was a martyr for her Christian faith. The Greek translation of *Christine* is a "female follower of Christ." Saint Marie was the patron saint of laughter and joy. I am indeed a follower of Christ, who has a tenderness toward others, and I love to laugh, and I have joy! Thanks, Mom and my great-aunts who named me. God knew!

This baptism would be different. We were so excited about it. It was a full-body immersion in a heated mini-pool baptismal above the choir loft area so everyone could see and witness our baptisms. We would get dunked underwater! Mom went first, then my sister, then me. I was the shortest, so I stood on a stool to see over the edge. Being dunked, we learned, symbolizes being buried in the *old* life of sin, and coming up out of the water is having a *new* revived and restored life.

> In baptism we show that we have been saved from death and doom by the resurrection of Christ; not because our bodies are washed clean by the water but because in being baptized we are turning to God and asking Him to cleanse our hearts from sin. (1 Peter 3:21 TLB)

When we all finished, we hugged each other in the baptismal waters, and our pastor, Pastor Jackson, who had baptized us, gave me a kiss on the head. Everyone cheered and the choir sang.

Baptism is a beautiful picture of new life in Christ. It is not earned through works and is not intended to secure a place in church membership by a certain age or a certain measure of good deeds done. On the contrary, baptism is instead God's loving grace, through Jesus' gift of salvation on the cross, being poured out over a living person, once trapped and dead in sin and now alive.

> For it is by grace (God's remarkable compassion
> and favor drawing you to Christ) that you have
> been saved (delivered from judgment and given
> eternal life) through faith. And this (salvation)
> is not of yourself (not through your own effort),
> but is the (undeserved, gracious) gift of God.
> (Ephesians 2:8 AMP)

Once we committed our lives to Christ and were baptized, everything changed for us. The dark cloud that overshadowed Mom had disappeared. She was more alive and seemed happier and more joyful than she had been in the past, and our lives seemed to move in a more positive direction with more purpose. We felt excited about this new life we had stepped into and the support and love that came with it.

New People Who Loved Us and Family Who Were Always There

Most significant on my young heart in those early months, after asking Jesus into our hearts, was the impact of people we didn't even know leaving anonymous bags of food and clothing on our doorstep. I asked Mom, "Who would do this?" We were all a bit shocked in disbelief that people would serve us in such selfless ways. It's something I'll never forget.

The Lord knew we needed help. We were living on food stamps, and our living conditions were such that our apartment had huge sewer cockroaches. I remember jumping from one piece of furniture to another to avoid stepping on one that might scurry across the floor in my path. They freaked me out!

These kind-hearted people even helped us get into a nicer place to live that wasn't infested with bugs. Much of our rent that first year was paid for—wow! The way they served us unconditionally left a deep imprint on my soul that would be the cornerstone of my heart that I'd follow all the days of my life. It was how Jesus treated and loved others, loving the hurting, the forgotten, the hungry, the outcast. That's who we felt we were at times, but God changed all of that. He showed us love in such practical ways.

Mom's friends' Bible-believing church became our church. We wanted to be there every day the doors were open to take in everything they had to offer. We were there Sunday mornings for Sunday school and church, Sunday night church, Monday night dinner and outreach to families, and Wednesday night children's choir and church. (My love for singing grew from those early years of being in the children's choir, and I'm so very thankful.) It was our home away from home, with people who became our family, our newfound church family.

Mom's friends' prayers weren't about pulling Mom from one church or denomination to another. They were instead about showing the persistent love of the Lord to Mom, an emotionally frail person in need of a doctor of the soul. They met her right where she was, introducing her to Jesus, who heals all wounds. My sister and I are eternally grateful for those two unknown prayer warriors who faithfully prayed for our mom.

And without fail, our extended family always loved us in such beautiful ways. Their sacrifices to us were such a gift, filling our childhood with wonderful memories. Support from friends and family who showed up in our lives were indicators that God always knows exactly what we need right when we need it. He is such a good, good God!

> And my God will supply every need of yours according to his riches in glory in Christ Jesus. (Philippians 4:19 ESV)

I Am a Child of God

In my enthusiastic young faith, I wanted everyone I knew to meet this Jesus who loved us so profoundly. Even when I felt scared or confused, He calmed my anxious heart. He was the real deal! He was mine, and I was His. I was His child, a daughter of the almighty King.

The song "No Longer Slaves"[3] says so much about the condition of a heart ready to release all to Jesus. A newfound relationship with Christ is so rich and hopeful that no matter the brokenness from the past, God heals and delivers a person through His Son, Jesus! There is such power and beauty at the cross of forgiveness with new life in Christ. Here are some of the song's lyrics. Turn it up on your streaming device. It's awesome.

> You surround me with a song
> Of deliverance from my enemies
> 'Til all my fears are gone
> I'm no longer a slave to fear
> My fears are drowned in perfect love
> You rescued me, I am a child of God

I'm so thankful Jesus saved me! He is the air I breathe. I owe Him everything. That is why you're holding this book in your hands. His love is greater than any pain I endured or will endure in years to come. He was and always is pursuing me. He's pursuing you too!

> That God was reconciling the world to himself in Christ, not counting people's sins against them. And he has committed to us the message of reconciliation. (2 Corinthians 5:19 NIV)

I can always look back and thank God for the faith heritage He instilled in me. And I'm forever grateful He turned my eyes to Christ, for I was a lost soul in need of a Savior. Jesus was thirty-three and single and had an eternal purpose. He loved me that much, and He loves you that much too. He gave His all on the day history changed forever.

> The biggest moment in all of history was 33 AD when God reconciled Himself to mankind through Jesus who died to save people from their sins.[4]
>
> —Luke Simmons, Lead Pastor,
> Ironwood Church

Closing Thoughts

After writing this chapter, it became clear to me that I needed to hone in on questions such as, what makes these Christians tick? As well, I needed to address topics that helped me gauge the waters of faith, from understanding my relationship with Christ to understanding why that relationship is important and why the Bible is important, along with how a church helps you grow. Expanding upon such themes turned into chapter 10. It has probably become *the* most important chapter in this book. If it hadn't been for Jesus intervening in my heart as a child, I wouldn't have a story to share with you at all! God saves the lost. He is the author and finisher of our faith. Amen and amen.

> Jesus, the author, and finisher of our faith, who for the joy that was set before Him endured the cross. (Hebrews 12:2 NKJV)

He is the whole reason for my story. It is His story lived out in me, just like He is writing your story for you to share. Don't ever hesitate to share your story. Someone may very well need it! They will relate to you as you show them what God has done in your life. I can look back now and see how God was in the middle of it all, from my days as a little girl at church with Grandma Mary to those two praying friends of Mom's, all the way to present life, this day, this moment. He is always there and never misses a beat! I'm so thankful God stuck it out with me and saw me through. Thank you, Lord.

He'll see you through too. Just trust Him.

> Trust in the Lord with all your heart and lean not on your own understanding; in all your ways acknowledge Him, and He shall direct your paths. (Proverbs 3:5–6 NKJV)

Thank you, Jesus, for Your vast, unfailing love that never fails. Amen.

> Your love, O Lord, reaches to the heavens, your faithfulness to the skies. Your righteousness is like the highest mountains, your justice like the great deep. You, Lord, preserve both people and animals. How priceless is your unfailing love, O God! People take refuge in the shadow of your wings. (Psalm 36:5–6 NIV)

CHAPTER 10

What Religion Am I?

Whenever I'm asked what religion I am, my answer is heartfelt. It is always my desire to convey my deep love for Jesus over being a religious person. People who are not religious might associate religion with judgment and narrow-mindedness. As you can see from my faith journey of meeting Jesus as a child, God used all those different faith experiences and beautiful, loving people along my life's journey to get to my heart and help me know the core of God's love. God uses that which He may—some to plant, some to water, some to toil, some to pluck—but it was Jesus who opened my eyes.

People are genuinely more interested in knowing what you believe, how you define Jesus, and why He matters to you. If religion is seen as a big set of unattainable rules, then religion is an idol and an obstacle to getting to Jesus, rather than a relationship with Him. Jesus came and changed all of that! A phrase related to parenting by author and speaker Josh McDowell speaks to this notion: "Rules without relationship lead to rebellion."[1] How true that is! If a parent disciplines without love or doesn't have an established relationship built on trust, is it any wonder a child dismisses that parent later on in life? It's the same with our relationship with God.

If we don't feel loved, we'll feel judged. Many dismiss God because all they see are rules and not a relationship. Let love be what they see in you.

> Judge not, and you will not be judged; condemn not, and you will not be condemned; forgive, and you will be forgiven. (Luke 6:37 ESV)

> Treat others as you want them to treat you. (Luke 6:31 TLB)

> Instead, be kind and tender-hearted to one another, and forgive one another, as God has forgiven you through Christ. (Ephesians 4:32 GNT)

I Am a Sinner Saved by Grace. I Am a Christian

Think of it this way: religion, even at its best attempt, falls short. Its sole purpose is mankind's attempt to get to God. A relationship, on the other hand, flips that upside down. Relationship with Jesus is not man-made but God-given! He gave Himself. He gave *relationship* as a free gift, not to be earned but to be received. When you're handed a wrapped gift, you naturally open your hands to receive that gift. You didn't earn it or ask for it; it was given to you, and you gladly receive it (or you reject it). This gift is the free gift of Jesus, no strings attached! You receive Him as your own, or you reject Him. To receive a gift, you unwrap it and delight in what's inside. To receive the gift of Jesus is to receive the gift of salvation, free to you. It's paid for by Jesus' own blood that He willingly gave to you, and it reveals the heart of God, lovingly embracing you and wrapping you in His grace. He gives you hope and love, as a father gives to a child. God has adopted you into His family, ready and willing to walk with you all the days of your life and to have an intimate and personal relationship with you on this new journey of faith to which He calls you. Without a doubt, Jesus is *the* best gift you will *ever* receive—eternity guaranteed!

The 2017 movie *The Case for Christ*[2] (based on the best-selling book by the same title) is the true story of Lee Strobel's life as an atheist journalist. He spent much of his early career trying to disprove his wife's Christian faith and to prove that Jesus didn't exist. It's a movie for everyone, especially if you've ever pondered the existence of God. He wrestles with facts to come to his conclusion—I'll let you watch or read for yourself. It's a well-made movie worth your time, even if just watching the trailer to gain an understanding of what he went through in his search for truth. In the movie, the statement "He was either a liar, a lunatic, or Lord" is pondered. Perfect segue. Who do you say He is? What are you going to do with this Jesus, this free gift? If your heartstrings are tugged, would you take this free gift? It is waiting for you and ready to be unwrapped!

The short answer to the question of my religion is that I am a sinner, saved by grace. I am a Christian, which means "Christ-follower," a Jesus lover. But for those who want to go deeper, Jesus accepted me in my brokenness. I didn't have to clean myself up to receive His gift of salvation that poured over me through His unconditional love and forgiveness. I live every day in the freedom of Christ and His redeeming love for me.

> Christianity does not teach a works-based salvation. You are justified by grace through faith in Christ alone. A Christian obeys not to maintain salvation, but obeys out of love and gratitude, and acts as the new creation they are because of the relationship they have in Christ.[3]

> And if by grace, then it cannot be based on works;
> if it were, grace would no longer be grace. (Romans
> 11:6 NIV)

The piece below speaks to the condition of a lost soul in need of a Savior. It's from a class I took at church called Bible Boot Camp (the class name alone, right? It was a *very* intense course but was super-good! I'd definitely recommend classes like this that help you learn more about God and the Bible.)

> Whatever we live for has control over us. It may
> be career, possessions, appearance, romance, peer
> groups, achievement, good causes, moral character,
> religion, marriage, children, friendships, or a
> combination of several. We do not control ourselves.
> The things we live for enslave us with guilt (if we fail
> to attain them), anger (if someone blocks them from
> us), fear (if they are threatened), an unhealthy drive
> (since we must have them), or despair (if we ever lose
> them completely). This means, then, even the most
> irreligious people are really worshipping something.
> Whatever thing or things from which we choose to
> derive our value become the ultimate meaning in our
> lives—thus it serves as a 'god' and gives us a sense
> of worth or 'righteousness' even if we don't think in
> those terms. Even the most religious people are not
> really worshipping God. Religious people may look
> to God as Helper, Teacher, and Example, but it is
> their moral performance which is serving as their
> Savior. They are just as guilty and self-hating if they
> fail it, just as angry and resentful if someone blocks
> it, just as fearful and anxious if something threatens
> it, just as driven to be good. So, both religious and

irreligious people are avoiding God as Savior and Lord but in different ways. Both are seeking to keep control of their own lives by looking to something besides God as their salvation. (*The Gospel—A User's Guide Introduction*, Bible Boot Camp) [4]

Because sin entered the human heart in the garden, we are relentlessly prone to our sin nature all the time; we are constantly in bondage of our sin. A sinner—that's all of us—sins. "As it is written, there is none righteous, no not one" (Romans 3:10 KJV). A sin, simply put, is going against God, knowingly or unknowingly. When you know so, you feel it in the pit of your gut but do so anyway. No matter if it is big or small, all of it separates us from God. There is nothing we can do to save ourselves.

All have sinned and fall short of the glory of God. (Romans 3:23 NIV)

Only God can rescue His creation from their sin by becoming that blameless, perfect Lamb through His Son, Jesus, when Christ enters the scene as the new covenant in the New Testament. Jesus is God's perfect, righteous, and divine plan, who came as our Redeemer, the chosen Messiah, to free all who would believe and call upon His name, so they no longer are captive to their own sin but freed from their transgressions. Jesus, the spotless Lamb, takes away our sins (Jesus, the Passover Lamb—1 Corinthians 5:7).

The Passover Lamb

The parallel of atonement for sins between the Old Testament and the New Testament is astounding! When God rescued His people from the hands of Pharaoh, He used a spotless lamb.

In Exodus 12, God told Moses to order the Israelite families to sacrifice a spotless male lamb and mark their doorposts across the top and along the sides with its blood. That night, God would execute judgment upon Egypt by passing through the land to strike dead all firstborn of both people and animals in Egypt. Death would "pass over" the homes with the lamb's blood. Today, a Passover Seder dinner commemorates what the Lord did for His people.

> This is a day you are to commemorate; for the generations to come you shall celebrate it as a festival to the Lord, a lasting ordinance. (Exodus 12:14 NIV)

Jesus is God's ransom (a payment to set a prisoner free), who sets people free from their sins. He paid our debt through His blood on the cross. Jesus has an everlasting love and lived a sinless, purpose-filled life—even unto death. He is the perfect Lamb of God.

> He was oppressed and afflicted, yet He did not open His mouth; He was led like a lamb to the slaughter, and as a sheep before its shearers is silent, so He did not open His mouth. (Isaiah 53:7 NIV)

> The next day he (John) saw Jesus coming toward him, and said, "Behold, the Lamb of God who takes away the sin of the world!" (John 1:29 ESV)

He freed people from their sins, such as in the Old Testament when a spotless lamb was used as a sacrifice to cover one's sins. God changed the old law when God incarnate (which means taking on a bodily form) was conceived in the womb of Mary and was born—the Christmas "Emmanuel, God with us" story (Luke 2:1–20)—lived a perfect life, and died for the sins of mankind, and rose again—the Easter Resurrection story (Matthew 28:1–20). He is God. God, Jesus, and His Spirit are three in one. (Verses on the Triune nature of God: 1 Corinthians 8:6; 2 Corinthians 3:17; 13:14; Colossians 2:9; Isaiah 9:6; 44:6, John 1:14; 10:30; 14:16–17; Luke 1:35; Matthew 3:16–17.)

Jesus comes into the hearts of anyone who puts their trust and faith in Him. You're born again, which simply means you've turned away from your old way of life through the loving grace of Jesus, not through a bunch of rules but in a relationship with Him. Read Nicodemus's story in John 3:1–21. Nicodemus asks Jesus, "How can a man be born again when he is old? Can he enter a second time into his mother's womb to be born?" Fair question. See what Jesus tells him.

When Jesus had His last meal with His disciples before He went to the cross, it was on the night of Passover (the Last Supper—Matthew 26:17–30).

> He took bread, blessed it and broke it and gave it to His disciples, and said, "Take eat; this is my body." (Matthew 26:26)

> Then He took the cup, and when he had given thanks he gave it to them saying, "Drink of it, all of you, for this is my blood of the covenant, which is poured out for many for the forgiveness of sins." (Matthew 26:28–29)

Wine represented the new covenant, a new wine.

> I am the true vine, and my Father is the gardener ...
> Remain in me, as I also remain in you. No branch
> can bear fruit by itself; it must remain in the vine.
> Neither can you bear fruit unless you remain in
> me. (John 15:1, 4 NIV)

> I am the bread of life. Whoever comes to me will
> never go hungry, and whoever believes in me will
> never be thirsty. (John 6:35 NIV)

Christ was the spilled blood of a spotless lamb on the cross to
spare our lives, just as the spotless lamb's blood spared lives from
death and set free the captives of slavery during the first Passover.
His life now spares those sheep who call Him the Good Shepherd.

> I am the good shepherd. The good shepherd lays
> down His life for the sheep. (John 10:11 NIV)

We are all sheep, walking around aimlessly, not knowing
what's around the corner. We need a shepherd!

There Are Many Shepherds. Which One Will You Follow?

Washing Feet

> If you're not following the right shepherd, what will
> happen when trouble comes? If you're following a
> counterfeit shepherd, you're left for ruin. Isn't it
> worth considering if you're following the wrong
> shepherd to turn and run? If Jesus is indeed the
> Good Shepherd who willingly laid down His life

for His sheep (John 10:11), why, then, wouldn't you follow Him?

At the Last Supper with His disciples, Jesus initiates a picture of greatness by washing their feet—not how the world defines greatness but how this humble king, one fit for royalty, got down on His knees and washed their feet, displaying love in a lowly act of servanthood. His ministry would soon come to an end on earth, but He chose to display kindness, compassion, and gentleness. He took their dirt and filth upon Himself, onto a towel draped on Him, to wash them clean as an example of His final act of service yet to come. Taking the sins of the world upon Himself on a cruel cross demonstrated His deep love for us. He instructed His disciples to go out and do the same. And as followers of Christ, we are called to do the same, even if we're inconvenienced or even if it's messy. Like Jesus, always serve with love and humility. (Sermon notes from *Loved Walked among Us*, within the series *Jesus Washes His Disciples' Feet*, from John 13:1–17)[5]

How to Meet Jesus

If you've not had a personal experience with Jesus, pray to receive Him as your own right now. He loves you and wants to be your personal Lord and Savior. Jesus is the only way to truth, the only One who saves sinners. Attaining favor in one's religion will not save you. It's a man-made attempt to reach God. Only a relationship with Jesus—and Him alone—will spare a person's ultimate judgment. The thief on the cross is an excellent example of this point. By all accounts, he didn't lead an upright life by the standards of the law. Yet while the other thief hurled insults at Jesus, this man saw no judgment should befall this innocent man, whose life was flawless. He recognized Jesus as the Savior for whom the bystanders were looking. He said to Jesus, "Remember me when You come into Your kingdom." Jesus then said to him, "Truly I say to you, today you shall be with Me in Paradise." (The story in its entirety can be found in Luke 23:39–43.)

> Jesus told him, "I am the way, the truth, and the life. No one comes to the Father except through me." (John 14:6 ESV)

If you don't have a personal relationship with Jesus, don't delay! It's the best decision you will *ever* make. It will change your life and your eternity for the better! God doesn't want you to clean yourself up to prove your love to Him or try to be good enough for Him to love and accept you. Instead, He wants you to cry out to Him, "Help me, Jesus!" The moment you realize you can't do anything without the Lord in your life is the moment you embrace Jesus' finished work on the cross for you. Invite Jesus into your heart right now through a simple, childlike prayer, like the one I shared earlier when I was a child meeting Jesus. Let it come from your heart in your own words. He is listening!

> If you openly declare that Jesus is Lord and believe in your heart that God raised Him from the dead, you will be saved. (Romans 10:9 NLT)

> Everyone who calls upon the name of the Lord will be saved. (Acts 2:21 NIV)

The moment one turns to the Lord with an open
heart, the veil is lifted and they see. (2 Corinthians
3:16 TPT)

Welcome to the Family of God

If you just prayed a prayer of salvation to accept Jesus as your
personal Lord and Savior, welcome to the family of God! His work
on the cross is now all the victory in your life. Your news of having
new life in Christ is the best news there could *ever* be. Your story
is now God's story. Share it!

> Therefore if anyone is in Christ, he is a new
> creature; the old things passed away, behold, new
> things have come. (2 Corinthians 5:17 NASB)

> May I never boast except in the cross of our Lord
> Jesus Christ, through which the world has been
> crucified to me, and I to the world. (Galatians
> 6:14 NIV)

> We are therefore Christ's ambassadors, as though
> God were making his appeal through us. (2
> Corinthians 5:20a NIV)

Once a Christian, How Does My Life Change?

When you invite Jesus into your heart, the Holy Spirit takes up
residency in your life. If you belong to God, He is with you; He is
for you. You don't have to be afraid! You go from darkness to light,
weakness to strength, despair to hope, guilt to innocence, tears to
joy, and from death to life.

Thirty-Three & Single

> At one time you lived in darkness. Now you are
> living in the light that comes from the Lord.
> (Ephesians 5:8a NLV)

New life in Christ starts to melt away the yearnings of your old life while new affections for Christ start to take hold. No need to turn back. We are sinners saved by grace who need a makeover, a heart change. It's an ongoing process of God transforming us and rescuing us from ourselves at every turn. Christian artist, Tauren Wells, has a song called "God's Not Done with You."[6] The bridge speaks to this very point.

> He's got a plan.
> This is part of it.
> He's gonna finish what He started.
> God's not done, writing your story.
> God's not done with you.

What great encouragement! The work of the Holy Spirit comes inside of us to give us the power to overcome sin and temptation. We are sanctified (the process of being made holy) by the Holy Spirit when we learn to trust God more through the love and discipline of the Holy Spirit in our lives.

God wants you to trust Him at all times. He wants you to have complete reliance on Him for every breath you take and every thought you have, and He wants you to talk with Him (pray) about everything. He wants to be Lord over your entire life. The faith journey is a lifelong walk with Jesus, who is patient with you and never gives up on you. It is worth repeating: God is with you, and He is for you! When temptation from your old life creeps in, He will be there, providing a way of escape, freeing you from those things that keep you in bondage, and allowing you to walk, instead, in new life with Him.

No temptation has overtaken you except what is common to mankind. And God is faithful; He will not let you be tempted beyond what you can bear. But when you are tempted, He will also provide a way out so that you can endure it. (1 Corinthians 10:13 NIV)

Peeled Back One Layer at a Time

Like an onion, our lives have many layers that are peeled back, one layer at a time, through sanctification by the Holy Spirit. He transforms us, making us new, bringing forth Jesus to shine through our lives.

You are the light of the world. A city set on a hill cannot be hidden. Nor do people light a lamp and put it under a basket, but on a stand, and it gives light to all in the house. In the same way, let your light shine before others, so that they may see your good works and give glory to your Father who is in heaven. (Matthew 5:14–16 ESV)

We cannot be a light standing alone on a hill—no. Instead, our light shines through the community we are a part of. Why does that matter? Why not just be an island all alone? It begs the question: why be a part of something, let alone anything? More specifically, why attend church? Maybe a more personal question you're asking is, what's so important about church, and how does any of this pertain to me? Let's dig deeper.

It's important to understand that a church does not save you. Only God saves you. If God has tugged on your heartstrings to follow Him, He's calling you to be a part of where He is at work, where His Son sets people free from their sins through the teaching of His Word, and where His Spirit dwells among His body, whose gaze is set on Him. People are the church, and Christ is the head. Don't miss that—they go together like a ball and glove, cookies and milk, peanut butter and jelly, chips and dip. It's a beautiful picture of the marriage covenant. Christ is the bridegroom, and we are His bride, the church.

I attend a local nondenominational Christian church where I'm loved and fed (spiritually speaking), and I participate, but I have brothers and sisters in Christ the world over who I'll never know or meet this side of heaven who also put their trust in Jesus, follow Him, and love Him. We are a global church family—*disciples* (followers of Jesus)—comprised of every race, tongue, tribe, and nation.

> Christ, the Bridegroom, has sacrificially and lovingly chosen the church (comprised of all who trust in Jesus all over the world as their personal Lord and Savior), to be His bride " … as Christ loved the church and gave himself up for her, that he might sanctify her, having cleansed her by the washing of water with the word." (Ephesians 5:25a ESV)[7]

Church is my fuel to get me through the week. The church is my family and community. It's where I learn from God's Word how to live my life to be more loving and kinder. His Word pours over me, and my faith grows. I go to a Bible-believing church where I am loved. Jesus meets me right where I am, in my mess, as He says, "Come to me, all you who are weary and burdened, and I will give you rest" (Matthew 11:28 NIV).

For certain, it's a much different conversation to have than answering, "What religion are you?" It takes their eyes off a place, denomination, and location and puts their eyes on that which matters most—Jesus!

Pray about a church you can get plugged into where you can be fed the Word of God (the Bible), the most essential and *only* ingredient needed as the foundational cornerstone when selecting a new church home that will grow your faith. A verse that speaks to the authority of God's Word says this:

> The whole Bible was given to us by inspiration from God and is useful to teach us what is true and to make us realize what is wrong in our lives; it straightens us out and helps us do what is right. It is God's way of making us well prepared at every point, fully equipped to do good to everyone. (2 Timothy 3:16–17 TLB)

Spiritualism

Knowing how important community is in a Bible-believing and teaching church, how does the church, His body (followers of Jesus all over the world), withstand differing views of spiritualism? And how do these viewpoints impact young adults today?

There's an interesting statistic on the matter. A Pew Research report surveyed millennials, ages twenty to thirty-five, in a large metro area of Arizona and neighboring cities, and found that "three out of every five classified themselves as 'none' about identifying with a religion." This means that more than half the targeted population, 61 percent, isn't engaged in any church life. "They've become the fastest-growing segment of people affiliating themselves with the religion category of 'none.' Other cities across the US would most likely sample similarly, expressing their concerns toward organized religions." (Luke Simmons, sermon notes). [8]

Some statements below are different reasons Luke (as a pastor) has heard of why a person doesn't attend church, and some statements added are some reasons I've heard from young adults over the years. Some reasons stem from church hurt where a wall goes up when you engage in conversation on the topic. Others have felt church isn't important or necessary. Do any of these resonate with you?

- Church isn't my thing, but I'm happy for you that you found something for you.
- There is no sense or need that I ought to go to church. My life is fine without it.
- I like my Sundays off. I work hard all week long and don't need to fill my day off with things like that. I have other things to do.
- Been there, done that. It didn't do anything for me before, so I don't need it now.
- Church is filled with hypocrites and judgmental people. I don't need that in my life.
- Church has no place for doubt. Too narrow and rigid for me, completely fake, not authentic, just not my thing.

(If one or more of these statements *does* resonate with you, I'd encourage you to try church again, even if it means trying a new church. Jesus, through a Bible-believing community, is there for you with open arms! If you don't want to go for yourself, go for the child within you who has an open heart, mind, and soul because God has *so* much for you and wants to meet you there! If you've been hurt by church in the past, I'm so sorry. I pray you find healing to move past the pain. People are there to help you grow from that place. Don't lose hope!)

With these types of statements, *spirituality*, like New Age, is undoubtedly a popular viewpoint that gains momentum for different spiritual paths, such as humanism (the belief that human needs and values are more important than religious beliefs; creates one's own set of ethics), pantheism (a doctrine that identifies God with the universe or regards the universe as a manifestation of God), polytheism (a belief in many gods), atheism (the absence of God), or agnosticism (neither faith nor disbelief in God; skeptic, doubter, cynic), just to name a few.

As spirituality maneuvers to cultivate culture, the global faith community around the world—made up of Christ-followers who attend Bible-believing Christian churches in person, online, in homes, or underground meetings in closed nations—have the important task of stepping up and telling the world how Jesus radically changes lives through hope. Now more than ever, with all the world events going on today, the world needs *hope*! People need hope. When people share Jesus with others, people come to know *hope* in Jesus. Such is the story in Acts 17:16–31. (Be sure to read it. It is super-good.) In it, Paul sets the example to point people to Christ, which was the better way to go than the idol-worshipping way they were practicing in their day.

Today is not a far stretch from Paul's day in Athens. People are intrigued with spiritual matters and want to engage in conversation. To that point, meet people where they are by finding common ground. Go as far as inviting them to church. Don't be afraid. Trust God. Just like Mom's friends back when I was a kid, invite people to church. I'm so glad they did! It starts with one person asking. A person may say no to your invitation, but at least you asked. The fun part is, they may say yes!

20% of those 61% surveyed, said they'd most likely
go to church if someone invited them, but no one

ever invited them. What an incredible opportunity the Lord has given us! God has put in the heart of man to connect with Him. (Luke Simmons, sermon notes) [8]

Without God, Life is Empty

Without God, there is a void we try to fill with everything under the sun. We fill it with hobbies, work, relationships, travel, worldly possessions, and so on, but nothing fits perfectly—only Jesus. That void, that hole, needs the right piece. Jesus is that missing piece. God, through His Son, Jesus, is the *peacemaker*. Help someone find his or her missing piece—the overwhelming love and unwavering *peace* of Jesus!

#JesusIsBetter

Pastor Trey, from a neighboring church that used to meet at a Harkins Theater—isn't that incredibly cool? They met at a movie theater! God is on the move everywhere—came to talk to our young-adult group a few times to share his life message of "#JesusIsBetter"[9]. Trey is the author of *The Non-Anxious Pastor*; as well, he has his own YouTube channel to feature faith moments. One video tells of a few unchurched people who were so moved when they first came to visit his church, Passion Creek. The outcome of God moving in their stories is truly beautiful.

A young adult girl in her early twenties:

I was depressed and suicidal. I tried killing myself once. I never learned about God or Jesus. I didn't know anything. It was like He didn't exist. When

I first came to church, I heard a message about Jesus that just laid it out, that Jesus died for my sins. That like just blew my mind! I started to get depressed again. It was really hard for me because when I did become a Christian, I thought I would never have to deal with that again. And so, with Jesus, I feel like He's already taken care of all this for me. He's already fought that battle for me.

A male vocal artist:

It was something that was new to me. I gave up everything that I thought was right before. Giving up those things never compared to the way I felt when I first came to church, which was unbelievable. I wanted to learn more about God. To realize that, you know, He is first, and it is an audience of one, and me being a singer, I've always been so used to an audience and wanting it to be a big audience. I always worried about how many people were in the audience, what they thought, and what they expected from me? I don't know how to handle it; you know what I mean? And that's something that when you go to church, and you can have a family and a community that you can share with, then all of a sudden, the struggle you go through in life, you have someone there with you. It really makes a difference!

A young-adult single mom:

It was hard for me to accept Jesus the first time I went to church, even though I wanted to, but I loved going, and I kept going. I just really wanted it to all make sense, but growing up with *no* answers, it was hard for me to just accept something right off the bat. My dream and my passion are guiding my family, and the ones I care about in my life and showing them that Jesus is the answer to all these things.

What a beautiful final line: *Jesus is the answer to all these things.* Amen and amen. If you are a part of that 61 percent, open your heart to what's out there for you with God. You won't be disappointed—I promise. Jesus *really* is better! Even if you're fearful of stepping into the things of God, He is there for you to grab hold of Him. It's like the message in Dr. Seuss's book *Green Eggs and Ham*—once you try it, you'll like it! In fact, you'll *love* it!

I Love God. I Don't Need Church

Let's look a little closer. Have you ever said, "I love God; that's enough, I don't need church." Opinions are fine, but what's important is what God says on the matter.

> To Him be glory in the Church and in Christ Jesus throughout all generations, forever and ever, amen. (Ephesians 3:21 NIV)

> Christ rules there above all heavenly rulers, authorities, powers, and lords; He has a title superior to all titles of authority in this world and in the next. God put all things under Christ's feet and gave Him to the church as supreme Lord over all things. The church is Christ's body, the

completion of Him who Himself completes all things everywhere. (Ephesians 1:21–23 GNT)

All of you together are in Christ's body, and each of you is a part of it. (1 Corinthians 12:27 NLT)

Let us rejoice and exult, and give Him the glory, for the marriage of the Lamb has come, and His Bride has made herself ready. (Revelation 19:7 ESV)

It is true that God loves the assembly of His body—the church, His bride—to be in fellowship with His Son, the bridegroom, Christ. Church may not be your thing or a place you feel called to, but I'd encourage you to check it out, especially if God designed it as Jesus' bride. His Holy Spirit, through His Word, is the authority over it, so it's definitely worth going. He wants to meet you there! You're not an island. God did not create you that way. You were made for community with others. You need others around you, and others need you around them! Don't miss out on what God has for you at church.

Community Is Essential

Find community within the church you commit to so you can build relationships with others. Look for a healthy, fruitful church where your faith will be challenged and uplifted through solid Bible teaching while joining others who are like you—broken and in need of a Savior.

Let us not give up the habit of meeting together, as some are doing. Instead, let us encourage one another even more. (Hebrews 10:25a GNT)

Through community, you will help each other when needs arise and will help those who are longing to know God's love and forgiveness at the cross.

> But God, being rich in mercy, because of the great love with which he loved us, even when we were dead in our trespasses, made us alive together with Christ—by grace, you have been saved. (Ephesians 2:4–5 ESV)

The following mission statement is painted on the wall in my friend Carolyn's church in Colorado. I *love* it—so well said:

> We Are Worship-Driven, Spirit-Led, Prayer-Dependent, Grace-Centered, Kingdom-Obsessed.[10]

"Pink-Spoon People"

Our pastor once gave an analogy for being a part of God's family. It made great sense to understand how our lives of faith in the body of Christ reflect Him and His kingdom to come. And it has to do with ice cream. (Yum—I love ice cream! You too?)

> Never forget that being a part of a family, you carry the family name. Live up to it! Be ever mindful of who you represent. A new identity requires a new way of living. Be a part of the "Pink Spoon People of God!" You know those little pink spoons you get when receiving a sample of ice cream? Similarly, your life as a believer is like that. You are Pink Spoon People. Pink spoons give you a sample of real ice cream, not a substitute ice cream but the

real stuff. True too is your life. You are a sampling for the world to taste and see Christ! (Luke Simmons, "Committed to Life Change in a World of Low Standards", Ephesians 2:15; 4:1–4) [11]

"Pink Spoon People" T-shirts were even made. It's always fun to explain when asked, "What does your T-shirt mean?" In turn, I would ask you: do you consider yourself a pink-spoon person? When you evaluate your life, does Christ shine through, not in any unrealistic way, but does authentic joy resonate in your life, even during hardships? Does kindness come through in despair? Does hope in a future with Christ give you true peace? As I type these questions, it's a reminder to me to be authentic in my faith walk. A fake faith is easy to spot. Can people trust you to genuinely care? Not every day is rosy, but is Christ my joy-filler? Is He your joy-filler? May the posture of our hearts always be, "Set me aside, God, so others see You."

A lot of times, people crave what you have—the joy and peace they see in your life. When you share about Jesus and what He means in your life and invite them to church, which may be the first time they've ever been invited, their souls will be touched. Perhaps they'll be renewed by God if they've been away from Him for some time. Your faith will be encouraged as well. Trust God with the results! As previously mentioned, I'm so glad Mom's friends invited us all those years ago. They were living out their pink-spoon lives, joyfully and prayerfully. I'm so glad they were. God was beautiful through them. They were a taste of the real thing!

Like Jesus, Meet People Where They Are

Next time you are asked what religion you are, share who Jesus is to you. Like Jesus, meet people where they are. Find out where they're coming from and what their longing for God is. If Jesus is indeed your treasure, treat Him as such, and share Him with others. When you love someone, you talk about that person. Talk about Jesus. Don't be afraid. If others don't know Jesus, share His love by simply sharing how much He loves them and wants to meet them right where they are.

When God's at work in someone else's life through a relationship with Him, it's a beautiful thing to witness. It is such a humbling privilege to walk alongside a person who is committing his or her life to Christ—truly the most amazing thing you will *ever* experience. If you've ever held a newborn baby, you know the excitement of holding that precious new life. It's the same joyful exhilaration you'll experience when seeing new life born in Christ. Be ready to be used by God at any time and in any place, and He will show you the people around you who are just waiting for someone to love them in Jesus.

Why Is the Bible So Important?

It's helpful to understand that Jesus and the Word of God complement one another. The written Word of God is His love story to a lost world. Two Instagram posts say it well: "Many books can inform you, but only the Bible can transform you!" and "The Bible may hurt you with the truth, but it will never comfort you with a lie."

> All scripture is breathed out by God and profitable for teaching, for reproof, for correction, and for training in righteousness, that the man of God may be complete, equipped for every good work. (2 Timothy 3:16–17 ESV)

The Bible isn't an old, irrelevant history book. It is as relevant today as the day it was written. It is what God has given to any who will read it and believe it—His words to live by today.

> For the word of God is living and active, sharper than any two-edged sword, piercing to the division of soul and of spirit, of joints and of marrow, and discerning the thoughts and intentions of the heart. (Hebrews 4:12 ESV)

"The Gospel is the key to conversion and ongoing change. It is both the A-B-C's and the A to Z of Christianity" (*My Faith Magazine*). [12]

The Bible is God's love story from start to finish, the gospel, the good news, nothing added or subtracted, alive and well today. The band Burlap to Cashmere, in the lyrics to their song "Basic Instructions," uses the word *Bible* as an acronym to describe God's Word: **B**asic **I**nstruction **B**efore **L**eaving **E**arth. And indeed, it is just that and so much more—medicine to soothe a weary soul!

> There are two ways to read the Bible. You can read it narratively which is: creation, fall, redemption, and restoration, as well as topically which is: God, sin, Christ, faith, not works.

> The Bible tells of God's creation, its fall and His redeeming the lost to Himself from the Old Testament pointing to Jesus, the Savior of the World, in the New Testament. The Bible displays His ultimate authority through love over feelings, opinions, and practices. The Bible, also referred to as the Word of God, is infallible, which means it makes no false or misleading statements and is

inerrant, which means it is without error or fault in all its teaching. (Bible Boot Camp/notes) [13]

In summary, the Bible is divinely inspired writings that are the foundational framework of Christianity. Here are NIV verses that speak of how awesome God's Word is:

- As for God, His way is perfect: The Lord's word is flawless; He shields all who take refuge in Him. (Psalm 18:30)
- For the word of the Lord is right and true; He is faithful in all He does. (Psalm 33:4)
- Your word is a lamp for my feet, a light on my path. (Psalm 119:105)
- You are my refuge and my shield; I have put my hope in Your word. (Psalm 119:114)
- The unfolding of Your words gives light; it gives understanding to the simple. (Psalm 119:130)
- Every word of God is flawless; He is a shield to those who take refuge in Him. (Proverbs 30:5)
- The grass withers and the flowers fall, but the word of our God endures forever. (Isaiah 40:8)
- Jesus answered, "It is written: 'Man shall not live on bread alone, but on every word that comes from the mouth of God.'" (Matthew 4:4)
- Therefore, everyone who hears these words of Mine and puts them into practice is like a wise man who built his house on the rock. (Matthew 7:24)
- Heaven and earth will pass away, but My words will never pass away. (Matthew 24:35)
- In the beginning was the Word, and the Word was with God, and the Word was God. (John 1:1)
- You are already clean because of the word I have spoken to you. (John 15:3)

✦ If you remain in Me and My words remain in you, ask whatever you wish, and it will be done for you. (John 15:7)

Why So Many Translations?

When asked why there are so many translations and how that is OK, it's helpful to understand what translations are and what they are not. Translations are the textual language of the Bible to a given audience "of which there are many audiences and many different kinds of readers."[14] What translations are *not* are additional gospels.

Various translations are definitely appreciated when dissecting scripture, as it helps to get all the different takes and angles of a given verse or passage. I'm so thankful for all the translations available when, for example, I'm doing a Bible study. I've been especially thankful for various translations while writing this book!

There are online sites, such as biblegateway.com or biblehub. com, where you type in any verse or word and receive all the translations of that verse, allowing you to read the verse in its full context, as well as see commentaries supporting the verse and given passages. They're awesome and definitely worth checking out, as well as others out there to help you dig deeper.

Bible translations are different phrasings that stay true to the core passage. They are a beautiful gift to every reader so all people can know and understand God's Word. Translations are available in almost every tongue and tribe the world over, translated into almost every language, even in the most remote villages. Getting Bibles to places, especially closed nations, is a full-time ministry to those who are involved with Bible distributions, sometimes putting their own lives on the line. They are such a huge blessing to the world that is hungry for God's Word!

> And he said to them, "Go into all the world and
> proclaim the Gospel to the whole creation." (Mark
> 16:15 ESV)

The Inerrant and Infallible Word of God

It is evident that the inerrant (without error or fault) and infallible
(not false or misleading) Word of God, the Bible, is very important
to God.

Filter out whatever *isn't* from God's Word when you're reading
or watching something online, following someone on social media,
or listening to teaching or preaching on spiritual concepts. Be
discerning. Here are some verses on how God doesn't tread lightly
on these topics.

> As we said before, so now I say again if anyone
> preaches any other gospel to you than what you
> have received, let him be accursed. (Galatians 1:9
> NKJV)

> I know that everything God does will last forever;
> there is no adding to it or taking from it. God
> works so that people will be in awe of Him.
> (Ecclesiastes 3:14 CSB)

> Beware of false teachers who come disguised as
> harmless sheep but are wolves and will tear you
> apart. You can detect them by the way they act,
> just as you can identify a tree by its fruit. You
> need never confuse grapevines with thorn bushes
> or figs with thistles. Different kinds of fruit trees
> can quickly be identified by examining their fruit.

A variety that produces delicious fruit never produces an inedible kind. And a tree producing an inedible kind can't produce what is good. So, the trees having the inedible fruit are chopped down and thrown on the fire. Yes, the way to identify a tree or a person is by the kind of fruit produced. (Matthew 7:15–20 TLB)

God's love story is complete in His Word, through His Son, Jesus Christ, on the cross, who died and rose again so those who put their trust and faith in Him will be saved. There is no other way to God. Not through good works or religion but only through a personal relationship with Jesus.

Enter through the narrow gate. For wide is the gate and broad is the road that leads to destruction, and many enter through it. But small is the gate and narrow the road that leads to life, and only a few find it. (Matthew 7:13–14 NIV)

Let Jesus Be Your Treasure

Christ is so freeing! He is better than anything this world can or will ever offer you. His is a relationship that is personal, pure, and perfect.

And we have come to know and to believe the love that God has for us. God is love, and the one who remains in love remains in God, and God remains in him. (1 John 4:16 CSB)

It's a wonderful journey. Join Him for the ride of your life, now and into eternity.

> If then you were raised with Christ, seek those things which are above, where Christ is, sitting at the right hand of God. Set your mind on things above, not on things on the earth. For you died, and your life is hidden with Christ in God. When Christ who is your life appears, then you also will appear with Him in glory. (Colossians 3:1–4 NKJV)

> This God is our God forever and ever. He will guide us from now on. (Psalm 48:14 ICB)

A beautiful piece shared by our pastor, inspired by Isaiah 53, asked a very fundamental question: "Have you seen Jesus?" This is a profound question for every heart to evaluate. His response was, "Jesus is the treasure!" I loved his piece so much that I wanted to include it here for you to embrace just how awesome Jesus is! With permission to share from Pastor Luke Simmons, here is his piece:

Jesus, My Treasure! Who He Was, Who He Is

> Jesus was the friend of sinners, the one who challenged false religion and comforted those who were crushed by it. The one who saw people— truly saw them—and still moved toward them in tenderness. The one who touched lepers, comforted doubters, healed the hurting and fed the hungry. He was angry with the hard-of-heart but patient with the slow-of-heart. He could befriend

the elites and everyman. He taught with authority, confounded His critics, and made everyone think. He never watered down His message just to make people happy. He was tough and tender, heroic and humble. He had the power to calm the raging sea and to crush His enemies, yet He allowed Himself to be crushed in the sea of judgment for sin He did not commit. On the cross, He forgave His enemies and looked out for His friends. He was pierced for our transgressions. He was crushed for our iniquities. Upon Him was the punishment that brought us peace and by His wounds, we are healed. All of us like sheep have gone astray and the Lord has laid on Him the iniquity of us all. Surely, He is the Son of God.

Have you seen Him? He's the treasure! He's the joy! He's given Himself to you so you can find life, so you can find forgiveness and healing and hope! So, you can have GOD! [15]

Dipping Back into My Story—Life after a Breakup

Dipping back into my story, we find more brokenness. But now you know—a foreshadowing of God working through all my mess yet to come and how He never, *ever* lets us go. I was saved, but I still ventured off and did life my own way. Why do we do that? If that is you, please stop! Learn from me. It's not worth it! Sin may be harmless, or so you think; you're not harming anyone—but you *are* harming yourself, for starters—or you think sin is fun (in the moment), perhaps. But no, it is not. There are consequences. There are *always* consequences—always! When you're walking with Jesus instead, the Holy Spirit helps you do the right thing because doing the right thing is the right thing to do, as opposed to doing the wrong thing. Plain and simple, Jesus is better.

Forgiveness

If you've been sinned against, you know the consequences are real. Let me tell you how very sorry I am for the pain you carry or have carried. Know that Jesus is there to hold you and move you to the next stage of healing. God calls us to forgive, even if it sounds impossible. Christ is our example. He forgave those who betrayed Him, beat Him, and mocked Him. By His strength, we can endure, and by His stripes, we are healed! And with His help, we can forgive. First and foremost, forgive yourself. Then, forgive the person who has hurt you. Until you do that, you will remain in a pattern of hurt. Even if they're no longer around, release them to God through forgiveness to be freed from fear so they no longer have a hold over you. He will help you. It may be the hardest thing you ever do, but when you forgive, you let go of that nagging grudge that has imprisoned you, that bitterness and hate that has consumed you toward that other person. You will finally be free.

> Be kind to one another, tenderhearted, forgiving one another, as God in Christ forgave you. (Ephesians 4:32 ESV)

What Makes You Angry?

A lot of stuff probably makes you angry. But God calls us to change and turn from our anger, our dismissive attitudes, our pride, our arrogance, our selfishness, and our judgmental spirits—the list goes on. In His eyes, all of this is sin. It puts our eyes on ourselves and takes our eyes off God. Christ freed you and freed me from all of this. Walk in that new life He's given you.

Since I was hurting from a broken heart, I chose to stay in that pain, making me have a rebellious spirit and not trust God or others completely. God calls us to repent and turn from our sins. Choose forgiveness and walk in freedom. As Jonah told the people of Nineveh, "Turn back ... turn from your wicked ways" (Jonah 3:8 GW).

If you tell yourself (or someone else tells you), "Don't do this" or "Don't do that," listen to your conscience and stay clear of trouble that will trip you up. As a child of God, never dismiss the prompting of the Holy Spirit as to what is right over what is wrong. Don't confuse it with the snares of legalism, being judgmental and self-righteous. Instead, be in a right relationship with Christ and His finished work on the cross for your sins. Head in a new direction, free from your past.

God always lovingly redirects us, just as a loving parent would do. He's our Dad, redirecting His children when they are on the wrong path.

> Christ has a grip on me! One thing is for certain: It is not our grip on God that keeps us safe, but the power of Jesus' grasp. "Christ Jesus has also laid hold of me" (Philippians 3:12 NKJV). (In His Grip/ODBread)[16]

Our Dog (Current Day) on a Walk

When our dog Lil' Rock was younger, he was notorious for wanting to chase bunnies in the desert wash behind our house. He'd see (or smell as only a dog can) a bunny and would nearly rip my arm off to get to it. But I had hold of the leash. I would lovingly but firmly pull him back and remind him, "No, we're not going that way; we're going this way." Unbeknownst to Lil' Rock, there was a busy road up ahead, and if he had run in that direction, he could've been run over. Worse yet, he could have died. Plus, that bunny will outrun him every single time!

As years have passed, he's come to learn the freedom of the extended leash and knows he can enjoy his walks with a great view of bunnies frolicking along the wash, without the chaos of getting tangled in a prickly bush or getting run over if he were to break from the leash. There are even times when, closer to home, I'll take him off leash, and he'll stay right by my side, knowing what awaits him after our long walks—home sweet home, where his food, water, and bed await him. Training started all over again when our daughter Tatum got a new puppy, an Australian shepherd named Quinn. Oh, the energy, excitement, and fear of daily walks for a puppy begs the question—who do you trust to lead your life? Are you trusting your own instincts or are you trusting God? He has a path specifically for you to follow. Will you trust Him with your life?

God allows us to choose that which we may, but He desires we stay within His will, as His ways are always better than our own. If we stray away, He's there, lovingly pulling us back. We return like the lost prodigal son and—wouldn't you know it?—a hot meal, a hug, and a warm bed await us. (A great story to check out is the Parable of the Lost Son in Luke 15:11–32.) We come back to God asking for His forgiveness, time and time again. All the while, He loves us unconditionally, time and time again, forgiving us like a good father does, guiding us back to Him.

We are not perfect, nor are we called to be. Only God is. We are forgiven and called to be image-bearers of Christ, such that we are kind and caring, loving, and forgiving of others. We can't do any of this on our own, but we can when we set our gaze on Jesus. He changes us, our habits, and our old nature, just like our dogs when we go on walks. We learn we can trust Jesus and stay by His side all the days of our lives, where we are safe from harm and can enjoy the life He's given us.

More Mess in Life Ahead

As you'll see in the chapters ahead, God allowed me to fall, all to have me stay clear of trouble and follow Him. Every time, God was there to rescue me from myself. I was saved! I had an assurance of my salvation and my eternity one thousand times over, but I was a wanderer. Can you relate?

Wanderers are like the Israelites, wandering in the wilderness. I was wandering. Wherever was I headed? Wherever are you headed? Don't walk your own path. Sin is dangerous, just like that busy road where you can get run over or, worse yet, get killed. He sees the road ahead; we don't. It is best to just follow Him and not make a mess of things. I was stubborn and had to learn the hard way. I pray you aren't stubborn, but most likely, you are. We have this trait in common; it's called being human. Only God can rescue us from ourselves.

Pick yourself up, hold on to God, and save yourself the headache and the wasted years. Stay clear of the roadblocks ahead. Just trust Him. I know it may seem hard, but honestly, it's not. It's such an easier way to live life when you stop running from God, fighting against God, and turning your back on Him. Remember, He is for you. Run to Him. He's far better qualified to run your life than you are, so trust Him. You'll be *so* glad you did.

Blessed is the one who trusts in the Lord, whose confidence is in Him. They will be like a tree planted by the water that sends out its roots by the stream. It does not fear when heat comes; its leaves are always green. It has no worries in a year of drought and never fails to bear fruit. (Jeremiah 17:7–8 NIV)

Let the morning bring me word of Your unfailing love, for I have put my trust in You. Show me the way I should go, for to You I entrust my life. (Psalm 143:8 NIV)

Full Access to God Any Time

Never, *ever* forget you have full access to God, any time, any hour, any day! Remember, you're His child. Go to Him.

In the Old Testament, access to God in the tabernacle and the temple was strictly limited. Only the high priest could go in through the curtain and offer sacrifices in the Most Holy Place, and then only once a year (Leviticus 16:2–20). But at the very moment Jesus died, the curtain of the temple was torn in two from top to bottom, showing that the barrier between man and God was destroyed forever (Mark 15:38). Because of Christ's sacrifice for our sins, all those who love and follow Him can come into His presence at any time. He has given us the right to access Him anytime. "Lord, thank You for paying a price to enable me to have unrestricted entry into Your presence! Amen"

Access to God's throne is always open. "Let us draw near to God ... with the full assurance that faith brings." Hebrews 10:22 (NIV) (ODBread, *Come In*, 3/9/16)[1]

This is the confidence we have in approaching God: that if we ask anything according to His will, He hears us. (1 John 5:14 NIV)

He Is Always There. Run into His Loving Arms.

Just as a child goes to his father, God is there for you, waiting to sit with you and hear from you. Talk to Him. Spend time with Him, and embrace Him. He is *always* there! Run into His loving arms.

CHAPTER 11

Mom Gets Married

When I was thirteen and my sister was fifteen, Mom married Allen, who became our stepdad. We adored him then and still do to this day. She met Allen in our church's "Singles Again" ministry, which became a beautiful network of support for us. After church every Sunday, we'd join other families and go out to eat lunch. Once a month, we'd do fun things together, like bowling and mini-golf. We were a big family doing life together.

They had their wedding in the lovely home of the Carter family, a dear family from church who adopted us as their own and whose daughter, Tonya, became a lifelong friend (she was the one who loaned me her pageant gown in college). Other than being a flower girl when I was little, Mom's wedding was the first wedding I ever attended. Their ceremony was my first experience of what a Christ-centered union looked like, giving honor to the Lord as being the head of their household. It was officiated by Pastor Jackson, who also prayed with us when we accepted Jesus, baptized us, was always encouraging us in our newfound faith, and was now there for us when we became a blended family.

We went from being a family of three to a family of seven, just like that. It was all so exciting! My sister and I gained two brothers and a sister, all of whom we're still close to today. My two sisters, Stephanie and Michelle, are two of my dearest and closest friends. I can call them at any time, day or night, and they are there for me, just as I am there for them. Looking back, I know God was in all the details of our lives.

We weathered a lot as a newly blended family, transitioning from one family to two combined. Mom and Allen were instant parents to three teenagers in high school, one in junior high, and an almost tween under one roof—no small feat. Most difficult was having to navigate through the destruction of alcohol and drugs that one of my stepbrothers used, which caused a lot of havoc in his life and, as a result, our lives as well. He was in and out of recovery programs and landed a jail sentence, which became the turning point in his life. We survived it all, by God's grace, but it was a very difficult, destructive, taxing long haul that took a toll on our entire family. As an adult, he turned his life around for the better, and we are all thankful for second chances in his life.

I suppose my connection with a boy during this season of life, someone who was interested in me and my life, was a welcoming distraction when the tensions at home were high. It gave me something and someone else to think about. As well, I was super busy keeping up with my school schedule and activities, holding down a job at Farrell's Ice Cream, and babysitting. This all kept me focused and away from home a lot.

Having a boyfriend also provided a getaway for me during my downtime. We'd meet for walks, get ice cream, or meet up at his sister's apartment, which often sat empty, as she worked a lot. Not a good place for two teenagers in love (or was it lust?) to be alone. I never realized that having a boyfriend would cause so many problems down the road. I jumped in too fast and too soon. I was thankful, looking back, that God always was my anchor. Being involved in youth group, church choir, and Young Life at school gave me a sense of stability that God had a hold of me, but sadly, I never felt a deep conviction over becoming so serious so young. It was as if I was living a double life. I never realized the choices I'd make as a teenager would have such severe consequences later on in my life, becoming the crux of my broken heart.

My mom and sisters were there for me when all came crashing down. When Mom found out the whole story, she was crushed. She didn't want what happened to her to happen to me. She was in high school when she got pregnant with my sister. She dropped out to be a mom and wanted to do the honorable thing and get married. Two and a half years later, another baby was on the way—me. Mom was just shy of turning twenty and my dad was nineteen when I came along. With two babies underfoot, the hardships they encountered—with little to no money and living in a shed in the back of my dad's parents' property—was more than they could handle. Divorce followed shortly thereafter. I was two.

I have early memories as a young school-aged girl of fabricating stories of my dad's whereabouts, as divorce was a bit taboo in those days. Sometimes, I'd tell of his being an astronaut and being on a trip to the moon or a pilot who was flying out of town. I was a bit of a daydreamer, or so I was told, and spent time staring out the big picture window at our elementary school. When I was asked what I was looking at, I described the pictures I made out of clouds. Perhaps what I really longed for was a glimpse of my dad—maybe he really was up there in the sky somewhere, flying in a plane.

Even though my dad wasn't in the picture in my earlier growing-up years, my grandmothers (mentioned earlier), aunts, and uncles were very helpful in raising me and my sister. Our sweet cousins on both sides were always fun playmates for us. When the movie *Steel Magnolias*[1] came out—about a core group of women helping each other through a hard family time—I always said that Grandma Mary, Aunt Bonnie, Aunt Michelle, and Aunt Ione were the *Steel Magnolias* women in my life. I grew up with many fond memories of my uncles—from Uncle Dave teaching me to ski and allowing me to live with them when I student taught, to Uncle Gary, a veterinarian, whose vet clinic I loved to visit, contributing to my love of animals to this day, and Uncle D. C.'s love for the Wildcats, which would be my future alma mater, which was always heartwarming. (I've since lost two aunts and two uncles in the years that have passed. All their sweet care for us will never be forgotten.)

How was it that with all this support, I chose to make my own decisions that would later cost me? Lesson learned. You might have layers of support, as I did, from your immediate or extended family who love you. Talk to them about big life decisions. Don't keep secrets from them, and don't dismiss their counsel. They care deeply about you. When following your own path, there will be consequences, and those closest to you will feel your pain.

My mom knew how much I was hurting after my return trip from Amarillo and was thankful I finally came to her with the truth—a few years too late, but she understood my pain nonetheless. My sisters were there for me as well. Even though I chose my own path at times, they were supportive and loved me when I hurt. They had their share of difficult heartbreaks, but each of us always came back to the one who never leaves us and never gives up on us, and that is the greatest love we all knew and could always rely on.

What I'd Tell a Younger You—Be Cautious! The Trap of the Internet

Fast-forward—it's been very important for me, as a mom who raised teens, to talk openly to them about their worth in God's eyes, especially if they've felt sad about a relationship with a friend or if they have a wrong view of themselves. They are precious in God's sight, and so are you! I'd hate any of them—or any of you—to go through the pain I went through as a teenager (young adult) because of my poor choices. I thought I had it all figured out, but I didn't, nor do you. Even though you think you do, you don't! It might sound harsh, but it's the truth. A lot of learning about oneself must take place before taking on someone else's life and their emotional well-being at such a young age. There's an unhealthy pressure to have a boyfriend or girlfriend, especially with social media. That's when the value of family comes in. Have open lines of communication with your people who care about you, love you, and support you. They are your lifeline.

About the Internet—Here's the Truth!

Everything is so easily accessible today with a click of a mouse or a swipe or scroll on your phone through all the different apps, available at any hour of any day to be in direct contact with anybody across the globe. The influx of instant messaging fills up all your time. All the while, God's voice gets smaller and smaller as the world and the opinions of others get louder and louder. You must learn that your worth is from God, not from the number of followers you have, how many likes come your way, or the coolest way to outdo the next coolest thing. It's all exhausting and plays on your mental well-being if you don't have a healthy perspective. You must stop being so obsessed with your phone! Please, put your phone down. Put boundaries on how you use social media and time limits to monitor your time and intake.

Make wise choices of what *not* to look at and who *not* to follow. *Never* send private pictures, let alone inappropriate pictures, of yourself to anyone—*never, ever!* Don't receive or open inappropriate messages on Snapchat or other messaging apps. Internet trolls are watching your accounts, looking for vulnerable opportunities to get to you by playing on your innocence and by feeding you compliments that move you to have online conversations with them. They lure you into their deceptive paths, isolating you from your friends and family. They could be predators, sex offenders, or working for a sex trafficking ring targeting you! It's real, and it's dangerous. You must be aware of who you are talking to, and *never* meet up with someone you've met online from an unsecured site or who you think you know simply from the flattering words they've given you that drive you to a place of illogical thinking. Don't give your number out to anyone you don't know or trust. Don't let them know where you live or where you go to school. Be safe and cautious! Don't buy the lie that they are your friend, that they are safe, and that they can help you. *No,* they want to hurt you.

Along the same lines, don't get lured into looking at pornography. *No! Stop!* It's all a trap that will have you spiraling down fast. Pornography is the leading cause of desensitizing a person to rationalize what is real and what is not. It causes a person to objectify another person. The more unchecked the behavior, the more a person becomes an addict, craving even harder porn. It is dangerous and not God's plan for a relationship. It ruins people, relationships, and marriages. Don't get caught in its snares of destruction.

Social media and the internet will consume you in unhealthy ways. You *must* be smart! If you are on social media, be a positive influencer. Reflect Christ lived out in your life through your posts by simply being courteous and kind. Rise above the social media tide by spreading good, encouraging, and thoughtful messages. Teenagers and young adults must stay the course to establish healthy boundaries and have accountability to people in their lives who love them and will tell them the truth before they find themselves in a mess. Don't become obsessed by the world's standards of relationships and casual hookups that are all too impulsive and rampant. Trust me; you will escape heartaches later on. Be a person of integrity, and respect yourself and others. Be a difference-maker in person and online. You have the ability to set the pace of how to live a life that honors God, yourself, and your family. Be smart! Choose your interactions wisely.

The person you are in public should be the same person you are behind closed doors. Live a life you're proud of, a life of integrity and honor. The world is watching you. Let them see Christ, who lives in you.

Here's a verse worth repeating:

> You are the light of the world. A town built on a hill cannot be hidden. Neither do people light a lamp and put it under a bowl. Instead they put it on its stand, and it gives light to everyone in the house. In the same way, let your light shine before others, that they may see your good deeds and glorify your Father in heaven. (Matthew 5:14–16 NIV)

Years of Wandering Up Ahead

In the following chapter, you'll see that my light hid under a bushel. For a couple of years, I searched for love in all the wrong places. There certainly was a guy out there for me, and I was going to find him—or so I thought. Even if it meant more heartbreaks along the way, it didn't matter. I was determined!

Don't make that same mistake. Run instead to the prize that

lasts, the reward that stands the test of time. Run to Jesus. He's worth it all!

> Therefore, since we are surrounded by such a great cloud of witnesses, let us throw off everything that hinders and sin that so easily entangles. And let us run with perseverance the race marked out for us, fixing our eyes on Jesus, the pioneer and perfecter of faith. For the joy set before Him he endured the cross, scorning its shame, and sat down at the right hand of the throne of God. Consider Him who endured such opposition from sinners, so that you will not grow weary and lose heart. (Hebrews 12:1–3 NIV)

CHAPTER 12

Life after a Breakup

When returning home to start my second year of teaching, I chose to get more serious about my faith and get plugged into the young adult group I had occasionally visited at the church I was attending. About that same time, I concluded that men were interested in only one thing and that it'd be best for me to interact with guys in this group as friends only, as I wasn't there to date. To my surprise, there were nice guys who weren't jerks and were much more like brothers to me than guys I'd be interested in.

Sadly, out of my deep pain, I seemed to fall into old patterns of having a double life. I had my spiritual friends on Sundays but occasionally joined my coworkers for happy hour on Fridays and would go to the bars to go dancing on Saturday nights. As for alcohol, I was never enticed to drink like a lot of my peers. After seeing in our home, up close and personal, all the damage alcohol can do to a person, it was enough for me to choose to never go down that path. Instead, I'd order my Diet Coke or water with a side of chips and salsa.

Never feel pressured to buy a drink! Stick to what you are comfortable with. Best case scenario: order water. It's free, and it's better for you—a sure win all the time. (While we are on the topic, let's talk about drinking and God's viewpoint on it.)

Drinking: "What Are Your Thoughts, God?"

A question I received from time to time while shepherding our young-adult ministry was, "What do you think about drinking?" Since some were going to be turning twenty-one, they had a sense of curiosity in wanting to go out for their first drink now that they were of legal age. Since God's opinion matters most, let's start there.

Jesus' first miracle was turning water into wine at the wedding feast found in John 2. So, if Jesus thought wine was an OK beverage of choice, why would there be any harm in it? Let's explore further.

First, ask yourself, "Why do I want to have a drink?" Perhaps you'll hear yourself say, "It's my birthday, and I'm entitled to it." Most likely, you'll then want to post a picture of yourself with a drink in hand, along with a GIF or hashtag of sorts—"21 and legal"—to document the occasion. Without any pressure from anyone else, go deeper with this question. "Would my having a drink cause a person looking on to stumble in confusion?" If the answer is *yes*, then reevaluate your motive for wanting to have a drink and making that public, especially when it comes to that particular setting with that person or people. If the answer is *no*, then drink responsibly and in moderation, sharing your time with family or friends over a meal, a time of gathering, or a celebration. Know your limit, your choice of location, and the company you are with. Be responsible! God speaks strongly about this. Here are a few verses to consider:

> Constantly be on your guard so that your hearts will not be loaded down with self-indulgence, drunkenness, and the worries of this life, or that day will take you by surprise. (Luke 21:34 ISV)

> O my son, be wise and stay in God's paths; don't carouse with drunkards and gluttons, for they are on their way to poverty. (Proverbs 23:21a TLB)

> Beloved, I urge you as sojourners and exiles to abstain from the passions of the flesh, which wage war against your soul. (1 Peter 2:11 ESV)

We must talk further about this—it's that important! Never make a habit of drinking to get drunk. It's dangerous. And *never* drink and drive! Even though you think you are fine, you are not! Don't chance it. Getting drunk causes problems and, worse yet, causes deaths on the road. One of the friends I've dedicated this book to was eighteen-year-old Keli Rutledge, a young adult from our group, who was on her way to work at ten o'clock on a clear, sunny Arizona morning when she was hit and killed by a drunk and drug-induced driver. Losing her was an enormous loss that will always be felt. She was an amazing worship leader and an aspiring songwriter with an incredible voice, who had just won first place in Alice Cooper's statewide singer/songwriter contest. Keli's precious family was in such turmoil because of this other person's actions, especially since the defendant's case stayed open for well over two years after the accident. It caused *so* much havoc and pain.

A large section covered in any online safety driving course relates to consuming alcohol and driving. That's telling! Drinking and driving is dangerous and can kill people. Don't be a part of the problem; be a part of the solution. Your life matters as well as all those around you.

What draws a person to drinking? What draws you to drinking? If it's beyond the point of having a beer or two with friends while watching a game or a glass of wine with friends at dinner, and you have become a closet binge drinker or an alcoholic, privately or socially, perhaps you need to face the reality of what it's become. If that is you, reach out and get the help you need to stop your overindulging consumption before it stops you. You can't control this on your own. It's bigger than you!

Even a person who thinks they have their drinking under control may be drinking or using drugs to medicate themselves, thinking it will numb their pain and make their problems go away, only to hurt themselves and everyone who loves them. It won't cure your problems; it will only take you down a dark path you don't want to go down. Whether alcohol, drugs, or any other type of substance use has become your addiction, get the help you need. This verse puts things into perspective.

> Be sober-minded; be watchful. Your adversary the devil prowls around like a roaring lion, seeking someone to devour. (1 Peter 5:8 ESV)

The good news is, God won't let you stay there if you trust in His ways over your own. He wants to free you from this or any other vice you struggle with. Release your struggle to Him, and He will be your helper because He is faithful.

> God is faithful. He will not allow the temptation to be more than you can stand. When you are tempted, He will show you a way out so that you can endure. (1 Corinthians 10:13b NLT)

He's There for You. Run to Him.

Run to Him with your situation. I wish I would have run to Him when things got dark. For me, it wasn't a drinking situation, but just the same, it was me, trying to navigate life on my own, not even knowing what I was looking for, only to be let down yet again.

It is said that bad company corrupts good character (1 Corinthians 15:33), which is *so* true! Whatever your vice in trying to navigate life on your own, it's such a slow lure that you don't even realize you're getting sucked into it until it is too late, and you're too far gone, or so you think. Are you, really?

Why do we become entangled with things that trip us up? We are weak. Are you ever weak? I was weak. Where does our strength come from? We know it comes from the Lord, so why don't we lean on Him? In those moments when we're weak and vulnerable, lean in hard. He is our *only* refuge!

- God is our refuge and strength, a very present help in trouble. (Psalm 46:1 KJV)
- My grace is sufficient for you, for my power is made perfect in weakness. (2 Corinthians 12:9a NIV)
- And the Holy Spirit helps us in our weakness. (Romans 8:26a NLT)

Poor Choices

When I hung out at bars so I could dance with my friends, the hours slipped away. In settings like these, you come across a lot of people, guys and girls alike, getting drunk, and the air fills with smoke. Second-hand smoke is a real thing. The whole environment made me feel a bit dizzy. It seemed then that I'd meet the guys I knew were trouble for me, but I was always drawn to them. Being spun around a dance floor by a cute guy was fun, and the thought that a guy might actually like me for me made me want more time and attention from him. I actually thought there was a nice guy out there for me, and probably there was, but for me, it seemed to be the same pattern. What was wrong with men? Or was it me? Why were they so obsessed with casual hookups that crossed the line? Was I not heard? "I'm not interested in being a one-night stand!"

Why wasn't there any depth? Even if there was a second or third date, it seemed as if things went in one direction and one direction only, which made me resolve that all men were alike. They were everywhere—single-minded, sex-driven, immature, and without depth—making me more repulsed by them every weekend that I went out, but I kept going out. I was intoxicated by their affectionate ways toward me, and I fell every time. Why did I keep falling for this pattern, week after week?

I remember the frustration of going home, smelling like smoke and beer spilled on me, and having to wash my hair before church the next morning just to get the smell off my body. The lingering smell in my clothes from the night before filled my hamper. I felt dirty. I just wanted to bathe and be clean from it all.

> All of us have become like one who is unclean, and all our righteous acts are like filthy rags; we all shrivel up like a leaf, and like the wind our sins sweep us away. (Isaiah 64:6 NIV)

Put on the New Self

But instead, God reminds us:

> Put off your old self, which belongs to your former manner of life and is corrupt through deceitful desires, and to be renewed in the spirit of your minds, and to put on the new self, created after the likeness of God in true righteousness and holiness. (Ephesians 4:22–24 ESV)

Isn't it great to know that God is in the business of restoring and healing? Even when things seem dark, He is there, illuminating His bright love in us! God gives us a fresh start every day—day after day, month after month, and year after year. He loves us that much! His love is so vast and so healing.

CHAPTER 13

#MeToo Movement

The #MeToo movement had been around for years but took the nation by storm in 2018. Other hashtags (#WhyIDidntReport, #TimesUp, and others) followed suit when a vote for or against a Supreme Court justice nominee stirred the emotional heart of America. I remember the hearing well as it landed on my fifty-third birthday. Fifty-three is the capstone year of the overarching age span of my story—forty years of sojourning with the Lord on this topic of His love story, written out in my life.

I felt led to add this chapter because of what the MeToo movement (and this case in particular) brought to light. This seemed like the appropriate place to put this chapter after having just shared about the season I was in of needing to take off the old and put on the new self. I don't share my thoughts and experiences here to take a political stance on the matter or to show hostility toward any side or person, as that is not my place nor my character. How each person responds to outcomes in cases like these and to social concerns in general plays out differently for each person, based on his or her own personal experiences; it's between that person and God.

Cases such as these have shaped people's perspectives of what sexual assault looked like decades ago and what is not looked upon favorably in the workplace and on college campuses today. With a no-tolerance policy in place across the board, a new set of rules is emerging regarding what appropriate behavior looks like and how sexual assault cases are being exposed and victims are being heard.

Looking at the heart of the matter, rules may change but hurt still resides. Without minimizing anyone's pain in what they have gone through or experienced, I would encourage you, if you are hurting or upset on either side of a sexual assault case, to be assured that in Christ, there is healing and forgiveness at the cross. When a person experiences authentic physical and/or emotional pain that is brought on by someone else's actions, Jesus knows what they're going through. He is there to comfort the brokenhearted, the hurting, and the abused. He is pure solace.

Sometimes in moments of extreme hardship when you don't understand why things are the way they are, you may find yourself begging God to change your circumstances. Although the desire for things to change is heartfelt, consider, instead, going to God with an even deeper longing. *God, change me so I can handle these things you're walking me through.* Walking through difficult things means you have to have faith and trust in God that He is at work in your life and those circumstances around you.

> Now faith is the substance of things hoped for, the evidence of things not seen. (Hebrews 11:1 NKJV)

> When life is tough, have faith that God won't abandon you, but will walk with you. (Daily Bread, 2/5/22)[1]

Faith, at its core, means overcoming the fear that is holding you back to trust that which you do not know. We may be fearful of an unknown outcome or the way things might go, but with faith we have hope. Christian British extreme adventurer Bear Grylls, who scaled Mount Everest at age twenty-three, thanks God for being the navigator in all his adventures. He says this about faith over fear: "Both faith and fear may sail into your harbor, but only allow faith to drop anchor," and "With courage and kindness, you can conquer the world."

A similar line was said by Ella's dying mother in the movie remake of *Cinderella* in 2015[2] "Have courage and be kind!" It's a simple but profound way to live.

In the spirit of faith over fear, embraced with God's courage and loving kindness, I felt compelled to write my stories because I have a unique vantage point on the matter at hand because of my age and experiences. Perhaps all the heartache that was felt on either side, related to this particular case, is an opportunity for this generation to learn from the missteps of my generation. It's a start.

The Hearing

The Senate Judiciary Committee hearing of an alleged sexual assault and misconduct case had the nation in an uproar and cultural clash for weeks. Because of the nature of this case, the question on every senator's mind and every American watching was, did the allegation happen or not? How that question would be answered individually by each senator would determine the Senate's vote to confirm or not confirm the next open seat on the US Supreme Court. The judge in question was said to have sexually assaulted a classmate from another school while he was in high school at a party. Compelling testimonies were heard on either side of the case, with his denial of her claims to be true.

The judge graduated from high school the same year I did, 1983, which became the year in question. The decade captured the headlines because of all that unfolded from this hearing. It used to be quite taboo to talk about such things that happened in the past, but here it was, under a microscope for all to see. It was asked, "What was going on in the '80s? Has anything changed?"

How to sort through all those questions, decades later, is where the nation arrived. From that vantage point, I watched the hearings, knowing that however things panned out, the nation was riding a cultural tidal wave that was indeed shifting right before our eyes.

Movies in the 80s

Because of all the hype generated, movies from the 80s were talked about that shaped the culture of teenagers and college students in that day. It was noted in the hearing that the drinking age was eighteen and that these movies portrayed a culture of partying and alcohol consumption in excess, such as in *Animal House* in 1978 and *Revenge of the Nerds* in 1984,[3] which became very impressionable on students at that time. Ironically, *Revenge of the Nerds* was filmed at the university I attended. I was a sophomore at the time.

The movie was filmed all over campus, so it meant taking extra routes to get to classes. Some girls in my sorority were cast as extras in the movie and told of their long stretches of filming, with some scenes depicting parties that felt and looked similar to fraternity parties on campus, but notably, the movie's depiction was over the top, presumably for entertainment purposes. These types of movies became the norm of entertainment. Viewers would laugh or roll their eyes at assumed funny innuendos as the satire of stereotypes was brushed off as comedy. Missteps on the big screen were not categorized in how they'd be defined today. Today's definition of things such as sexual exploitation or assaults might have appeared differently back then. For example, a scene in the movie of the lead nerd, in a mask, having a sexual encounter with the opposing lead's girlfriend would be categorized today as rape by deception. The perception of the scene then was that the guy had smoother moves and got the girl. If the content of the movie made you feel uncomfortable, you'd look away, surmising that was just how things were. It was a satirical portrayal of fraternity life and the assumed sex-craved culture of college students that honed in on the stereotypes they depicted.

There was a sense of excitement and pride that the movie was filmed on campus. The overarching theme of the film was that the underdog fraternity wins the school's affection over the antagonizing fraternity, who belittles them throughout the movie, while the song "We Are the Champions"[4] plays as they triumph in victory at the end. They celebrate their heroic stance that their existence matters, and they'd no longer succumb to being bullied, which is an important message every generation needs to embrace—though in these culture-shaping movies, the backdrop was a party scene and all that went with it. Even growing up in the '80s, the party scene was the backdrop, including the sexual overtones, regardless of your participation in it or not.

Greek life, for me, was very different from what these movies depicted. Parties did not define my college experience, but I did go to a handful of parties, as a date with my then-boyfriend to his house fraternity parties. Themed parties were a big deal; if you were invited, it was kind of like being invited to prom. You'd dress up, and pictures documented the evening. Everyone had fun! And though we didn't embrace the evening activities of drinking, we had fun dancing and would simply leave when things felt uncomfortable for us; I'm sure others who felt the same way left too. How others chose to celebrate never affected or dampened our relationship with our friends.

The 80s culture then and the view on fraternity life in general did not define for me the good that came out of the Greek system. Fraternity and sorority house members came together to make a difference in the community on different causes we supported, and I was proud to be a part of those experiences. What encouraged me the most, though, was the ongoing Bible study I was a part of. We not only prayed for our house but for the Greek system as a whole. It was evident God was at work through answered prayers happening all around us. My sorority, Gamma Phi Beta, established in 1874, was founded on Christian principles, and I loved being a part of that! Our motto, "Founded on a Rock,"[5] was taken from Jesus' parable in Matthew 7:24–27 to build your house on a firm foundation of faith. It became the cornerstone of our study, to stay in God's Word, and a life motto to stay grounded on a firm foundation.

Many years later, when visiting campus during homecoming, I stopped by my old sorority. It was exciting to walk through the house to see all the rooms and take in all the memories. Mom Vest, now a widow, had retired, as she had spoken of doing so. I missed getting to see her but was so thrilled to hear that the Bible study she allowed us to host in her house suite had grown into a study beyond our house walls and now included other houses in the Greek system. My heart was so full when I heard this news. I thanked Jesus that indeed His presence was still very much alive.

It is so telling that a life lived for Christ makes an impact. I'm so thankful for the impact Mom Vest made on my life and so many other girls as well.

Sixteen Candles

The movie *Sixteen Candles* [6], a high school comedy love triangle that came out in 1984, was a huge movie, loved by everyone.

Any girl in that day was dreamy-eyed over the lead actor, whose character's name was Jake. The storyline was his pursuit of liking the unassuming, innocent girl, who was perceived as awkward with a nice smile, and his wanting to ditch his old ways with his girlfriend, who was not serious and only wanted to party. It didn't even register to viewers that anything was wrong or inconsistent with the times when he said of his unconscious girlfriend, "I've got Caroline in the bedroom right now, passed out cold. I could violate her ten different ways if I wanted to." And then his passing her off to another guy, saying, "Have fun," which the other guy does. The girlfriend, not recollecting anything that happened, woke up after being intoxicated and having passed out the night before, wondering why her hair and clothing were all disheveled.

In more recent YouTube interviews with the lead actors from this movie, they unequivocally state there are questionable parts of the film that would not sit well with audiences today.

When watching these movies, I found myself always wondering, *where are the parents?* No matter if you're watching films from decades ago or current movies, even those that are light-hearted, you must pay attention to what is in front of you, even if it means fast-forwarding through scenes, muting sections, or turning it off altogether. If you see a movie at the theater with questionable content, talk through the subject matter afterward with a parent or another trusted adult.

Along these same lines, if you're being pressured, struggling, or going through something, even if it feels small or seemingly insignificant, find that safe person to talk through hard things. Talking raw and real about the pressures you're going through is undoubtedly critical. If there is a trusted relationship built on love and respect when reaching out to your parents on anything you're struggling with or have questions about, there will always be an open line of communication between you. Even if you go through seasons of pushing back, you can always count on them to be there for you!

To parents reading this, parent-up when it's called for, put healthy boundaries in place, and, in everything, pray, pray, pray! Dig your heels into Ephesians 3:16–20 in praying over your children, no matter their ages, to have *inner strength* from the Spirit, that God would inhabit their hearts, and that they would trust Him and gain the vastness of His love that is deep and wide so they absorb the understanding that they're complete in the finished work of Christ. Through Him, they can accomplish more than they could ever ask or imagine.

MADD

Alcoholism is a serious problem, especially when operating a vehicle. MADD[7]—Mothers Against Drunk Driving—began in 1980 after a hit-and-run driver killed a thirteen-year-old girl. From that tragic loss, the mother of that teenage girl started MADD, a nonprofit, to support others like herself who were suffering the consequences of a drunk driver. In 1984, MADD lobbied for the National Minimum Drinking Act to change from age eighteen to twenty-one to take effect per state by October 1986 or lose their federal highway funds. Their efforts support victims at no charge while advocating for stronger laws and creating a future of No More Victims. When the drinking age was eighteen, underage drinkers were getting into parties, which, no doubt, was wreaking havoc on their systems.

A memory locked in my brain was when I was in junior high at a friend's house. A high school student lived next door. He pulled up to his house with other boys in the car and a girl in the back seat. I saw the girl lying down with beer bottles on the floor. Her face was as white as a ghost. I thought she was dead! The shock on my face must've said it all, as one of them said, "She's not feeling well so she's taking a nap." I thought, *this just doesn't look right or feel right*, as I saw her clothes were disheveled and her head was limp on a boy's lap. I didn't talk about it with my friend or anyone else and just kept it to myself, but I thought that something felt wrong. The girl passed out in the back seat haunted me for years.

Underage Drinking

Teens who drink are more vulnerable to addiction because the pleasure center of the brain matures before the part of the brain responsible for impulse control and executive decision-making. In other words, teenagers' capacity for pleasure reaches adult proportions well before their capacity for sound decision-making does. Students age 18 to 22, who admitted to binge drinking at least once a month, are prone to pass out, blackout, feel sick, miss school, and behave in ways uncharacteristic of them by injuring others or themselves, or damaging property. Drinking too much slows bodily functions to a dangerous level, causing one to lose consciousness. Young people who start using alcohol before 21 are more likely to be involved in violent behavior, start using drugs and become addicted to substances that are dangerous and illegal, attempt suicide, get in car accidents involving deaths when alcohol is a factor, engage in unprotected sex, or have multiple partners, and develop alcohol problems later on in life. (Help Guide)[8]

The Vote

The past cultural landscape was in question during the Supreme Court hearings to nominate the judge to the bench. With all these topics being discussed, the nation's view on partying and drinking were addressed. They wondered, was it worth peeling back the layers from decades earlier to see through that lens? Many concluded that things happened back in the day, but people change, and their lives move on to more productive things.

In conclusion, the FBI's further investigation into the allegations examined the evidence exonerating the judge. He was sworn in on October 6, 2018, as the 114th Justice of the Supreme Court. It was noted that what ended up being a very public hearing of "he said, she said" should have happened behind closed doors to protect the confidentiality of individuals and their families. Instead, the nation watched in the wings. It was hoped that as time went on and people moved past this case, individuals and their families would not be disgraced, there'd be healing in our land, and, as a nation watching on, we'd take into account how we treat others with our words and actions.

After the confirmation, fellow justices representing both sides of the aisle set the tone of how they planned to move forward with the new justice in a joint statement news release: "We have to treat each other with respect and dignity and with a sense of amicability that the rest of the world doesn't often share."[9] The harmony the courts shared was certainly a measure of rising above.

A Nation That Prays Together Stays Together

It certainly sets a healthy tone to live by when people self-check their behavior to be respectful. No matter the situation, God's message of reconciliation rings loud and clear for an individual heart and for a nation. He calls each of us to repent and pray, as real change happens when one turns from his or her sin and asks for forgiveness. As a nation, He calls us to pray for our elected officials and appointed positions, as He is our *only* hope, individually and collectively.

> If my people who are called by my name humble themselves, and pray and seek my face and turn from their wicked ways, then I will hear from heaven and will forgive their sin and heal their land. (1 Chronicles 7:14 ESV)

> I urge, then, first of all, that petitions, prayers, intercession and thanksgiving be made for all people—for kings and all those in authority, that we may live peaceful and quiet lives in all godliness and holiness. (1 Timothy 2:1–2 NIV)

How to Handle Chaos under Pressure

With the topic at hand, if you're hurt by someone physically or emotionally, or you've hurt someone physically or emotionally, no matter how big or small, each and every pain hurts deeply. Mishaps, chaos, and craziness will no doubt come knocking on your door in life. A pastor once said something that rings true of the world we live in: "You're either in a crisis, just out of a crisis, or will be in a crisis soon." How you choose to handle yourself, participate in, or walk away from things is a good measure of how you respond under pressure. How you choose to handle hardships as your world crashes in around you will determine the outcome of how you move forward.

Learning to take life in stride is one thing, but learning to lean on God is another level all its own. Hardships come in all shapes and sizes—from oversleeping and missing your alarm causing you to be late to class; to getting a flat tire on your way to work; to the unforeseen diagnosis you receive; to a hurricane destroying your home, to the ravages of a war overtaking you and your family; to someone you love dying. Any and all hardships are extremely painful and taxing to any person.

Hardships attack the very core of who we are as unforeseen pain takes its toll. In times like these, God wants to remind you to never dismiss that He is at work around you through difficult circumstances, even in your pain. He loves you that much. He is there for you and wants you to call out to Him in prayer.

- I will redeem you with an outstretched arm. (Exodus 6:6b ESV)
- Do not be afraid—I am with you! I am your God—let nothing terrify you! I will make you strong and help you; I will protect you and save you. (Isaiah 41:10 GNT)
- Call to me and I will answer you. (Jeremiah 33:3a ESV)
- Let not your heart be troubled. (John 14:1a KJV)
- I have told you these things, so that in me you may have peace. In the world you will have trouble. But take heart! I have overcome the world. (John 16:33 NIV)

What an awesome assurance! God never misses a beat. He is always there, and He cares and loves you so deeply and so perfectly.

What's Happened Since Then?

A watching nation has seen such incidences happening in every industry, where a high-profile individual later regrets his or her actions from something inappropriate that happened, sometimes even decades earlier, especially when alcohol and drugs were in the mix and unsolicited sexual advances, one or more times, has cost the person everything—career, relationships, reputation; some even serve jail time.

When a high-profile case surfaced in 2019 of a billionaire committing suicide in jail after being arrested for his operation of running a sex trafficking ring of teenage girls, grooming them for sex acts for himself and high-profile clients, it was a shock to the nation. It's a wake-up call for parents to be proactive and ever-vigilant to know who their children's friends are and who they are talking to. To teens and young adults, as mentioned earlier, be wise and discerning to do the same, especially on social media. There are internet trolls who are looking to lure you in by manipulating you to explore things that you aren't naturally inclined to do. Don't fall for their trap.

The horrific effects of human trafficking, such as depicted in the 2023 movie based on a true story, *Sounds of Freedom*,[10] exposes sex trafficking as being the fastest-growing international criminal network the world has ever seen. America is its number-one consumer, telling of what a *huge* problem this is! With its lewd activity, laced with drugs and abuse, it's unthinkable. Rape, prostitution, and the tragedy of suicide are real and are on the rise. We need to be vigilant and watchful to step in when we see something that doesn't look right. As the saying goes, *if you see something, say something*, and pray for those in harm's way. Lives are on the line every day. We can't turn a blind eye.

An online interview[11] tells of a young adult woman who was born into sex trafficking, the only life she's ever known. She wants to escape this life but fears her owner will kill her or force her to kill herself. Her personal story rattled me to the core of how horrific this is. The unthinkable and unimaginable pain she's endured represents countless others just like her out there. Their stories must be heard and brought to the forefront! Several Christian organizations are on the front lines of fighting sex trafficking. Their work is noble and is making a mark, but so much more needs to be done. Learn ways you can get involved to upend this crisis. The first step is to be aware.

Seeing Sex Trafficking Up Close

I saw a girl once in a grocery store on a cold winter's night, wearing an off-the-shoulder midriff sweatshirt, short shorts, platform stiletto heels, and heavy makeup. A few rows over, I saw an older man looking at a magazine; he appeared to be very aware of his surroundings. I brushed by her, making sure I made eye contact with her, and whispered to her as I passed by, "Are you OK?" She looked up at me in shock and under her breath, as if rehearsed, said, "I'm fine." She then quickly looked over her shoulder. I reported my observation to the store manager, who took note of the situation and had their store security watching. When she went to leave, the man was a few steps behind her. The store management gently approached her to see if she needed assistance with her groceries as the man walked quickly by. She looked scared but a bit relieved as she stood near the security guard with a police officer now on the scene. I walked quietly past where they were talking while praying for that beautiful girl, who was now safe, praying she'd be freed from her fear and healed from all the wrongs done to her.

As for how it all turned out, I don't know, but God knows and was there! May all who fear the grip of these heinous atrocities know that God is there and is with them. And when they cry out to Him, may they sense His peace and presence. "Do not fear, for I am with you" (Isaiah 41:10a NASB). Let's take a moment and pray for these victims.

Dear Lord, please protect these children, teens, and young adults who are thrust into this horrific lifestyle. Comfort them when they cry out to You. Give them hope that they are truly loved by You. Free them from their bondage and from cruel hands who hurt them. Help them search for You, find You, and know You. Let them know You're there to rescue them. Give us eyes to see those who are hurting and meet them where they are to love them in their pain. We pray all these things together in one voice and in one accord, in Jesus' precious name we pray, amen.

A Cultural Shift

My takeaway from the #MeToo movement is that when you bring your story to light, however that looks and plays out for each person in his or her given situation (*be it privately with a loved one, with a counselor, in a small group, or maybe going public*), a part of you that has been hidden and in secret, even for decades, begins to heal. Your story may even help someone else along the way who is hurting. When people see how God sustained you through your hardship, they may be encouraged to bring their stories to light to heal and, *most importantly*, to have closure.

After much prayer, I've felt God impress upon me to share my stories. As mentioned, I don't share my stories to make a political stance, to attack anyone, or to get revenge. As a follower of Christ, I wanted you to hear my accounts to encourage you if you have lived in silence, whether you're male or female, to let you know there is healing at the cross. Christ's power will heal your brokenness and set you free from your pain. Maybe you feel it was your fault for having been in that situation in the first place or that no one will believe you. Instead, be encouraged.

By His wounds we have been healed. (1 Peter 2:24b ESV)

So if the Son sets you free, you will be free indeed. (John 8:36 NIV)

A Story of God's Protection in an Assault

Before sharing my stories, I must first share a story I heard once that I'm certain will stay with you, as it has with me all these years. I'm not sure if it's a true story, but it certainly lines up with how God works. God will do *whatever* He chooses to do, any day, any time, anywhere, amen! It certainly speaks of God's mighty protection. It is a story of God's presence being more powerful than an enemy who wants to destroy you. It illustrates, in a spiritual way, how the Lord works. Be vigilant in all circumstances and always pray, for in Him, you *are* strong.

Prayer is bringing your helplessness to Jesus.[12]
—Pastor Luke Simmons
(Ephesians Series. "Be strengthened by Jesus in a world bent on making God seem small.")

Some verses that speak to this:

+ Be alert and of sober mind. Your enemy the devil prowls around like a roaring lion looking for someone to devour. (1 Peter 5:8 NIV)
+ For the weapons of our warfare are not of the flesh but have divine power to destroy strongholds. (2 Corinthians 10:4 ESV)

+ Put on the whole armor of God that you may be able to stand against the schemes of the devil. (Ephesians 6:11 ESV)
+ Finally, be strong in the Lord and in the strength of His might. (Ephesians 6:10 ESV)

The Story

> A woman was asked to identify a man in a jail lineup who she'd seen in an alley (and who was later caught in a home invasion and rape). She pointed at the man without hesitation. When questioning this individual about the woman in the alley and why he *(thankfully)* didn't attack her too, he said, "Two large men were walking on either side of her who would've taken me down fast, so I stayed frozen, hoping they wouldn't see me." When the woman was asked about the two men with her, she said she was alone but that she had started praying when she saw a man at the end of the alley.

Wow! I still get goosebumps just recalling that story. You too? I know, right? Can you just picture how that must have appeared? She had her *very* own personal bodyguards hand-delivered to her by God Himself! Not just one but two! That's *so* awesome! Here are a few verses on God's protection:

+ I lift my eyes up to the mountains, where does my help come from? My help comes from the Lord, the Maker of heaven and earth. (Psalm 121:1–2 NIV)
+ The Lord is my protector; He is my strong fortress. My God is my protection, and with Him I am safe. He protects

me like a shield; He defends me and keeps me safe. (Psalm 18:2 GNT)

✦ God will put His angels in charge of you to protect you wherever you go. (Psalm 91:11 GNT)

Forgiveness through Jesus

My stories are my complete disclosure of what happened to me. I'm so thankful Jesus has healed me from these hurtful incidents. First and foremost, I needed to forgive those who assaulted me. Only by God's grace could I have ever gotten to a place of forgiving my offenders, all of them, even though I never saw them again. Had I not released them to God in forgiveness, they'd still have a grip on me now. "Hatred stirs up strife, but love covers all offenses" (Proverbs 10:12 ESV).

If my sharing brings healing to you, I'm hoping you'll continue the conversation of how this generation can move forward in more productive ways, including the hard task of forgiving, as Jesus calls us to do. It is not easy to forgive someone who has violated you or hurt you, but it was what Christ demonstrated on the cross. He even cried out, "Father, forgive them; for they know not what they do" (Luke 23:34a KJV). Jesus demonstrated insane love right there! He's the author of forgiveness, and even though you could never forgive on your own strength, God helps you. When you do, you will be freed from the hurt and fear their acts have over you which sometimes turns into hate and bitterness. That rage inside of you, if not released to the Lord, will eat you alive. Forgiving may even come in the form of you forgiving yourself and releasing your past to the Lord. God restores brokenness. When you submit the broken pieces of your life to Him, He restores you completely.

The first to apologize is the bravest. The first to
forgive is the strongest. And the first to forget is
the happiest. (ipost.christianpost.com)[13]

I know it sounds hard and perhaps impossible to do, but God is
by your side. He will help you if you need to apologize to someone
or forgive someone. He will help you get past your situation so
it won't ruin your life anymore, and you can move forward once
again. He helped me get past mine, so with a heart of reflection, I
share these stories. They do not define me, and they do not control
me. God's redeeming blood has washed over me, and I am free, as
are you, in Christ as our Savior. There is healing at the cross.

For by the blood of Christ we are set free, that is,
our sins are forgiven. How great is the grace of
God. (Ephesians 1:7 GNT)

Reflections Before My Stories

Even though we don't always understand why bad things happen
to people, we can be assured God is there, just as He was for me
during the first three accounts I will share. His hand of protection
was woven into each one of my assaults, protecting me from what
could have been worse. I don't say that lightly to dismiss others
whose accounts have been similar or worse, but I say this to let
you know that even in the day of not knowing who to tell, in my
naivete as a child, as the talk of "stranger danger" wasn't a thing
yet, I was assuredly in the loving hands of God. Each time I cried
out to Him, He heard my cry, He comforted me, and He assured
me that I was not alone.

The later accounts happened when I had my Pollyannaish take
on the world—of assessing all people as decent, respectable, and

kind. That was the beginning of my understanding that we live in a fallen world, sin is rampant all around us, and people hurt people. But on the flip side, God was telling me, "Pray for those who abuse you" (Luke 6:28b ESV), and so I did, remembering that "All have sinned and fallen short of the glory of God" (Romans 3:23 ESV).

Yes, that included me. I was a sinner and needed a Savior to forgive me and rescue me, just like the shepherd leaving his flock of ninety-nine to rescue His one lost sheep. I was that lost sheep in need of a shepherd. Though things can get dark sometimes, and we can get tangled in the mess of this sinful world, God gently reminds us, "But take heart, I have overcome the world" (John 16:33 ESV).

Assaults by a Stranger

First assault: I was eleven years old in the sixth grade. I was out on a bike ride with my dog, near the back of my school. A baseball game was going on in the distance. I stopped to watch while my dog wandered off, exploring. A man, parked in a large town car next to oleanders that were as tall as a massive wall, called out to me, asking who was playing. I offered the information I knew, talking to him through his passenger-side window. The motion of his hand caught my eye. I suddenly felt scared and unsafe. He was a large, strong man who was only half-dressed, exposing himself in inappropriate ways, all the while telling me he could drive me home. I felt paralyzed at this rude awakening! He lunged aggressively toward me to pull me through the window. His grasp was an inch away from me when I realized what was happening and snapped out of shock and jerked away fast.

I jumped on my bike, calling for my dog. She had no idea what had just happened. She sensed the urgency and was alert to get us home. My legs were limp like noodles trying to pedal. I felt like I was in slow motion, not moving at all. The entire time, my heart pounded out of my chest as I was praying, "Jesus, protect me. Jesus, please protect me." At one point, I turned around to see if he was following us. Thankfully, he was not! I finally reached our house a few blocks away. I steadied my shaking hands to unlock the door, something I did every day as a latchkey kid, letting myself in the house, with Mom at work and my sister still at school. Once in, I locked the door behind me. With deep gasps of sobbing, I curled in a ball, huddled in the corner, trying not to be seen below the front window ledge. My dog licked my tears, helping me calm down, while every breath was on repeat—"Thank you, Jesus! Thank you, Jesus! Thank you, Jesus!" I was so thankful He saved me from something that could have gone horribly wrong.

Second assault: I was working at Duke Studios Photography when I was student teaching and was closing the studio alone. A man came in and locked the door behind him, exposing and expressing himself in front of me. The same image came flooding back in my mind from when I was eleven as he talked profanity to me and made sexual advances toward me. I was shaking but was praying to keep it together. I talked calmly to him, telling him that he was making a mistake and that he was probably a nice person who just needed to be reminded that his mom and God loved him and that he needed help. I nonchalantly reached for the phone below the counter, locking my eyes with his, not looking away for even a second. My attempt to dial 911 on the push-button phone failed as my mind went blank, and I dialed 411 instead, which is information. The operator asked if it was an emergency, at which point I said yes, and she immediately connected me to the police. That got him scared, so he grabbed my purse that was sitting on the counter and ran out the back door. My heart was pounding, just like that earlier time when I was curled up in the corner, crying.

I ran and locked the door and waited for the police who arrived about fifteen minutes later, which felt like an eternity.

While waiting, I called my mom to tell her what had happened. She prayed for me, which helped me feel calmer. I knew God was there, and I wasn't alone! I once again thanked Jesus for rescuing me from something that could have gone terribly wrong. My purse was later found in the dumpster behind our building with my wallet stolen, which had my debit card, license, and seven dollars in cash in it. Remarkably, the card and license were later found scattered down the alleyway.

Third assault: I was out jogging at dusk—something I did almost every evening, so I knew my running path well. I was just finishing up, cooling down with a brisk walk. Out of nowhere, near the dark corner of our apartment complex, a man jumped out of a bush and grabbed my chest while talking in sexual terms as he lurched toward me. I screamed at him, pushing and shoving him with all my might, a strength I didn't even know I had! No one was around to see what happened. Thankfully, I was able to push him away and ran as fast as I could to my apartment. None of my roommates were home that night, but Jesus was there! I cried as my heart pounded in fear, just like when I was a little girl. I thanked Jesus for rescuing me once again. I didn't report it, as I was tired from a long day, and going through a police report when I didn't have a description to give sounded taxing. I was restless, with one eye open that night, but reported the incident the next morning to the apartment management, and they filed a police report.

Two Other Assaults

The next assaults happened during the season when I was going out with guys I'd met. I never thought to tell anyone what happened, as I figured I had gotten myself into these situations. In both incidents, my Diet Coke was tampered with. I was drugged and date raped. I remember being fully present in my mind leading up to those incidents, remembering where I was and what I was wearing. Each time, there was dancing and a nice dinner with a supposedly nice man I was enjoying time with. Was I so naive that his advances didn't signal to me that he was hopeful for more to come that evening? Did he assume since I did not drink, I wouldn't get drunk, and by drugging me, he'd get his way? It was an undercut scheme to take advantage of me.

Waking up the next morning in an unusual place, with my clothes torn halfway off, was a nightmare! It was awful! It was shameful! I wondered how I got there and who this person was—and in one case, two crashed out next to me. I was mortified! How could this have happened? Why couldn't I remember anything? God, help me! All I could do was scramble to find my car keys and drive away as fast and as far as I could, praying that a shower would wash away the pain and the humiliation, all the while being haunted in my mind, vaguely remembering hearing one say, "Where did you find this one?" This was beyond horrific! Who did they think I was? A prostitute?

And the next time they called, I hung up the phone until they finally went away. I told no one, as I felt dirty and ashamed, and I didn't want to remember. I hoped it was all a bad dream. It left deep scars only God could heal.

Please Tell Someone! You're Not Alone!

I have never shared my stories with anyone publicly or told all of them in one space, only bits and pieces here and there if someone was hurting and needed to know they aren't alone, but God prompted me to share them here. Maybe someone needs to hear them, and maybe that someone is you. If you've been sexually assaulted, I am so very, very sorry that happened to you! You may feel terribly shocked, afraid, or even emotionally numb. Whatever you're feeling, even if it happened a long time ago and you've suppressed your emotions about how it affected you, please find someone to talk to about this. If you know immediately of an assault or rape, go to the police or the hospital so you can be checked out for harm done to you. Without fail, run to Jesus with your pain, write in your journal, and cry out to Him. He is there!

From experience, I can tell you that healing is in His hands. Talk to people who care about you—a trusted friend, a parent, a pastor at your church, or a counselor at your school. Should action need to be taken, they will guide you in those decisions. If you'd like to reach out to me, I am here for you and would love to pray for you. In the end, ask God to give you the strength to use your pain for good and for forgiveness.

Though I did not seek counseling, as my thoughts entangled me with shame, regret, and embarrassment, I did talk (prayed and journaled), most importantly, to God about everything. As a believer in Christ, you have the Holy Spirit dwelling within you. He is your helper (see John 14:15–26).

> He will give you another advocate to help you and be with you forever—the Spirit of Truth. The world cannot accept him, because it neither sees him nor knows him. But you know him, for he lives with you and will be in you. (John 14:16b–17 NIV)

His presence in my life counseled me, loved me, assisted me, and supported me. The same is true today. The Holy Spirit counsels me, loves me, assists me, and supports me, twenty-four/seven. He's always available, always there—my constant companion! And He is there for you too.

> He is the great paraclete (the Holy Spirit: an advocate, intercessor, comforter) who offers the very things so many people tend to seek in therapy. That is why, when it comes to seeking a counselor, a Christian counselor or therapist is paramount for walking through difficult things with you, as they are committed to the Holy Spirit's leading and directing you in understanding God's truth and will pray your life forward in wisdom and help you gain freedom from the disparaging chains of your past. To counsel apart from His mighty power is to quench the Holy Spirit. (Summarized notes from Biblical Counseling Coalition, post by Lee Lewis, 2016.) [14]

Those two assumed dates that went horribly wrong were wake-up calls from God for me to get away from the nightlife that was filled with such luring obstacles and pitfalls that left me empty. I gained a very important perspective that the Holy Spirit taught me through those assaults and that was to be responsible for my own actions. (In saying that, I don't want to minimize or misrepresent what others have gone through, as each case is different. But for me, it was what ultimately changed my behavior.)

I cannot control the actions of others, but I can control my actions and how I respond to things. If something felt wrong, and it did, I could have—and more importantly, I should have—left, but I didn't. My naivete and being enticed by the attention was intoxicating to my emotions, and I fell for the bait. I know these incidents were not my fault, but if I had made better choices in the first place, I could have avoided all of these hardships that ensued. I had more to live for than what the world offered in relationships.

It was all the same, and I needed to make better choices in my life. Most importantly, I needed to remind myself that I was bought with a price. Jesus paid it all on the cross! The same is true for you too. You are victorious through Jesus, who makes all things new. God is there to heal your wounds and make you whole.

Your Value and Your Worth

Have you ever heard of the value of a twenty-dollar bill? It goes like this: Take a brand-new, crisp, twenty-dollar bill and compare it to an old, crumbly, torn, and tattered twenty-dollar bill. Which has more value? Hmm … not a trick question. Yes, of course, they both have exactly the same value. They equate to the same amount, each having the exact amount of buying power equivalent to twenty dollars. Neither has more value than the other. Why ever, then, do we devalue ourselves because we have some bumps and bruises, literally or figuratively speaking? That is a lie we hear and sadly listen to. Remember, you're new in Christ!

> "But I will restore you to health and heal your wounds," declares the Lord. (Jeremiah 30:17 NIV)

> He was pierced for our transgressions; he was crushed for our iniquities, the punishment that brought us peace was on Him, and by his wounds we are healed. (Isaiah 53:5 NIV)

And what a beautiful perspective to lean into. As a child of God, let your hope and focus be on your future and what it will ultimately be—eternity with Jesus. Don't allow your past to dictate your present or your future. Satan wants to rob you of your joy. Satan loves a slow death—like a matador with his red cape to lure the bull, all while exhausting the bull until the plunge of his sword pierces his side, slaying him to his death. Oddly enough, my high school mascot was a matador. It made sense as a mascot to be the tough competitor, to finish strong, and to win on top, with cheers that depicted the win with chants of, "We are the mighty, Mighty Matadors!"

But as for matadors in general, I always had a difficult time with the despicable death of the poor bull. In the 2017 animated movie, *Ferdinand* [15], based on the beloved children's book, I authentically cried when his dad died. (So sorry for the spoiler there but a great movie to watch nonetheless.) Sad too were all the other bulls who went into the arena. It's just like Satan to lure us into the arena with his red cape, distracting us and getting our attention so we take our eyes off Jesus, not even realizing he's out for our lives—worse yet, he's out to destroy and kill us.

That's where prayer comes in. "Satan, get behind me. You have no power here! I am a child of God. My past does not define me. Flee from me. In the name of Jesus, I pray. Amen." And a quick side note on this point—Satan shudders at the name of Jesus. Your heart is released from the talons of his grip when you call out to Jesus, who will replace your fear, despair, attack, and ruin with His light and goodness. Darkness hates the light, just like a scurrying roach flees for cover when a light turns on.

> The light shines in the darkness, and the darkness
> can never extinguish it. (John 1:5 NLT)

A great novel I read as a young adult—and would highly recommend—that scared me senseless (but in a good way) will help you better understand the spiritual warfare that goes on around you, vying for your very soul. It's titled *This Present Darkness* [16], by

Frank E. Peretti and its sequel is *Piercing the Darkness*. Here are verses that speak to this:

> Submit yourselves, then to God. Resist the devil, and he will flee from you. (James 4:7 NIV)

> You dear children, are from God and have overcome them, because the One who is in you is greater than the one who is in the world. (1 John 4:4 NIV)

A View from the Car Window

A wonderful analogy I heard somewhere along the way and have shared countless times when encouraging people with wounded spirits says this:

When you drive a car, you have a rearview mirror. Its entire purpose is to let you see what's behind you. Notice its size. It's a small mirror so it won't distract you from the large front windshield, which gives you a clear view of all that's in front of you, pointing you in the direction you're headed. While driving, if you stayed focused on the rearview mirror and those things behind you, you'd eventually crash. What is behind you is behind you. What's in front of you is the new direction you're headed.

What a great life lesson! Learn from the things that are behind you—a peek in your rearview mirror of life—to learn from your past. If your past is laced with hardships, your new perspective looking forward will keep you from those past pitfalls. Instead, God calls you to keep your eyes fixed on Him, looking forward to all He has in store for you, which is heaven-bound!

Let your present be molded and shaped by what
you are to become in Christ, not by what sin did
to you in the past.

—Henry Blackaby [17]

You Are Priceless!

A must-see movie, inspired by true events, called *Priceless* [18], is
about a young girl caught up in sex trafficking and her deliverance
and freedom from evil hands. The 2016 film's lead actor is from the
Christian band For King & Country, whose song lyrics featured
in the movie speak from God's point of view about His creation—
you. It's a compelling message that no matter what you've gone
through, you have been bought with a price. You're forgiven, and
you are priceless! Believe it. Live it. Become it! Here are some of the
lyrics to their song "Priceless".

> That isn't who you are
> Don't you dare forget, that in the pain
> You can be brave
> I see a rose in bloom
> At the sight of you
> Oh, so priceless

Closing

However this chapter sits with you, I pray that something I shared
will resonate with you. If your own heart needs healing, or you're
walking with someone who is hurting in this area of pain—from
an assault, betrayal, abandonment, and the list goes on—may God
comfort you and them as you and they walk this journey of healing

while finding forgiveness at the cross and moving forward from this place. God is the truest and best treasure ever! He heals you, forgives you, restores you, renews you, and sets you on a new path. Amen and amen.

CHAPTER 14

Dating God

A s my disdain for wrong choices in men grew, my desire to be more involved in my young adult group grew deeper. It was evident I had put up a wall from being hurt in the past and needed healing, but as I grew further from those painful moments and experiences, I knew God was doing a work in my life. He still had to teach me about matters of my untrusting heart, which brought me to my thirtieth birthday and honed in on my obvious lack of trusting completely. Instead of unequivocally trusting God 100 percent in all things, I wavered and trusted in myself when I felt I knew better than God. When the first guy I was really interested in just wanted to be friends, I couldn't understand why the gut-wrenching pain of rejection, betrayal, and lack of self-worth came storming in again like a raging river, flooding my soul. I thought I had grown so much spiritually, and I had, but to process these same *feelings* and emotions from seven years prior would take an act of God to get my attention and reach my stubborn heart, which needed to be altered.

Life Lesson: Feelings are fickle! You can't trust your feelings. You just can't! They will lie to you every time. Only God's Word, the truth, will set you free! People's opinions or your mood that shift like the wind on any given day can't set you free from your feelings. Only God's truth can. He'll guide you on how to handle your ever-changing feelings and uncover the many layers you are hiding behind.

As with the onion analogy earlier, we have multiple layers. Some of these layers are brought on by our own choices that cause self-inflicted wounds, some by others, but all in all, layers close off our ability to hear from God. But in His kindness and grace, God gently peels back one layer at a time. After long and tedious days, months, years, or even decades of shedding layers from our bruised hearts that have become embittered, God prunes us and shapes us into His image. That is when He gets to our core—our center. Shiny and new, Christ sprouts inside of us as He takes root in our hearts, and we blossom, becoming a lamppost for others to see Christ in us. We are now ready to face the world with a newfound hope and perspective. God calls us to be patient and to trust Him as we walk this journey of faith with Him. God was surely there to see me through, and He is there to see you through too. We are all works in progress. Be still and know that He is God! He loves you and is doing a good work in your life. Amen.

He who began a good work in you will carry it on to completion until the day of Christ Jesus. (Philippians 1:6b NIV)

Had I had this kind of wisdom back then, I believe I would've avoided so many of these pitfalls. Thankfully, God was moving on my heart, big time, and His mighty love was taking hold! His hand was clearly seeing me through and giving me clarity of what was right in front of me—and that was Him. I was concentrating more than ever on my relationship with God. Choosing to live a life of integrity and spending intimate time with God would take a heart of intentionality. I was up for the challenge. I was all in, and I was ready.

Choose a Life of Integrity

If you're a follower of Christ, choose to be a person of integrity. Be ever mindful of your conduct, actions, activities, and whereabouts. And if need be, change your conduct, your actions, your activity, and your whereabouts because what you put into your life is what comes out. Resist the temptation of places, things, and/or people who are toxic and cause you to stumble or are your obstacles, even if it means getting those places, things, or people out of your life altogether so you make better and wiser choices for yourself.

> Never forget, you're a reflector of Christ. That alone should set the precedent for how you live your life privately and publicly.
> —Luke Simmons, "Pink Spoon People" sermon[1]

Date Nights with God

Instead of joining coworkers for happy hour or joining friends to go dancing, I was finally comfortable telling them, "No thanks." It wasn't anything against them or their choices; I just knew that, for me, they were past traps I needed to avoid.

Life Lesson: It's OK to say no. You don't have to say yes to every invitation. Save your *yes* for the best plans, and everything else is optional. It's a great way to live your life—without the pressure of feeling obligated to go everywhere you're invited. Saying no is OK.

Instead, I enjoyed my own plans alone with the Lord. I'd pick a night when my roommates weren't home and would have a date night and meal with God and would play worship music. (For me, worship music has been a continuous lifeline to Jesus. I *love* worship music and can't get enough of it. Worship music helps me breathe. If you've never experienced Christian music, give it a try! You might just *love* it. Your soul will be renewed—guaranteed!)

I would dance with Jesus as if he were physically present with me—either fast or slow, whatever the rhythm was, we danced.

> Let them praise His name with dancing; Let them
> sing praises to Him. (Psalm 149:3 NASB)

I'd then have a time of communion with the Lord by putting a blanket down on the carpeted living room floor. I would have a small loaf of bread, tear it into bite-size pieces, and eat them, remembering His body, broken for me and all He had done for me, while I ate in remembrance of Him. I would drink grape juice in remembrance of His offering of forgiveness flowing over me, and then I'd spend time in prayer.

Having communion with Jesus, spending time in His Word, dancing and singing with worship music, journaling, and praying were some of the most precious and sweetest times I've *ever* had with the Lord! I referred to it as my season of "dating God." He met me every time, and it was beautiful!

A Little Bit About Communion

(Follow-up from an Earlier Chapter)

Communion (an act of sharing or holding in common; participating) is a time when believers (people who believe in Christ and put their trust in Him) reflect on what Jesus did for them on the cross by symbolically having a meal in remembrance of Him. At some churches, you may go forward to receive the elements of bread and juice (some serve real wine), or the elements may be passed around to you. Some churches may offer Communion every week, while others may offer it during special occasions. In my situation, I was having communion on my date nights with God. If you'd prefer to have a few sips of wine (in moderation) with the Lord at His Communion table, this is certainly an appropriate time and place for it, if you're of legal age. And as Paul instructed, do not drink of the cup in an unworthy manner that would be sinful against the body and blood of the Lord (1 Corinthians 11:27), but reflect on matters of the heart before the Lord, confessing any sin, coming to the table humbly before Him. How, when, and where you have Communion are secondary details to the symbolism of what Communion represents.

Remembering all Christ did on the cross when He died for your sins, believing He was raised from the dead (Easter), accepting His life, death, and Resurrection as a free gift of salvation that cannot be earned but is received—these are at the heart of Communion. He was the sacrificial Lamb, the substitutionary atonement for our sins, and His new resurrected life is ours to receive if we simply ask Him into our hearts and believe. The Last Supper was the last meal Jesus had with His disciples before He died. Jesus is God, the Triune God—the union of three, Father, Son, and Holy Spirit—is one.

> In the beginning was the Word, and the Word was with God, and the Word was God. He was in the beginning with God. (John 1:1–2 ESV)

> And the Word became flesh and dwelt among us, and we have seen his glory, glory as the only son from the Father full of grace. (John 1:14 ESV)

> But the advocate, the Holy Spirit, whom the Father will send in my name, will teach you all things and will remind you of everything I have said to you. (John 14:26 NIV)

> And (He) will help you and be with you forever. (John 14:16b NIV)

He is omnipotent (having unlimited power, able to do anything).

> And He is before all things, and in Him all things hold together. (Colossians 1:17 ESV)

He is omnipresent (being present everywhere at the same time).

> When you go through deep waters, I will be with you. When you go through rivers of difficulty, you will not drown. When you walk through the fire of oppression, you will not be burned up; the flames will not consume you. (Isaiah 43:2 NLT)

Jesus' Last Meal

Jesus knew this was His last meal with His friends, and used strong symbolism to foreshadow all that was to come. He gathered them, and together, they shared one last meal. Here is what happened.

> Now as they were eating, Jesus took bread, and after blessing it broke it and gave it to the disciples, and said, "Take eat; this is my body." And He took a cup, and when He had given thanks He gave it

to them, saying, "Drink of it, all of you, for this
is my blood of the covenant, which is poured out
for many for the forgiveness of sins." (Matthew
26:26–2 ESV)

Paul's account of this story to the church in Corinth said this:
"As often as you eat and drink ... do this in remembrance of me"
(1 Corinthians 11:24–25).

Jesus used bread and wine as a symbol of the new covenant
poured out for the forgiveness of sins and new life that is eternal—
life after death—to all who believe. No longer would the old law
apply of a lamb being sacrificed for the forgiveness of sins. Jesus
became the ultimate substitution, the priceless Lamb who takes
away the sins of the world, and in that, we worship, celebrating all
He has done, at the Communion table.

The Lord's Supper is an act of worship. Come to
the table focused on the Lord and partake in the
elements that are central to the Gospel message.
(John Piper, *Desiring God*)[2]

Having Communion with God, breaking bread, drinking juice
(or wine) in remembrance of Jesus and His forgiveness, and praying
with songs of worship in your heart is such a precious and cleansing
time that you will treasure. Have a date night with God! You will
have such a blessed time, rich in fellowship, with your precious
Lord and Savior, a night that will fill your spirit and leave your
soul satisfied, desiring more and more of Him—exactly how a
relationship should be!

Quality Time with Jesus Is Better than Anything

If you are single, I urge you to spend quality time with God. You will *never* have this type of alone time with the Lord in your life, ever. For such a time as this, your singleness is a gift; enjoy it! It will enrich you in ways you'll never regret. Right now, it's just you and God. Most likely, you will meet someone someday, all in God's good timing, but this time with the Lord, at this moment, you will never have again as it is right now. Lean into this time. It's His gift to you! Don't sulk in your aloneness. I did, and it only made me long for more of what I didn't have and thought I needed. Everything I needed was right in front of me. When I finally released my desires, all I longed for was more of God. My time with Jesus became so rich and was so *very* precious.

Relish every moment during this window of time. It will be gone in a flash. Even though it feels like an eternity, it is not. He wants your whole heart and wants to meet you in this private place in your life to have oneness with Him. You will never be sorry you did. It's a time you'll always look back on with great fondness. Plus, it will set the precedent for your intimate time with God in the future seasons of your life. Once you establish the beauty of alone time with God, you will crave it for the rest of your life; I guarantee it!

Time alone with God is a powerful thing. You will get to know Him. Establish these solid habits now that will last for your lifetime. Journal throughout this season with God so you can look back, years later, and read all that He has done for you and all the things He taught you as you trusted Him.

When you get to be my age, I promise that you'll look back on those precious years that were just you and God and will be eternally grateful. Enjoy them!

Praying for Your Future Spouse

I started praying for my future husband during those date nights with God. I prayed that whoever he was, that his walk with the Lord would grow deeper every day. I prayed God was preparing him to meet me someday and that he'd accept me for who I was in the Lord. I prayed that he would love Jesus more than anything else. I prayed he was kind and had a servant's heart.

But I also was getting to a place of being content with being single. My heart's longing could no longer be a transaction with God. "I'll love You, God, if You do this for me." Or "God, I promise I'll always serve You if You find someone for me." No, that's not how God works. God is God regardless of what we think we need or want. God is not to be bargained with, nor is He interested in our trying to buy His love and affection by trying to earn His approval through works. Step aside, and let God be God because we are not. In fact, without Christ, our works are like filthy rags. This verse was shared earlier but worth revisiting:

> All of us have become like one who is unclean,
> and all our righteous acts are like filthy rags; we
> all shrivel up like a leaf, and like the wind our sins
> sweep us away. (Isaiah 64:6 NIV)

We won't ever measure up to anything good in God's eyes. He died for that sinful pride of ours that's choking us from living lives of freedom. Freedom in Jesus is the good news that saves us from ourselves. He is our Savior, He is our hope! Put your faith in Jesus in every aspect of your life. He knows you and the desires of your heart, so trust Him. His ways are *always* better than our own! Amen.

As I embraced this truth, I knew that if God would choose to answer my prayer to meet someone special someday, it would be completely His doing, as everything up until this point was not working the way I had planned. I continuously intervened, putting my agenda above God's and putting my wants ahead of what the Lord was working out in me. It seemed now I was finally succeeding at a relationship, the one true relationship above all others, the one that would last forever, the best there could ever be, an intimate relationship with my sweet Savior, which included an ongoing dialogue and prayer throughout the day.

I highly recommend you watch the 2015 movie *War Room*.[3] It tells the story of an elderly woman who converted a closet in her home into a prayer closet she called her "war room," as she explained, any battle you have going on belongs to the Lord. She passed on her prayer legacy to a stellar career woman who had a struggling marriage and was about to lose everything. The woman desired a prayer life like this endearing woman and took her advice to pray and cry out to God to salvage her marriage. I won't share the ending, but she learns that God answers prayers His way, whether that's for or against your request, hopes, and/or desires. He is always there for you, no matter the outcome. Most importantly, He desires to spend time with you when you take time to pray!

Without fail, make this the best season ever by shifting your eyes off yourself and onto others. Join Jesus by spending time with Him and serving Him by serving others. Watch where He is at work and join Him. It will change your life and perspective in beautiful ways.

> Now may the God of peace ... equip you with everything good that you may do His will, working in us that which is pleasing in His sight, through Jesus Christ, to whom be glory forever and ever. Amen. (Hebrews 13:20a–21 ESV)

Along the lines of serving others, the following is an awesome piece I received in a Bible study that speaks to loving others first. It includes great principles to live by, straight from the Bible that encourage us to be others-focused, always!

One Anothers

> Greet one another, comfort one another, forgive one another, build one another up, serve one another, bear one another's burdens, encourage one another, meet with one another, be kind and tenderhearted toward one another, receive (welcome) one another as Christ received you, care for one another, minister to one another, show hospitality to one another, pray for one another.
>
> —Revive Our Hearts Ministry[4]

Radio deejay Shannyn Caldwell at Family Life Radio, author of *The Healing Season*—which tells of her parents dying in a tornado (a powerful story) and how God the mighty healer mended her brokenness—encouraged her listeners during a Compassion Child radio segment to act by being difference-makers, reminding them, "You've been given so much; give back. These children desperately need your help! You are a lion! Roar, baby, roar!"[5] What a great reminder. Instead of being focused on our own needs, focus instead on the needs of others. We are made for a purpose, and like Christ's example, we should serve and help others. It's our greatest calling. Love others before yourself!

> Clothe yourself with compassion, kindness, humility, gentleness and patience. (Colossians 3:12b NIV)

> In humility, value others above yourselves, not
> looking to your own interests but each of you to the
> interests of the others. (Philippians 2:3b–4 NIV)

Shannyn and the morning team encourage my heart, as do other deejays, Lauree (love that funny girl @radiolauree) and Carlos from K-Love. Christian radio lifts me up daily through worship music and sermon broadcasts. Fill your heart with streaming apps—FLR, K-Love, and Air1 are my favorites. Artist and sermon podcasts are great too. You'll be so encouraged by the worship and daily truths that are taught.

Have Gratitude

Also, have a heart of gratitude rather than a bad attitude. It will change your overall perspective every time. Whenever you find yourself in a bad mood, check your attitude. Be intentional; shake off that chip-on-the-shoulder attitude that is weighing you down. Change your physical posture at that moment from being slouched over to pulling your shoulders back, standing up tall, and asking God to forgive your bitter heart. Release whatever is eating at you, and think instead of those things you are grateful for and blessed with.

Before you know it, your bitterness will turn to joyfulness, and you will be ready to enter into a new day with a smile on your face and a skip in your step. Try it! It takes your eyes off yourself so you can see clearly who is in front of you, to love them, and to serve them with a heart of joy and kindness. Even if your days or the circumstances around you are tough, be secure in knowing God's got you! He's not going to let you go. Because of that assurance, set your gaze on Him, and watch your mourning turn to dancing.

Give thanks in all circumstances; for this is God's will for you in Christ Jesus. (1 Thessalonians 5:18 NIV)

Paying It Forward

Years had passed since I joined the young-adult group after the breakup that flipped my world upside down. At one point, I told my pastor that I would be moving on, as I was now an older single in the group, though he encouraged me to stick around to disciple younger girls coming up behind me. He knew my past story would help them better understand that Jesus is their first love above anyone or anything else in their lives. I agreed to stay to share with them what God had done in my life. I knew there wasn't anything more important for me to do with my time than to pay it forward and share with younger adult ladies that God loves them and has a plan for their lives. There is nothing more rewarding in this world than to pour into another person's life with gospel truth. God shows up when you spend time helping others grow in their faith when they are hungry for more of Him.

First Thing in the Morning, Have a Meet-and-Greet with God

Let this verse be the anthem over your life:

Let the morning bring me word of Your unfailing love, for I have put my trust in You. Show me the way I should go, for to You I entrust my life. (Psalm 143:8 NIV)

The first verse of Jeremy Camp's song *Give Me Jesus*[6] (an all-time favorite) can set the tone for your day. Everything else is secondary:

> In the morning when I rise, give me Jesus!
> You can have this whole world, just give me Jesus.

An old high school church-camp song comes to mind that even had hand motions:

> Love Him in the morning when you see the sun arising.
> Love Him in the evening 'cause He took you through the day.
> And in the in-between time when you feel the pressure coming,
> Remember that He loves you and He promises to stay!

Amen. Before climbing out of bed or reaching for your phone or coffee, greet God with love, and say hello! A simple greeting will start your day off right. *More on prayer, up next.* Let His name be the first name from your lips. Remember, if you're in a relationship with someone, you spend time with that person. The same is true with God! Take a few minutes to meet with God by turning your day over to Him. He is the *most* important appointment of your day! When you come to God first, before your crazy day begins, He'll help you sort through things, prioritize your thinking, and give you guidance in your day. Give Him words from your heart. Take in the moment, this new day—breathe, inhale, exhale. Greet God with words about your day. Here's an example:

Good morning, precious Lord. Thank you for a peaceful night's rest. Thank you for giving me this new day. I place my schedule in Your hands. I trust You with it as You see fit. Guide my steps today. Holy Spirit, give me eyes to see who You want me to love and serve today, and may I do so joyfully. Help me to put their needs above my own. Forgive me in the ways that I've opposed You. Make my heart right and pure before You. Thank you, Lord, for new mercies this day. Protect me in Your care. This is Your day; do with it as You will, and help me to trust You in the process. I love You so much! In Jesus' precious and mighty name, I pray. Amen.

Then, take a few moments, even if brief, to get a dose of feeding from God's Word. It can be something like a "Daily Bread" devotion or an online devotion on your phone, a Psalm or chapter from your Bible, or meditating on a verse that will stay with you throughout the day from a Bible app. Don't jump on social media before meeting with God. Talk to Him first! Pray and journal. He's listening.

Trust Him completely and be confident in the way He leads you. He has a purpose for you, even though you don't think He does. He might not reveal it to you right away but don't lose heart. Stay the course, and trust Him. Each day that you spend time with God, you will crave more! You might do a full Bible study, or take a class to dig deeper, but getting started is a great place to be. Read His Word daily. The Bible will be fuel for your soul.

The steadfast love of the Lord never ceases; His mercies never come to an end; they are new every morning; great is Your faithfulness. (Lamentations 3:22–23 ESV)

So we do not lose heart. Though our outer self is
wasting away, our inner self is being renewed day
by day. (2 Corinthians 4:16 ESV)

About Prayer

Prayer is talking to God. It's a relationship. He delights in our
coming to Him to talk, to listen, to share, and to be still. (Below
are some sermon notes on prayer from teaching pastor Seth Troutt
to help you start your prayer journey with God.)[7]

In the same way, the Spirit helps us in our weakness.
We do not know what we ought to pray for, but the
Spirit Himself intercedes for us through wordless
groans. (Romans 8:26 NIV)

+ Prayer must constitute your complete devotion, constantly
conversing with God in all manners of your life.
+ Prayer is the cornerstone of your faith. It is communicating
on a regular basis with the God of the universe, who loves you
completely and wants to hear your heart.
+ If prayer isn't your comfort zone, perhaps your thoughts are to
pray lofty prayers. Honestly, those are just wasted words if not
honest and raw.
+ Start by journaling your prayers and asking God for direction
in those areas.
+ It is such a joy to see God answer prayers. He's waiting for you
to talk with Him.
+ Don't miss out on the most important person in your life by
standing idle and never conversing with Him. He's there. Just
start talking!

- Don't be prayerless. Don't let a level of confidence and sinful rebellion keep you from praying.
- Connect with God by being attentive and honest and allowing the Holy Spirit to intercede on your behalf.
- Even if it means the moans of your guttural heart crying out, Jesus meets you in your incompetence.
- To admit, "I believe. Help me in my unbelief," is like Doubting Thomas in his unbelief. More often, we need to cry out, "Lord Jesus, have mercy on me. I am a sinner." That's a moment of truthfulness to God of the distraught and disordered desires of our hearts.
- Walk in dependence of your Savior!

CHAPTER 15

Questions of Purpose and God's Will

As God was consistently sorting through matters of my disgruntled heart throughout those years, another place He was shaping and molding my character was through my employment, which was a huge part of my young adult story. For any young adult, a job is critical. Not only does a job pay the bills, but it also helps clarify one's dreams and passions. God uses individuals' jobs and/or careers as a training ground to equip them, inevitably preparing them for all that's ahead in life. I can look back now and see how God used all my work experiences to teach me more about Him, His faithfulness, and His purpose in my life.

God ultimately connects all the dots in your life, even when you don't necessarily realize they all have a purpose in the first place. He never wastes an experience or an encounter to draw you to Him. As a believer, when making life decisions, it's critically important to keep Jesus at the helm to navigate the waters of life, while you ponder such questions as:

+ Who am I, and where am I going?
+ What is God's will and purpose for my life?
+ How do I know if I'm in God's will?
+ Who should I talk to about the decisions I am facing with school, work, and my future career?
+ How do the gifts God has given me play a part in my decisions for my future?

These are just a sampling of questions that young adults may have spinning around in their heads at any given time. For that matter, these are great questions for people of any age to ponder when evaluating their life purposes and goals. Let's look at the entire picture before we dive into what we're supposed to do with our lives.

A change of mindset often is a great place to start. Let's say, for example, you're flipping burgers, feeling insignificant, and wondering, "How will this job ever change anything?" Instead, pause a moment and be thankful that you have a job! Any opportunity you're given is an opportunity to learn new skills and gain personal growth, as well as to be a light to those you work with by simply being present, attentive, hardworking, and kind.

That also applies to school. You may find yourself asking, "Why do I have to learn this stuff? It will never apply in the real world." Instead, look at the environment God has placed you in with your classmates and teachers, and pray, "God, help me be a student who truly cares and desires to authentically learn. Let Your love flow through me to be kind, helpful, and respectful always. Amen." Treat school as your job. God will show up and shine through you in beautiful ways! He has so much to teach you when you are physically and mentally present and attentive in class. Be an active listener by responding, participating, and engaging. Above all, be kind.

How to Make an Impact in Our Ever-Changing World

Trying to grasp how to make an impact for good is a bit daunting and overwhelming, especially in our ever-changing world that feels hostile and often cruel. Wars breaking out over parts of the world are both jarring and devastating, let alone difficult to make sense of during these perilous times. It's truly heartbreaking to watch the news streaming twenty-four/seven, seeing the pain and suffering of hundreds of thousands, even millions, of lives being uprooted over territories. Not to mention school shootings, deaths, drugs, suicide, human trafficking, hostility within differing communities, and anger all around, it is all a reminder that we live in a fallen and broken world.

Each person has a role to play for the good of humanity to be compassionate. God is always working out His plan through His people. We have to watch where God is at work and join Him. With regard to all the painful tragedies brought on by people inflicting pain on others, may we be ever mindful and in tune to be compassionate, to pray for those suffering, and to come to their aid with help, however that may look. Being the hands and feet of Christ in all circumstances brings hope to a hurting world.

Ultimately, there is only one MVP and He died on a cross on a rescue mission for humanity and He has commanded us to go defend the weak, protect the poor, and to help those who are hurting. And let me tell you something, there are a lot of people around the world who are hurting which means we have a big job to do. Let's go get our job done!

Tim Tebow,[1] "Sports Impact of the Year"
2022 K-Love Awards

Claire at Pepperdine

Claire, a young-adult friend from our group, shared on social media that when she attended Pepperdine University, her school community endured devastation when eleven students were shot and killed by an active shooter at a local dance club near her college, one of whom was an acquaintance of her friend. The next day, more rattling news came when the university and neighboring counties were surrounded by the 2018 Woolsey Fire that rolled ferociously through seventy thousand acres overnight. Students were temporarily housed in safe shelters on campus while the fire was kept at bay and fanned off from school buildings.

Those were incredibly scary incidents—students' lives were threatened and fear set in by flying bullets and flaming fire on all sides! Claire shared how prayer between students and administration held them together and that holding on to hope was their solace and anchor to carry on. Her faith sustained her and encouraged those around her during those dark days that they encountered.

What or Who Is Shaping You?

Guest pastor Dr. Mike Goheen, author of *The Drama of* Scripture,[2] preached from a passage in Ephesians and started his message with these questions: "With life flying at a person so fast from every direction, what is shaping you? Is it the gospel, or is it the culture?"

He went on to note how Ephesians responds to those questions:

> He made known to us the mystery of His will,
> according to His good pleasure which He set forth
> in Him, regarding His plan of the fullness of the

times, to bring all things together in Christ, things
in the heavens and things on the earth. (Ephesians
1:9–10 NASB)

His point was that we may not know what the future holds,
but we know who holds the future—God does. And God is
worth trusting with our lives. Dr. Goheen closed with these final
questions: "Who gets to narrate the earth? Who gets to narrate
your life? Those are life-altering questions! How would you
respond?

CHAPTER 16

He Leads, We Follow—
God, the Ultimate Boss

This chapter is filled with nuggets of truth I've collected along life's way to encourage and challenge you as you ponder your direction and purpose and the decisions you make. Chapter 17 describes my job experiences where these principles played out in my life and how God wove them together as only He can do.

When you were a child, were you ever asked, "What do you want to be when you grow up?" A preschool teacher friend, Ms. Nicole, asks her preschoolers this question every year before they are promoted to kindergarten. Wearing handmade graduation caps, with a mic in hand and deep in thought, they answer her question—everything shared from wanting to be a police officer, a nurse, a pilot, a teacher, or an occasional princess, cowboy, or Superman, to name a few. It's adorable! Every adult in the room captures their child's unscripted response on their phones, taking in the moment, snapping photos and videos. What was your answer when asked that question?

Did a person or an experience influence you with a dream of

becoming (fill in the blank)? Or maybe you're still figuring it out. Was a dream ever derailed or crushed altogether? Maybe you're still trying to make sense of it all, as it feels as if everything you worked so hard for and dreamed about came crashing down. If that's your situation, don't lose heart!

For a very long time in my young adult years, I had hopes of becoming a full-time worship leader and traveling with a band as a vocalist, thinking that was the direction God had for me. God, however, had other plans in mind for me that didn't look like that, although He did fulfill my desire involving worship and singing in other ways.

Never get discouraged; there is hope in loss. And never allow envy or jealousy to creep in; don't wish you had what others have in their positions or see your dream played out in their lives. Instead, be their biggest cheerleader in their accomplishments. It's not yours to touch or be concerned about, so don't get caught up in misguided feelings. I've learned along the way that you never lose your love or passion toward a gift. God just shapes it in other ways. Always be expectant and hopeful of how He will shape those dreams. A great line I learned once at a worship conference rings true: "Bloom where you're planted." It refers to all areas of your life. Look where God has placed you in life, and start there. The dream is usually not too far from that starting point.

Life from God's Perspective

No matter your age, you'll always be on a quest to figure out what you're doing with your life. As life moves forward, life experiences will shape your passions and pave the way you will go. All experiences will sharpen your skill set and hone in on your gifts while your dreams and desires take hold. It's a natural progression of how life moves forward—but have you ever considered life from

God's perspective? He may very well have a plan for your life that looks completely different from what you envisioned. Could it be that your dreams and the direction of your life are always changing? How do you feel about that? Giving God complete control means letting go. Are you up for the challenge?

Life Happens

A quote made famous by former Beatles singer John Lennon in his 1980 song "Beautiful Boy (Darling Boy)," written for his son, says this:

> Life is what happens to you
> While you're busy making other plans

Isn't that true? We get busy doing what we think we're supposed to do, and suddenly, life happens when we're busy making other plans. We need margin in our lives for those unexpected moments that show up *all the time!* A large part of life's journey is learning how to go with the ebb and flow of life and roll with the punches but, most importantly, to understand how God operates in your life. It is critical to learn how to hold on loosely to things that are important now or that you think are important because anything can happen at any time. Whatever might be yours one day may be gone the next.

At the end of the movie *Mr. Holland's* Opus,[1] Mr. Holland, the band teacher, is retiring and is honored at a surprise assembly in the school's auditorium that is packed with the entire school and previous band students. He is overwhelmed by their kind gestures, and when asked to say a few words, he takes to the podium to thank his wife and their son, who is deaf, singing and signing this song to him—"Beautiful Boy." He impacted countless lives along the way, including his son. Together, they learned the power of music that surpassed Mr. Holland's dream of becoming a composer and writing his own symphony. His dream was always set aside, as everything was always vying for his time and attention. A previous student, now the governor of the state, shares how Mr. Holland gave her confidence to do things she never thought she could do before. She tells him, "There is not a life in this room that you have not touched. Each one of us is a better person because of you! We are your symphony. We are the melodies and the notes of your opus, and we are the music of your life." All his past students join him on stage as he's handed a baton to conduct his orchestra as they play his symphony. (It's super-good. A must-watch!)

If we were to take this statement and apply it to being a part of God's symphony, it might read something like this. "There is not a life, Lord, that You have not touched. Each one of us is better because of You! We are Your Symphony. We are the melodies and the notes of Your opus, and we are the music of Your story!" We truly are His tapestry that He is constantly weaving together until its completion. What a privilege and a joy to be a part of God's symphony! You may be going in one direction, but He will direct your path that is all His own. It may feel like a loss of a dream or a path, but hold tight. He has you and will take you there.

When All You Have Is Jesus

When difficult situations arise in life, such as a loss you can't understand, or when you don't have control over a situation, a story worth embracing is the life of Corrie ten Boom, who knew great loss. Corrie was from a Christian family who harbored hundreds of Jews during World War II to protect them from arrest during the Holocaust. By all accounts, they saved nearly eight hundred lives. She and her sister, Betsie, were later imprisoned for ten months.

Betsie later died in that camp from starvation and lack of medical care. Betsie's last words to her sister were, "We must tell them [the other women in the camp] that there is no pit so deep that He [God] is not deeper still." Two weeks later, Corrie was released due to "clerical error," which was a miracle in and of itself, after laboring alongside these women at farms and factories for all that time. She later learned that thousands of those women were exterminated at the hands of their captors at the concentration camp where she was held. In her bestselling book, *The Hiding* Place,[2] later made into a movie, she penned these words reflecting her experience: "You may never know that Jesus is all you need until Jesus is all you have!"

What a profound statement made by a woman who lost everything except life itself. With God, you need not be fearful or lose hope when hardships come your way. Though we are human and will experience deep, sometimes agonizing pain in loss, be encouraged; the Lord is with you.

> The Lord Himself goes before you and will be with you; He will never leave you nor forsake you. Do not be afraid; do not be discouraged. (Deuteronomy 31:8 NIV)

If you've experienced the loss of a loved one or any other type of loss, I am so, so sorry and extend my deepest condolences and prayers to you. I can't imagine your pain. I know it must run deep. Know that God is there with you in your loss, holding you and crying with you. He is your strength in times of sorrow.

As time passes in the ebb and flow of life, be encouraged; the heart will heal or—best-case scenario—will adjust, and you'll see God at work in your loss. The love of Christ will overtake you, and you'll live again—a hope that can't be explained. In life, there will be good days and bad days, laced with twists and turns, but no matter the hardships you go through, you're never alone. God is there every step of the way to guide you as you move forward in the big world of unknowns. He'll help you make decisions that come to you at every turn. Trust Him. Follow Him. He will lead you.

> He heals the brokenhearted, and binds up their wounds. (Psalm 147:3 ESV)

> Having a rough day? Place your hand on your heart. Feel that? That's called purpose. You're alive for a reason! Don't give up! (Anonymous Instagram post)

God's Call on Your Life

Embracing this notion that life is unpredictable, and the plans we make may or may not pan out, allows us to be open to God's perspective of being flexible and tuned into His heart, which is to love others before self. So, even when you don't know what direction you're headed in when a loss throws you off, or you're just fumbling along in life in general, God has control of the situation and calls us to trust Him. He has a calling on your life and is there to guide you.

There is no higher calling than to lead the life the Lord has assigned to you. Embrace your assignment, this *great adventure* chosen for you, and press it to the limit. God has made your entire life your calling! We tend to think of our callings as our vocations, some significant job God gives us to do with an identifiable, and preferably esteemed, title. Our primary, core calling is to love God with all we are and to love our neighbors as ourselves. (Luke 10:27) And this calling incorporates everyone we interact with ... from morning till night. That's one reason Jesus tells us, "...do not be anxious about tomorrow" (Matt 6:34a ESV). (John Bloom, *God Has Called You*)[3]

God's main concern isn't that you do things for Him, but that you delight in Him. Delight should fuel our doing, not doing our delight. (John Piper, Desiring God.org.)[4]

The Great Adventure

Embrace this great adventure! The song "The Great Adventure"[5] by Steven Curtis Chapman (a Christian artist who was hugely popular in my young-adult years and still inspires hearts today), hit number one on the Christian music charts for numerous weeks in a row in 1992 and was Song of the Year in '92, as well. He reenergized a live audience again in 2019 at the Dove Awards with the same song, encouraging them, and all of us watching, to be passionate about seeking God every day.

God desires you to know Him personally, giving you joy in your journey. See each day as an opportunity to spread your wings and fly, trusting Him in the process. Here are some of the lyrics to his song:

Started out this morning in the usual way
Chasing thoughts inside my head of all I had to
do today

I opened up the Bible and I read about me
Said I'd been a prisoner and God's Grace set me
free
I saw a big frontier in front of me …. "Let's Go!"
This is the Great Adventure!

His Plans Above My Own

God is at work all the time through His people. It's not about the pressures of trying to be extraordinary for God. He's the extraordinary one! He's the one doing extraordinary things through ordinary people—us—the way He's made us. How cool is that? So often we ask God to bless our dreams, plans, and goals without emphasizing, "though Your will Lord, not mine." We simply reduce God to being a genie in a bottle. God has taught me in my faith journey that when I make Him small, I get blindsided and disappointed.

If you've ever wanted to abandon God because you feel He doesn't care about you or love you because He didn't give you what you asked for or wanted; if you've felt disheartened and disillusioned, saying, "I'm not going to believe in God anymore," it's worth taking a self-check in that moment. Are your eyes on you or on God? People walk away from God when they feel hurt by Him. Instead, when you allow God to be God in your life, fully and unabashedly, you will see things from His perspective. He may involve you in what He is accomplishing, as His plans will always be above your plans. He chooses to bless efforts, dreams, and goals because He is a generous and loving God.

But if those plans are self-seeking and misguided attempts to override His plan in your life, you are choosing your own path. I've been there and done that, as you've read, and it doesn't work out best. Following His way is *always* the better plan!

"For I know the plans I have for you," declares
the Lord, "plans to prosper you and not to harm
you, plans to give you hope and a future. Then
you will call on me and come and pray to me, and
I will listen to you. You will seek me and find me
when you seek me with all your heart." (Jeremiah
29:11–13 NIV)

Be available with a tender heart to be the hands and feet of
Christ at any moment He nudges your spirit. Then, when something
extraordinary happens (the daily miracles all around you), you will
see God at work in the most beautiful and gentle ways. When you
encourage others, for example, with a simple smile or are genuinely
kind toward them, it shows that you authentically care about them
and their situation. In that moment, it is Jesus shining through you
that reaches them deeply. When others know you care, it helps lift
a burden and may even give them a glimpse of God at work in the
middle of their pain. If you're tuned in to what God is doing all
around you, you may very well witness a miracle, giving you the
opportunity to rejoice and give praise where praise is due. It's all
His doing! He's the miracle worker, the truly extraordinary One!
An outward expression of love driven by a deep, abiding inner
expression of care to see others above yourself is the person who is
Christlike and servant-minded. Be that person.

Be the person who fixes the crown of another in
their moment of glory without telling the world
that it was crooked in the first place, and you were
the one who fixed it. (anonymous Instagram post)

He Gets the Credit

There may be moments in your life when you'll get to wear a crown of accomplishments, hear your name announced on the loudspeaker, or become the person people look up to for inspiration because of what you've said or done. Should those moments in life happen, remember that God gave those to you, not for your glory but to point others to Him. He gets the credit! Jesus never took credit for things but directed all eyes on His Father in heaven. Did you know that even Jesus didn't do anything without God willing Him to do so first? Jesus lived His entire life in absolute dependence upon His Father.

> For I have come down from heaven, not to do My own will but the will of Him who sent Me. (John 6:38 ESV)

> Do you not believe that I am in the Father and the Father is in Me? The words that I say to you I do not speak on My own authority, but the Father who dwells in Me does His works. (John 14:10 ESV)

Hours before Jesus was arrested and later betrayed and crucified, He prayed to His Father that He Himself would be glorified to bring glory to His Father, revealing the deity of the Son of God as He lifted His eyes to heaven and said,

> Father, the hour has come; glorify Your Son that the Son may glorify You, since You have given Him authority over all flesh, to give eternal life to all whom You have given Him. And this is eternal life, that they know You, the only true God, and

Jesus Christ whom You have sent. I glorified You on earth, having accomplished the work that You gave me to do. And now, Father, glorify Me in Your own presence with the glory that I had with You before the world existed. (John 17:1–5 ESV)

What a powerful model from Jesus Himself, who looks to the Father in everything He does, even to the end of His life here on earth, and gives God praise in all He does. It's every reason we, too, should look to Jesus, who is one with the Father and longed to do His Father's will over His own, even when saying these words: "Father, if You are willing, take this cup from me; yet not My will, but Yours be done" (Luke 22:42 NIV).

When you receive God's free gift of salvation through His Son, Jesus, He sees you through Jesus' Resurrection and righteousness. When you get a clear picture of how God sees you—"To all who believed Him and accepted Him, He gave the right to become children of God" (John 1:12 NLT)—you then see things that make His heart beat. He opens your eyes and heart to see where He is working and what matters to Him. When coming to your Father, as a child comes to their dad, ask for things with the understanding that what matters to your Dad, matters to you—"Your will, Lord, not my own!" Your affections shift because your care increases by God moving in your life! It's a beautiful thing.

Jesus Is the Center and the Purpose of All History

"When it comes to people in the Bible, we see God's bigger picture and His love story written for us. Each and every one of the Old and New Testament stories draws us to God's way over our own and points us to Jesus, the center and purpose of all history. Jesus was the plan all along. His narrative swallows up all others. He is God's power, faithfulness, and compassion on display to the world. This is His narrative, and He is the only true hero! See in the narratives of scripture and in your own narrative, the strong, wonderful, and benevolent sovereignty of God."[6] (Arnold Ruiz)

The Power of Jesus

Jesus is the vine, the true vine, and apart from Him, we can do nothing! The way to follow Jesus is not through our goodness, or our good works. Jesus is the only good one! We lack the goodness that only Jesus provides. From Him, we bear fruit. The fruit grows from the vine to be pleasing to the gardener (God), and to share with others, just as real fruit does, (pleases the gardener and is good for others). May we bear good and pleasing fruit, never to outgrow God, but to stay abiding and remaining in Him.

'Jesus + nothing = EVERYTHING!!' That means we can't add anything to God's work, nothing! It is complete in Jesus. He is the bigger and better plan! (Pastor Josh Watt, sermon notes, John 15; Ephesians 5:1–5)[7]

God's Bigger Plan in Esther, Noah, and David's Lives and Others

God has you in your very spot in life for a purpose! Never underestimate what God is doing in your situation. Rather, trust God and obey Him wholeheartedly. Think of Esther in the Bible, who became queen. God strategically placed her in the right place at the right time, allowing her influence to complete His plan to save a nation. Wow! That's incredible! Notice, it wasn't Esther's doing. It was all God.

Esther was humble and followed the Lord's prompting. Likewise, allow the Lord's prompting in your life. Be humble and never insist that God put you in a position you think you deserve or you think you can handle. It might not be what He wants you to do, which may lead to your own ruin. Taking matters into your own hands is manipulating the situation, making you god over your own life. Let God be God. He is far more capable of accomplishing His kingdom's purposes than you are. His heartbeat is *love* throughout His biblical story. Let His heartbeat be your heartbeat. Love conquers all! Learn to wait on the Lord. Be still.

There are countless stories in the Bible of God drawing people to Himself, such as Noah, Abraham, Moses, David (a man after God's own heart), Mary, John, Peter, and Paul, just to name a few. In their very ordinary lives, God intervenes, drawing them to Him. He allows them to be participants in His miraculous plan, the gospel story, which is God's love story to humanity—redeeming a lost world unto Himself through His abiding love, paid on a cross to live with Him, the Triune God (Father, Son, and Holy Ghost) in glory! We are all a part of that bigger plan that He is still at work moving on individuals' hearts, drawing them to Him, and allowing us, as He chooses, to be a part of His plan—not our plan but His.

A Clearer Picture

Through that lens, His plan is always in motion to reconcile the lost unto Himself by putting compassion in the human soul. God wants us to see clearly a picture of Christ as He moves toward pain and suffering. Might we do the same by having compassion for the hurting and lost, the devastated and the afflicted. We are invited to be a part of where God is at work by helping point others to find hope in hopeless situations and find comfort in Jesus in their pain and suffering. It's what Jesus did! He moved toward the hurt. Love like Jesus!

- Don't look through people and pass them by. Look at people with tender eyes as Jesus did. Meet people where they're at.
- Feel compassion. Move toward the situation, the problem. If a friend were to literally fall in a hole, you would, of course, pull them out. True of all references, help people.
- Act—pray. Take that person and their hardship to the Lord who loves them and wants to care for them.

(Tyler Johnson, sermon notes)[8]

God Is at Work All the Time

Understanding God's purpose through His people demonstrates that God is at work all the time. He moves mountains and puts dreams and passions in His people, inspiring them and encouraging them along the way. No matter the task, He will equip you, but always be mindful of who is accomplishing the work. It is God! Never get ahead of Him. Follow His lead.

> Many are the plans in a person's heart, but it is the Lord's purpose that prevails. (Proverbs 19:21 NIV)

> "For My thoughts are not your thoughts, neither are your ways My ways," declares the Lord. (Isaiah 55:8 NIV)

When God achieves His purposes in His ways through His people, God will be glorified. It is foolish to think we can accomplish God's work by using the world's methodology and values. God's ways are redemptive, loving, and compassionate. His ways bring cleansing and forgiveness and build people up.

God's plan for the world is more important than telling God what you are planning to do for Him. He will purify your life and make you into a clean vessel for His service. When we develop our own plans aside from God, implement our own strategies, even place those plans on others, the result in our limited knowledge and power will bring with them exhaustion.

(Excerpts and notes from *Experiencing God*)[9]

Do Things God's Way

Do not get ahead of God. Learn to surrender your schedule to Him trusting that His timing for all things is perfect! [10]
—Dr. Charles Stanley, In Touch Ministries
(Beloved pastor to so many around the world; passed away on April 18, 2023, at age ninety.)

Don't try doing things for God in your own strength by trying to flex your spiritual muscles and "will" your life forward. Those were the zealots God spoke of in the Bible, such as the Pharisees. Their zeal was founded on legalism and not on knowing God. Their works were futile and, in God's eyes, dead. They promoted a cause that made their hearts proud and arrogant. Verses that speak directly to this point show the severity of being religious over having a relationship with Jesus as Lord and Savior of your life. Here, Jesus explains the difference between a true follower of His and one who is false.

> "Not everyone who says to me, 'Lord, Lord', will enter the kingdom of heaven … On that day many will say to me, 'Lord, Lord, did we not prophesy in your name, and cast out demons in your name, and do many mighty works in your name?' And then I will declare to them, 'I never knew you; depart from me, you workers of lawlessness.'" (Matthew 7:21–23 ESV)

> Jesus said to him, "I am the way, and the truth, and the life. No one comes to the Father except through me." (John 14:6 ESV)

> Enter through the narrow gate. For wide is the gate and broad is the road that leads to destruction, and many enter through it. But small is the gate and narrow the road that leads to life, and only a few find it. (Matthew 7:13–14 NIV)

Whew! God doesn't mess around with this stuff! He wants your heart—your whole heart! He wants you to stop trying to earn your way to heaven with your good works. He can't be fooled. He's God! When you follow Him, He'll direct your path. You just need to commit your life to Him and trust Him. An old children's song says it well: *"Trust and obey, for there's no other way to be happy in Jesus, but to trust and obey."* For when we put our trust in Jesus, He calls us to obedience, and in that new life of trusting and obeying, we are secure in His loving arms, surrendering our will and our plans over to Him completely. We no longer have to worry. We turn our cares over to the Lord. He carries us through anything and everything. He is God almighty, Lord of our lives!

Walking by Faith

As believers, we can get off track in trying to unpack God's will for our lives. That's when trust comes in, and walking by faith starts to make sense, such as this quote from quotespedia.org:

> Faith is like WIFI. It's invisible but has the power
> to connect you to what you need.

When you're born again (a transformed life by God, old life to new life), you enter into a love relationship with Jesus, God Himself, at which point the counselor, the Spirit of truth, takes up residency in your life. He is always present to teach you and direct you. He draws you to Him. Once your heart is set on God and His activity, God may present a situation to your spirit that nudges you toward a person who is pondering or inquiring about spiritual matters. Know, in that moment, that God is drawing that individual to Himself. He is the only One who can do that. When your heart is sensitive and in tune with His heart, you'll respond to God at the slightest prompting to join Him. The Spirit will lead you. God may have you in that person's life, or situation, for a reason—perhaps to just be still and present with them, to listen and pray with them, or to encourage them. Perhaps God is prompting you to lead them to Christ. God will lead; you just follow.

When trying to keep up the pace on your own strength, you will miss all this because your eyes are on yourself and your own agenda.

And in those moments, you get off track and are completely drained and out of focus. These are moments God gives you to regroup with Him, to step back, breathe, and reconnect with your first love—Jesus! Trust that His plan is always best. God's purpose is bigger than what we can understand, so in that, we can trust Him and rest in His loving arms and purpose for us.

> As the heavens are higher than the earth, so are My ways higher than your ways and My thoughts than your thoughts. (Isaiah 55:9 NIV)

Be in God's Will

Who is more valuable to a company? The boss or the custodian? In God's eyes, they are equally valuable. No matter the position you have, He desires you to value and love others, just as He values and loves you! "We love because He first loved us" (1 John 4:19 NIV). God's interested in the heart! It's not about what a person has to offer God. God does not need us to accomplish His will. He chooses to invite us into His purpose to reconcile a lost world unto Him by stirring our hearts to serve others well and to love boldly. Who better to be an example of serving than Jesus Himself?

> For even the Son of Man came not to be served but to serve others and to give His life as a ransom for many. (Matthew 20:28 NLT)

Maybe you'll be called to run a company someday, start a ministry, or climb Mount Everest. Or maybe you'll be called to hug a crying child, make a meal for a neighbor, or be there when a friend is hurting, to listen and care. One season of life, you may very well be that president of a company, and the next season, you may be home, raising a family (or doing both simultaneously, as God has made us multifaceted, while keeping lots of balls in the air at any given time). What it all boils down to is that God doesn't look at the title(s) a person has. He looks at the heart. He places useful, caring, and loving hearts of service all over the globe. No matter the gravity of work at hand, great or small, it all matters to God. As a child of God, He is calling you to action. God calls us to Himself, first and foremost, to be in a relationship with Him. Join Him!

How Your Attitude Should Honor God

Before continuing with the plans God is doing in you, around you, and through you, let's pause a moment to understand how your attitude (mentioned earlier but worth revisiting) and your conduct in the workplace (or at school), affect everything important that you do. Straight up, work is work, no matter how glamorous it is (or is not), and regardless of whether it may or may not be enjoyable. You may wonder, "Why am I here in the first place?" or "Whatever good will come out of my role in this position?" Though those are good, honest questions, notice they both show I-isms. It's a good reminder that it's not about you!

There will be seasons in your life that will shape you, mold your character, define your skill set, adjust your attitude, and/or simply remind you of God's provision for you. In any of these scenarios, be grateful He's blessed you with a job (or getting an education). Be a good employee (or student) because you're not serving man; you're serving God. Refrain from complaining, hunker down, and get to work!

Without a doubt, a key ingredient to the success of any person, no matter his or her life status, is attitude. Attitude is everything! Your attitude will dictate your life. A good attitude will determine your day. Be mindful that, "A joyful heart is good medicine, but a broken spirit dries up the bones" (Proverbs 17:22 NIV).

A framed quote at home says it well:

> The longer I live, the more I realize the impact of attitude on life. Attitude, to me, is more important than facts. It is more important than the past, than education, than money, than circumstances, than failures, than successes, than what other people think or say or do. It is more important than appearance, giftedness, or skill. It will make or break a company … a church … a home. The remarkable thing is we have a choice every day regarding the attitude we will embrace for that day. We cannot change our past … we cannot change the fact that people will act in a certain way. We cannot change the inevitable. The only thing we can do is play on the one string we have, and this is our attitude … I am convinced that life is 10% what happens to me and 90% how I react to it. And so, it is with you … you are in charge of your attitude. Choose well. Make your attitude count today!
> —Charles Swindoll[11]

If you find yourself in a bad mood or feeling cranky (a state of being angry, frustrated, or annoyed), ask God to change your attitude. It matters! A sign that hangs in my daughter's room that is the last thing she sees when she heads out the door has been very impactful in the way she treats others:

> Everyone you meet is fighting a battle you know nothing about. Be kind! Always! (anonymous)

Be Obedient in Your Work

The level of obedience and reverence you have toward the Lord in your kind and caring ways should be the same level of respect you have toward your bosses and/or employers: "Obey them ... serve wholeheartedly, as if you were serving the Lord, not people" (Ephesians 6:6a, 7 NIV).[12] Treat your employer with the utmost respect, and give attention to your job, as everything you do is for Jesus. You are a reflector of Christ on a mission from God. (If you are not a Christ-follower, invite Him into your life. He is there with open arms, waiting for you. He will give you guidance in your life and work to be purposeful in all you do. No matter the task, large or small, it all matters to God.)

More insight on this topic from an Ephesians 6 study by Luke Simmons [13]

1. How to work under authority: Work obediently always following Christ. Do your job and do it well!
2. Work with sincere respect. As the military says, "Salute the rank, not the person." (Ephesians 6:5)
3. We work to be seen by Jesus, not by people! You're working for an audience of One! Don't cut corners. Don't work for the eye service of man. Work hard because it's the right thing to do!
4. Jesus notices and rewards. He is eager to please (Ephesians 6:8).

a. How to work when you have authority (boss, manager, department head, in charge):

b. Serve and manage people well who work for you. Follow steps 1–3. Above all be kind, thoughtful, and servant-minded to everyone. Have a good attitude that is reciprocated by those around you. You, too, are under the authority of Jesus. Follow His ways to set the tone in your workplace (Ephesians 6:9).

    i. Show respect.

    ii. Don't threaten.

    iii. See yourself under the True Master. Steward well that which He put you in charge of so at the end of your life, it is said of you, "Well done, my good and faithful servant" (Matthew 25:21a NIV).

A Study in My Twenties

When I was in my later twenties, I went through a Bible study, "Experiencing God," with a group of professional ladies that shaped our hearts in profound ways on how we approached everyday life and work circumstances. People need people. "As iron sharpens iron, so one person sharpens another" (Proverbs 27:17 NIV). Growing and spurring one another on in the faith as working young adults deeply impacted us and gave us a view from God's perspective. Here are a few takeaways from notes I kept:

➤ Your relationship with God must come first.

➤ God wants you to enter each day by seeking Him. Out of that relationship, you will experience Him guiding your life.

➤ The plans God has for your life are based on what He is doing in the world around you.

➤ Discovering God's greater plan helps you know what He wants to do through you.

➤ If you're experiencing a time of spiritual dryness in your life, you may be trying to do things on your own that God has not initiated.

➤ Don't focus on your talents, abilities, and interests to determine God's will. Instead, seek God's will, and watch Him equip you for whatever assignment He gives.

➤ For Peter, Andrew, James, John, and Paul (see Matthew 4:18–22; 9:9; Acts 9:1–20), God gave minimal details about their assignments. He simply said, "Follow Me."

➤ Adjust your life to Him so He will do what He wants to do through you.

➤ Today, our world desperately needs to witness what God wants to accomplish.

➤ The outcome does not depend upon a person being unusually gifted, educated, or wealthy. The key is the indwelling presence of God doing unusual things through a willing servant.

➤ Renounce a self-focused approach to life and turn the attention and control over to a God-centered outlook.

➤ Self-centeredness is a subtle yet common trap.

➤ The world praises self-reliance. Trusting God may make no sense from a human perspective.

➤ It's easy to trust God at one moment and fall right into self-reliance later.

➤ God-centeredness requires a daily denial of self and a submission to God.

When You Walk with God, He Leads the Way

What a true statement! You have to choose to follow His lead. If you choose not to follow, you may be met with resistance, like our dog Lil' Rock (mentioned earlier). If he tries to go one way, he'll be met with resistance to redirect him to go the right way.

> A person's heart plans his way, but the Lord determines his steps. (Proverbs 16:9 CSB)

What a powerful verse! God determines our steps.

If you're not sure the path you're traveling on is the right path, be in God's Word for direction, pray about it, make a list of pros and cons about the decision you're facing, and seek godly counsel. If you find He is opening a door of opportunity for you, move in that direction. If that situation remains fluid and you are assured He has placed you there, humbly thank Him and move forward. Serve Him where He places you, and follow His next steps.

> In the same way, let your light shine before others, so that they may see your good works and give glory to your Father who is in heaven. (Matthew 5:16 ESV)

Jesus, the True Miracle Worker

If the opportunity you've pursued doesn't pan out, don't be alarmed. God has something else for you. The feeding of the five thousand is such a story (see John 6:1–14). The disciples saw hungry people and weren't sure how to feed them. At that moment, they witnessed a miracle!

Jesus took what the disciples had collected from a boy's lunch— five loaves and two fish—and fed the multitudes. It was a miracle indeed! They didn't know how it happened, but they knew who the miracle worker was. "We don't know *how*, but we know *who*, and His name is Jesus!"[15] They were in awe! Could you just imagine?

And miracle after miracle, He took the impossible and made it possible! He is the true miracle worker all the time, then and now. If you trust in Jesus, you can trust that He will work it out, whatever the hardship or the feeling of lack of direction in your life, through the good days and the bad, He has a plan. Trust Him!

Trust God's Plan

God may call you to a specific job or a specific assignment for perhaps one person or even one situation. You may not know the ins and outs or the how, but you know the Who, so keep trusting! Don't miss Him in action. Always watch and be ready with great anticipation. God does the impossible with one yielded vessel. Here I am, Lord; use me.

> In 1 Kings 18:16–39, Elijah made his life available for God's use. God did a powerful work through him that impacted a nation.[16]

> Now may the God of hope fill you with all joy and peace in believing, that you may abound in hope by the power of the Holy Spirit. (Romans 15:13 NKJV)

God's Economy

When God presents an opportunity to you, be mindful that the work is a gift from God. Treat it as such. Be grateful! Working to earn a living to support yourself, to pay your own bills, and to save for a car (for example), or a place of your own someday are great goals to strive for, but if money becomes your only focus, your eye is on the wrong prize. It's important to understand that making money is neither the goal nor the treasure—God is.

> No one can serve two masters. Either you will hate the one and love the other, or you will be devoted to the one and despise the other. You cannot serve both God and money. (Luke 16:13 NIV)

God created you for work, so learn to respect His financial system for your life. Since God's economy and the world's economy are completely different, how you navigate through it is critically important to understand. To begin with, don't think so highly of yourself that you run over others, intentionally or unintentionally, striving to be on top, thinking you're self-made, created in your own making—because you're not. That mindset will only lead to destruction.

> Pride goes before destruction, and a haughty spirit before a fall. (Proverbs 16:18 ESV)

As a believer, you are merely a steward of what God has given you to manage, as it is all His in the first place (more on stewardship, ahead). Therefore, be mindful to not become an obsessed consumer on a quest for self-fulfillment.

In God's economy, it's not about status or how much you make; it's about so much more. If those are things the Lord has blessed you with, do not flaunt them in front of others. Instead, privately and quietly, without fanfare, seek ways to be a blessing to others and give generously to the Lord.

Remember, you're created to work, and through you, He is pouring Himself out to others to know His love and saving grace. That work can be in the professional arena or in your home as you serve and love your family. Seasons of life will change, but God will never change in calling you to serve, no matter the job. You may get paid for it, or you may not. He knows, and there, you can rest. Trust that He will take care of you and your needs as you diligently do the work to which He's called you. The following verses are certainly not a pass to sit idle; instead, they are saying not to let *stuff* always be your emphasis. Jesus' own words describe it this way:

> Look at the birds in the sky. They do not plant seeds. They do not gather grain. They do not put grain into a building to keep. Yet your Father in heaven feeds them! Are you not more important than the birds? Which of you can make himself a little taller by worrying? Why should you worry about clothes? Think how the flowers grow. They do not work or make cloth. (Matthew 6:26–28 NLV)

> Do not worry. Do not keep saying, 'What will we eat?' or, 'What will we drink?' or, 'What will we wear?' The people who do not know God are looking for all these things. Your Father in heaven knows you need all these things. (Matthew 6:31–32 NLV)

Prepare for Rain

No matter if you make a little or a lot, steward the riches God has given you. First, tithe. (Tithe to your local congregation. Tithing is a biblical principle to give back to God's work in the local church.) How much to tithe is between you and God. In the Old Testament, it gives a reference point of giving 10 percent of your first fruits. That's a good place to start. No one is looking, only God. You won't be docked points or called out if you don't give a certain percentage. That's legalism. God wants your heart, and out of your heart for God, He fuels your giving. Then, if you have extra beyond what you need for daily living, for paying your bills, and for what you're saving for, consider giving to others in need in a manner that is pleasing to Him.

There's an awesome scene in the movie *Facing the Giants*[17], that illustrates this point perfectly. In the movie, the head football coach is anonymously gifted a brand-new truck and is completely overwhelmed by the kind gesture. Prior to that moment, everything seemed to be collapsing all around him. He admitted his struggle to a praying man in their school, who proceeded to tell him this story:

Two farmers desperately needed rain, and both prayed for it, but only one of them went out and prepared his fields to receive rain. Which one do you think trusted God to send the rain?

The coach says, "The one who prepared his fields for it."

The praying man then says, "Which one are you? God will send the rain when He is ready. You need to prepare your fields to receive it."

That is *so* good! God calls us to do the same, to be prepared in all seasons of life. Prepare your life fields for rain! By doing so, you will be ready for anything that comes your way, good or bad, because you're prepared spiritually, mentally, and physically, knowing that no matter what, God is with you. He is in control, and He knows your needs. Call out to Him!

Prepare your fields. Rain is coming! This is twofold because there is a harvest of lost souls out there. Prepare the crops in all seasons. Jesus said to His disciples, "The harvest is plentiful but the workers are few" (Matthew 9:37b NIV). Be on Jesus' team. Prepare the fields! As well, prepare for what's around the corner that only God knows is coming, the good and the bad. Life will come at you full speed! If you aren't prepared for it and all the hardships that come along in life, it will hit you like a ton of bricks, and you won't be prepared. Gear up with God so you are ready for anything that life throws your way.

If you're in a season of drought or of plenty, God wants your eyes on Him at all times, giving Him praise, no matter the circumstances. Since shifting sand comes with rain, stand firm on the solid rock of Christ to withstand the chaotic world around you, externally and/or internally. The chorus of an old hymn rings true:

On Christ the solid Rock I stand,
All other ground is sinking sand.
All other ground is sinking sand.[18]

Be prepared—rain is coming!

(As I finish typing this section, I'm also on the phone with the doctor, scheduling surgery for thyroid cancer. I didn't see cancer coming, but God did, and He is here with me as I go through this season. You can trust He is with you in every season, even those you never saw coming. I'm a little nervous, but I know He's with me! And I know He's with you too with whatever you're facing. Let's be brave together, brave in the Lord! He's got this!)

(p.s. A few months have passed since I typed the above. I'm happy to report that I'm cancer-free! Surgery went well and all cancer was removed! God was so kind to heal me. Thank you, Jesus!)

And What about Those Credit Cards?

When a credit card in your wallet or an app on your phone makes it too convenient to purchase something for which you don't actually have the money, then perhaps you don't need that something in the first place. The interest you accrue on that item will double or triple the amount it actually costs you if you don't pay it off in a timely manner. Better to put the credit cards aside or take down the app until the balance is paid off. If tempted to use your cards, put them in a Ziploc bag with water and freeze them; then the block of ice has to melt before you can use them again. At that point, you most likely won't bother. If more extreme measures are needed, do some plastic surgery—cut up those cards, close those accounts, and pay off what you owe. Learn the principle of saving. Be patient by saving for that item that you think you need so badly. Patience is a virtue!

> But the fruit of the Spirit is love, joy, peace, patience, kindness, goodness, faithfulness, gentleness, self-control; against such things there is no law. (Galatians 5:22 ESV)

Perhaps God is teaching you to have self-control and gain an appreciation of waiting and not splurging on stuff you don't need in the first place.

Darci Willems, a young-adult teacher who was in our group in her early twenties, shared a post on her Instagram account when she was single about her financial struggle and how she conquered her battle. She came out stronger and happier for having paid off her debt and was thankful for getting a handle on things that mattered most in her life. I know her story will resonate with someone out there. Thanks for sharing, Darci! (Darci's now a wife and mommy of two darling little girls. It's been such a joy to watch her life grow from this place in such beautiful ways!) With permission to share, here is Darci's story.

Two years ago, today, I walked into Kohl's as a seasonal worker (*a second job*) starting my first shift. I had mountains of credit card debt, a car loan, and wasn't sure what I'd live on, or how I would afford to live on my own without a roommate.

When people would ask me what my credit card debt was from, I could only reply with 'stuff' because I wasn't even sure myself ... it was stuff I thought would make me happy, stuff that I thought would make people like me, stuff that I thought would give me relationship ... but all that 'stuff' left me feeling nothing but empty ...

No one had any idea about my debt because I became so good at hiding it. I finally told my parents and brought it to the light ... I was embarrassed and ashamed.

After many tears, lots and lots of prayers, and reading, I quickly realized all that stuff I was buying would never fulfill me ... the only thing that could fill me would be a deeper relationship with Christ and to know that He is the prize.

So, two years later, I have no credit card debt, I've bought a condo, and will have my car paid off 2.5 years early, all because I stopped seeking the things of the world (that will only leave me empty) and started to seek God first. "But seek first the kingdom of God and his righteousness, and all of these things will be added to you." (Matthew 6:33 ESV)

Set Free

When it comes to breaking a cycle of debt and the mindset that leads to debt, we must be set free. And this freedom comes from Jesus. He transforms our selfish desires into truly aligning our hearts with God's desires. As we break free from the distractions and expectations of this world, we begin to experience true freedom—laying aside worldly pleasures that entangle us and embracing the freedom of God that gives light and hope.

> God changes our "Want-o-Meter." We go from wanting our selfish desires to wanting what God wants! "We were once slave to sin, but now set free …" (Romans 6:17–18, in summary)
>
> —Luke Simmons

Jar Analogy

A great visual on important and nonimportant "stuff" is a jar analogy, which is especially relevant with all the choices vying for our attention on the internet and through social media. Here's how it goes.

+ Take a large mason jar; golf balls or ping-pong balls; beads or small objects; sand; and water.
+ Put the balls in first. Decide then, "Is the jar full?" (Yes, it is full. But is it?)
+ Now take the beads and pour those in. As it is, they'll fill the gaps where the balls cannot fit. "Is the jar full?" Yes, there is no more room.

- Then take the sand and pour it in slowly. As it is, it fills all the open spaces in the jar that neither the balls nor beads can fit.
- Last, pour the water in. Sure enough, water covers it all.
- The analogy goes like this:
- The large items represent the important things: God, reading His Word, worship, prayer, family, church.
- The small beads represent the next tier of important things, such as school, work, friends, sports, activities, hobbies.
- The sand represents all the other stuff: internet, social media, apps, Netflix, video games, and on and on and on.
- The water then comes through and essentially touches everything in the jar (such as the Holy Spirit touching everything in your life).
- Now try this same experiment by first pouring the sand into the jar. When you try to put the balls in next, wiggling them down into the sand, the sand will overflow and make a mess.

The takeaway:

When you crowd out the most important things in your life with those things that are fun things to do, the important things are pushed aside completely. Reprioritize your life if it's out of order. Focus on the important things first.

How very true that is. If you aren't paying attention to what you're putting into your life, even if it's good stuff, it will overtake everything else that is important and will crowd out God and the relationship He wants to have with you. Everything you put into your life comes with a cost, financially and emotionally (yes, very often there's a price tag included). Choose wisely what you put into your life.

If things are consuming and occupying your entire being other than God, consider it God's wake-up call to reprioritize your "important" stuff. It takes *major* intentionality to make changes with those things that are consuming you when it comes to setting new boundaries with your time and energy. If social media, for example, is a huge time-waster, try putting more God in your life and less of all the other stuff. It will make all the difference in your world. Be intentional! Pastor Greg Laurie, author of *Jesus Revolution* (also a movie), makes an excellent point:

> What if we consumed God's Word like we do social media?
> It would change our lives!
> —@gregelaurie[19]

Financial Peace

It's important to have a vision of your financial goals and overall future dreams. Dave Ramsey[20] offers a "Financial Peace" university program worth checking out. His course will teach you how to pay off debt, make a budget and stick to it, and build wealth that is meaningful to your future, and it will help you develop habits to give generously as you've never given before. Several young adults I know have taken this course and are glad they did. It's helped them get a handle on their finances before they take on the next chapters of their lives.

> A man with sight is blind without a vision.
> —Helen Keller[21]

Helen Keller, a truly inspirational woman who was blind and deaf, defeated the odds by earning her bachelor's degree. She was an American author and lecturer. Said of Helen at her memorial service in 1968, "Ms. Keller was the woman who showed the world there are no boundaries to courage and faith."

What Are You Holding on To?

Denzel Washington[22], an Oscar-winning actor and Christian, raises millions of dollars a year for several organizations, including the Boys and Girls Clubs of America. They had a big impact in shaping his character in his childhood years, so he loves to give back to them, even serving as their spokesperson. Once asked in a news interview about his philanthropic efforts and why he's so motivated to give such substantial donations, he responded with a thought-provoking question: "Have you ever seen a hearse pulling a U-Haul?"

Great point! We surely can't take stuff with us when we die, as was the thought and the practice of ancient Egyptians, whose tombs and pyramids were filled with their worldly possessions for their supposed afterlife.[23]

> For we brought nothing into the world, and we can take nothing out of it. (1 Timothy 6:7 NIV)

All that remains is our relationship with God and with others, which is eternal. You either believe in Jesus, or you don't. It makes an eternal difference where you land on this topic. When it comes to our money, possessions, and all earthly-related things, He invites us to have an eternal perspective always.

> For where your treasure is, there will your heart be also. (Matthew 6:21 NIV)

Who Is Your Treasure?

The Bible has *a lot* to say about money, wealth, greed, contentment, and a variety of other topics as they pertain to one's finances and spiritual life. Why does it do this? Could it be that Jesus wants all of you and not just a little of you?

> Jesus talked a lot about money. Sixteen of the 38 parables were concerned with how to handle money and possessions. In the Gospels, an amazing one out of ten verses deals directly with the subject of money. The Bible offers 500 verses on prayer, less than 500 verses on faith, but more than 2,000 verses on money and possessions.[24]

Jesus is talking to each one of us to find out where our hearts' loyalties lie. What is most important to you—things on earth or things that last long after you're gone? He wants to know—is He your treasure?

Verses That Speak on Finances

Here are a few verses that speak on the topic of finances. They are awesome life principles to help shape the way you handle your finances as a young adult that will sustain you for the rest of your life.

- Do not lay up for yourselves treasures on earth, where moth and rust destroy and where thieves break in and steal, but lay up for yourselves treasures in heaven, where neither moth nor rust destroys and where thieves do not break in and steal. (Matthew 6:19–20 ESV)

- Keep your life free from the love of money, and be content with what you have, for He has said, "I will never leave you nor forsake you." (Hebrews 13:5 ESV)

- Glorify God with all your wealth, honoring Him with your first fruits, with every increase that comes to you. Then every dimension of your life will overflow with blessings from an uncontainable source of inner joy! (Proverbs 3:9–12 TPT)

- For the love of money is a root of all kinds of evil. Some people, eager for money, have wandered from the faith and pierced themselves with many griefs. (1 Timothy 6:10 NIV)

- In everything I did, I showed you that by this kind of hard work we must help the weak, remembering the words the Lord Jesus himself said: "It is more blessed to give than to receive." (Acts 20:35 NIV)

- The Lord sends poverty and wealth; he humbles and He exalts. (1 Samuel 2:7 NIV)

Let's look at Job again, who was mentioned in an earlier chapter, and Paul, to see how this last verse played out in their lives.

Job's Story

God saw Job through excruciating and difficult times. One might read Job and wonder, where was God and why didn't God intervene on Job's behalf? It must be noted that God was there. God remained faithful at the beginning, middle, and end of his story. God remained silent a good part of the time, but when God spoke, He spoke! And God was heard.

Job had no such context for his suffering. He had no idea his faithfulness in extreme difficulty mattered so much. But it did! Job teaches us that our response to testing matters, too. Like him, we often cannot see God's hidden purposes. Yet we can determine to be faithful and keep walking toward the Lord in the darkness ... This is the kind of faith that's pleasing to God – a faith that's determined to trust Him when He hasn't answered all the questions when we haven't heard any voice from the whirlwind.[25]

What can we learn from Job? To listen? To trust? To wait? Life and how it plays out may not make sense to you or me, but we can rest in knowing God is sovereign. He is in control, and He is in the midst of your situation as well.

There will be times when you will be stretched financially and emotionally, but take heart—God is there! He is ahead of you every step of the way. In those times of wondering if the Lord is there, never forget, and be encouraged that He is there! He is *always* there. He loves to surprise you when you think you can't carry on and to encourage you that indeed you can. He is there to help you! You can trust Him completely. Don't lose hope. Lean on Him.

Cast all your anxiety on Him because He cares for you! (1 Peter 5:7 NIV)

Paul in Prison

Paul, writing from prison, encouraged others amid his own personal circumstances.

Do nothing out of selfish ambition or vain conceit. Rather, in humility value others above yourselves, not looking to your own interests but each of you to the interests of others. (Philippians 2:3–4 NIV)

His personal testimony is a model for every believer.

But whatever were gains to me I now consider loss for the sake of Christ. (Philippians 3:7)

One thing I do: forgetting what is behind and straining toward what is ahead, I press on toward the goal to win the prize for which God has called me heavenward in Christ Jesus. (Philippians 3:13b–14 NIV)

In closing, he puts everything into perspective of how we should view our role in the world.

I have learned the secret of being content in any and every situation, whether well fed or hungry, whether living in plenty or in want. I can do all this through him who gives me strength. ... And my God will meet all your needs according to the riches of His glory in Christ Jesus. (Philippians 4:12b–13, 19 NIV)

(Footnotes from the NIV Study Bible in Philippians about Paul in prison) [26]

Job and Paul certainly had big-time trust! God calls us to trust Him in big ways too. He called His disciples to follow Him. Are you willing to follow where He leads? With confidence, can you say "yes" and "amen" to the following statements?

+ "Lord, wherever you send me, I will go."
+ "Lord, whatever Your 'will' is for me, I will accept."
+ "Tell your Mountain how BIG your God is!"

(anonymous Instagram posts)

It is true! God *is* bigger than *any* obstacle that comes your way. He will give you challenges to help you trust Him more in the process.

I once was lost but now am found,
Was blind, but now I see
—"Amazing Grace"

Mentors and Community

Solid Bible teaching was poured into my life during my young adult years by my pastor at the time, Tom Shrader, who helped me keep my eyes on Jesus as I moved forward in life. He made a huge impact on me and countless others as well. Being a part of a Bible-teaching church guided my life in the truth. Here's a little bit about Tom and some of his pearls of wisdom to encourage you.

Tom started a ministry for working professionals that I attended called Priority Living and also started a Bible-teaching church that I went to that birthed ten churches in Arizona. Tom went home to be with Jesus after battling cancer in 2019. Over 2,500 people were at his memorial service, as he had touched so many lives.

He had a radical transformation coming to the Lord in his thirties. No one in his office ever thought he'd be interested in the things of God until he asked them once if he could join them at their Bible study. He went that day, and God got a hold of his heart as he gave his life to Christ. The man teaching was Larry Wright, who became Tom's mentor. Tom's life pursuit from that day forward was to tell everyone he met how much Jesus loved them and died for them and how new life was theirs by believing and having faith in Him. In his later years, Tom shared, with a fervent heart, his longing to be with Jesus in heaven, driving home the point that life is fleeting, and the daily battle is real and not easy, but it will all be renewed. If he were here right now, Tom would ask, "Are you ready? Do you know Jesus personally?" Heaven awaits those who trust in Him!

At Tom's service, a video titled *In Memory of Tom Shrader*[27] was shared. In it were clips of him talking about heaven, along with younger pastors sharing about his influence in their lives. It's on YouTube, along with sermons Tom preached. A 2011 video shares his testimony, and another is of our pastor, Luke, sharing Tom's influence on our church, called, "What God Gave Gateway through Tom Shrader."[28] All are *so* rich in teaching. Dive in! Tom was known for his remarkable and witty one-liners, which were coined "Tom-isms." He had so many! Here are just a few favorites. Enjoy!

+ No matter how bad it gets, it can only last a lifetime.
+ Comparison leads to discontentment.
+ Changed lives change lives!
+ We're more sinful than we ever imagined and more loved than we ever dreamed.
+ Make the invisible Christ visible in your life.
+ God gave us one tongue and two ears; respect the ratio!
+ Transformed heart, informed mind, radical life!
+ Sin always takes you further than you want to go, keeps you longer than you want to stay, and costs you more than you want to pay.
+ For the unbeliever, this life is as close to heaven as you will get. For the believer, this life is as close to hell as you will get.
+ I'm pathetic! Anything good you see in me is Jesus!

+ I'd rather suffer in obedience than prosper in disobedience. Both are temporary.
+ We can't will ourselves to do right. We need a heart change. We need new affections to pursue.
+ Don't let this season of poor choices become a lifestyle. Change course. Follow Jesus.

In All Seasons, God Always Has a Plan

Mentors, pastors, and life coaches will help you, just like Jesus helped Peter when he got out of the boat (Matthew 14:22–33). It's a story that has really encouraged me to keep my eyes on Jesus. When Peter's eyes weren't on Jesus, he was scared and started to sink, crying out,

> "Save me Lord." At once Jesus reached out and grabbed hold of him and said, "What little faith you have! Why did you doubt?" (Matthew 14:30b–31 GNT)

When you're in those moments, do you sink or swim? I often sank, but God rescued me!

When my eyes were on my personal circumstances, my lack of staying focused 100 percent on work would spill over. But God, in His mercy, worked through me, despite my circumstances, to see His plan through. His plans will surely see you through too, as His ways are always perfect.

God's Plan Is Perfect

God puts us in places of employment, sometimes for a season or for a reason for personal growth or to join Him where He is at work in our lives or circumstances, never wasting an opportunity to help us grow. For me, everything came full circle to the very spot God used to bring healing to my heart.

His guiding hand allowed restoration, healing, and purpose through different jobs and experiences.

I always knew I wanted to be a teacher after spending a lot of time in my aunt's classroom, so I pursued those avenues. After a few years, God impressed upon me that I needed to trust His plan. The skills I gained in the classroom would open other doors. I often wondered how a girl with a degree in elementary education and a minor in music was afforded so many different opportunities. God continuously challenged me to trust His plans over my own.

Many times, I felt inadequate, underqualified, and a bit out of my element, so I did a lot of praying for God to help me. He was always so kind to equip me. As friend Ellen Marrs says, "Faith over fear wins every time."[29] A true statement indeed! The work journey I share in the next chapter is simply an illustration to showcase how God chooses to pave the way in a person's life, which is all His own doing, displaying His faithfulness, so in the midst of their lives, His goodness and glory are shown to them, and sometimes to others looking on.

I look back now and see how He opened doors for me that I wouldn't have been brave enough to walk through on my own. He was there all along, encouraging me and orchestrating the bigger picture, establishing building blocks that would take me on the path He had for me. He gave me courage and led me to this very moment to writing this book. I love how God strategically puts people in places to use the gifts He's given them to be a light in the workplace. In doing so, their authentic joy and kindness build others up with encouragement and love. He's always on the move, for His plan is perfect!

An Extra Chair and a Jesus Cam

A great verse I learned as a working young adult is, "Whatever you do, work heartily, as for the Lord and not for men" (Colossians 3:23 ESV). He is our ultimate boss! I took this verse to heart and put an extra chair in my workspace for the Lord. It became a visual reminder to me that He had a seat at the table with every client I met with and every meeting I had. He was present, helping me make the right decisions in every situation, as I would constantly converse with Him about everything.

As you can imagine, having the extra chair made for great conversation if anyone asked who it was for. As well, I added to the idea and had an invisible "Jesus cam" in the corner of my office to remind me to keep my actions above reproach in all my conversations, in person or on the phone, and to keep a check on my tone and attitude throughout the day, keeping my heart joyful.

He is working through you as well to draw others to Him, so stay focused on the bigger picture in motion. If putting an extra chair and an invisible Jesus cam can help you, give it a try!

I Am an Ambassador for Christ, Disguised as a ...

The definition of an *ambassador* is "a person sent out to be a public representative to a foreign land to represent and reflect their homeland."[30] What does that look like for a Christian? As it is, a Christian's spiritual citizenship is in heaven; therefore, as ambassadors for Christ here on earth, we have a message of reconciliation to deliver to a world living apart from God.

> We are ambassadors for Christ, as though God were pleading through us: we implore you on Christ's behalf, be reconciled to God. (2 Corinthians 5:20 NKJV)

A lyric from the song "The Commission,"[31] from the band Cain (an awesome two-sisters-and-a-brother band who wear matching outfits—so cute!), says it well. Their 2021 release of this song in the series *The Chosen*[32], (An incredible series on Netflix. Watch it, if you can. It's really good!) speaks from Jesus' point of view:

> Go tell the world about Me.
> I was dead but now I live …
> Where I go, you will go too, someday.
> There's much to do here before you leave.

Our friend Justin's Instagram description was, "I am an Ambassador for Christ disguised as a Land Surveyor." Justin lost his life from a car accident when he was only twenty years old. It was heartbreaking! Though, of the years he was here on earth, he left an incredible mark for Christ. As a land surveyor, he did his job with excellence. His entire company spoke at his Celebration of Life service, telling about the amazing, hardworking young man that he was—that he was always attentive to learning, enjoyable and fun to work with, and his outgoing personality was positive and uplifting to be around. The impact he made in how he treated people was a beautiful testimony of his life, always showcasing God's love to others. Given the opportunity, he had life-transforming conversations with several of them that always pointed them to know the love of Jesus.

Justin loved others well in Christ with his kindness and care. He certainly made a huge difference in people's lives, mine included. People saw the Christ who lived in him! I know if Justin were here today, he'd challenge you to be an ambassador for Christ. Next time you're asked what you do, in Justin's honor, say it loud and say it proud—"I am an ambassador for Christ, disguised as a [fill in your life status or occupation]."

"All of Life Is All for Jesus"

Your "fill in the blank" life status or occupation will change over time, as life assignments and life seasons are always transitioning, but as a follower of Christ, what will *never* change is that you will *always* be an ambassador for Christ, no matter your job title. How cool is that?

Every day of your life, until your last breath when God calls you home, you will *always* be on a mission for Christ. This calling is not a chore; *it's a lifestyle!* Our church's tagline, coined by our pastor, Luke Simmons, is, "All of Life Is All for Jesus."[33] It's on T-shirts, mugs, and posters. As I type this, I happen to be wearing my T-shirt right now. It is true; life really is *all* about Jesus! Amen and amen.

Mom often said when we were growing up, "We're like pilgrims passing through. Don't get too comfortable settling in. Our time here on earth will be brief, so set your eyes on where you're headed and your future home that awaits you." I love that! Thanks, Mom.

The older I get, the more people I know in heaven. A song that brings my heart peace in our ever-darkening world is the old hymn, "Turn Your Eyes upon Jesus."[34]

> Turn your eyes upon Jesus.
> Look full in His wonderful face!
> And the things of earth will grow
> Strangely dim,
> In the light of His glory and grace.

Yes, our days are numbered.

> Lord, remind me how brief my time on earth will
> be. Remind me that my days are numbered—how
> fleeting my life is. (Psalm 39:4 NLT)

Friends and family who trusted and followed Jesus and who are now in heaven certainly heard, "Well done, good and faithful servant" (Matthew 25:23a ESV). So, live your life with purpose and intentionality. Live your life, your "dash"—the little dash between when you were born and when you die (and only God knows when that is)—as a follower of Christ, every single day of your life. Live with expectation, purpose, and hope in the cross of Christ, and He will guide you through your life's journey with grace and mercies new every morning.

It's the New You!

When you become a Christian, Christ comes into your heart, replacing your old life with a new life.

> Take on an entirely new way of life, a God-fashioned life, a life renewed from the inside and working itself into your conduct as God accurately reproduces His character in you. (Ephesians 4:24 MSG)

Every day, put Christ into everything you do. Watch where God is at work and join Him. Remember, His plans are perfect. This mindset is true for every aspect of your life (e.g., where or if you'll go to college, which town you'll move to, where you will live, where you'll go to church, who you'll date, whether you'll marry someday or remain single, as Christ did, and so on). It's all about trusting God and knowing that He is looking out for you and has your best interest at heart. With confidence, you can trust His plan over your own. He's got this! He's got you!

> Be strong and take heart, all you who hope in the Lord. (Psalm 31:24 NIV)

As mentioned at the beginning of this chapter, a lot of my single adult years consisted of my working story, as I'm sure is true for you too. The following chapter is simply a backdrop of all God did through different work experiences He allowed me to be a part of, reminding me that He always has a plan for us to follow where He leads. There is nothing magical or impressive in any of my work stories. Anything that happened that was awesome was truly all God's doing. He will use you in ways you won't necessarily understand, sometimes until even decades later, so stay the course, and enjoy the journey He has for you.

For me, He used all my experiences to complete the story He was writing in my life to bring me to the very place where my heart healed. Each new opportunity opened the next door. I never fully comprehended what His plan was, but I see now the tapestry He was weaving, showcasing His love to me and displaying His glory.

Chapter 17 closes with sections titled, "Faith in the Workplace," "Balancing Faith in the Workplace," and "In This World, but Not of It." As a working young adult, I navigated these topics pretty well, thanks to Jesus, but other times, not so well. I was young and had a lot to learn about balancing work-life and not allowing work to become my idol. For a Christian, these topics are important in the workplace. The world is watching to see if you'll trip up, so be a person of integrity in your workplace, your relationships, and your purpose. From this point of view, may these sections encourage you as you navigate your faith in the workplace, God's got you!

CHAPTER 17

Career Life after Graduation and the Years That Followed

Teaching

absolutely loved being a teacher! I was transferred to the newest school in the district; it had just opened, and textbooks hadn't yet arrived. I needed to think out of the box for learning applications and decided to use the sports stats from the sports page of the newspaper for my math class. The remaining parts of the paper were used for other subjects. (Oh, to have had Pinterest back then!) I was nearing the end of my fourth year of teaching when I received a call from Marlene, my high school mentor from church when I was growing up. She was a great source of encouragement to me, always praying my life forward.

Newspaper

Marlene was the public relations director of a local news station and was approached by a colleague of hers from the local newspaper, asking her if she knew of anyone who might be a good fit for their newly created position of Education Coordinator; they wanted to hire a teacher. She recommended me to her colleague. Shortly thereafter, the director of this program observed my classroom, in which I used the newspaper for learning. When she offered me the job, I almost turned her down, as I never saw myself leaving the classroom. She quickly assured me that I'd still be teaching, but now it would be in classrooms around the valley, as an employee of the paper. How could I turn down such an offer? What an exciting opportunity! Plus, it came with a raise in pay that was a direct blessing from the Lord to help me pay off my student loans. I was in awe of God's provision!

Along with teaching in classrooms, I would oversee their education program and facilitate staff development courses in districts and local colleges. It was a dream job that literally landed in my lap! Teachers asked me all the time how I got so lucky to land such an incredible job. My answer was, "It was God! He gave it to me." He truly did! It was an exciting job, with a taste of two busy, fast-paced worlds—the classroom and the newsroom.

Not only was my boss, Jody, a great mentor to me, but our publisher, Mr. Schwartz, was a big support to our program, as he was a huge advocate for schools and the community. He also loved the Phoenix Suns and became friends with Suns' star A.C. Green and his education foundation, partnering us with his "Stay in School" campaign and his commercial, that I got to help coordinate with valley students.

We also were the sponsors of the Arizona State Spelling Bee. As the state coordinator, I joined our state winner and his mom for our first year in Washington, DC, for the National Spelling Bee. He made it to the second day of competition, which was amazing! And what an incredible experience it was to go to our nation's capital, somewhere I hadn't been before. The history of our nation and its early beginnings are so rich in faith—truly fascinating at every turn! If you've never been, plan to go.

Another opportunity came—to go to Russia with one of our photojournalists to tour schools and interview teachers in their arts and writing programs. Even though there was a language barrier and a sense of heaviness at times among the people we met, my desire was to smile and say hello and "God bless you" to every person I met. A word of kindness seemed to bring life to some who looked so heavy-hearted. (*And with a war there in recent years over territories in the region, it's a constant reminder to pray for all who are hurting and suffering, on either side. "Lord, let Your peace overcome war and conflict for people everywhere. Amen."*)

Laurie—the Columnist

The most significant moment at the paper was watching God draw someone to Himself. Laurie was an ambitious, well-written columnist, a young adult who once asked me, "Why are you so happy all the time?"

I told her, "The big guy upstairs keeps me going!" Our office building had two floors, so she assumed I was referring to someone in the sales department upstairs. When I told her, "The guy even higher up," she asked, "Oh, you're one of those?" Her curiosity got the better of her, so the newsworthy fact-finding reporter that she was dug deeper. It wasn't long afterward that she was open to visiting church with me one Sunday.

On her first visit, she'd meet her future husband, my friend from high school whose sister prayed for me in college! He'd always sit with his sweet mom, Lucy, who had a deep, endearing faith.

Laurie had grown up in church, which laid a faith foundation for her, but now, as a young adult, she realized she had a personal choice to make—would she follow Jesus or not? She once had little interest in the things of the Lord, but now she was choosing to be a Christian and live her life for Him. It was a beautiful transformation to watch her faith life grow from there. God was indeed at work in her life!

Sometimes, God may place us right where we are because individuals may need to see Jesus in us to get through their day. You may never know that someone is watching you, but as a believer, your life and how you live your life is *always* on display—*always!* Your attitude and integrity in the workplace are opportunities for Christ's love to flow through you in how you handle yourself, especially in high-stress situations. Just be who you are—considerate and kind to others—and people will be drawn to Christ who lives in you. If you have that mindset, it will keep you from getting complacent in the workplace and will remind you that you are there for a purpose—to love others well! Remember, you're an ambassador for Christ disguised as … (this time for me, a newspaper employee).

The Holy Spirit will direct you to certain conversations and relationships. Pray for opportunities. A seed planted in soil is watered and given nutrients and sunlight. As it grows, it's pruned, helping it thrive and mature into a beautiful plant. The same is true for the "God seed" planted in the human heart. The seed is watered, nurtured, and pruned. God does all those things, as the Master Gardener that He is, and He may very well allow you to be a part of a person's growth as He prompts you. We may never know where a person is in his or her private faith journey, but God knows.

> That person is like a tree planted by streams of water, which yields its fruit in season and whose leaf does not wither. (Psalm 1:3a NIV)

That amazing and talented writer and friend went on to become the religion editor for a large publication and is now a blogger and published author, with articles published in Chicken Soup for the Soul and other publications; as well, she's a public speaker at women's events. You can follow her at http://lauriedavies.life.[1] You will love everything she writes, each pointing you to Jesus. She's also the women's ministry director at the very same church where she and her husband, Greg, met. God "stories" are always being written, and hers (theirs) is another beautiful one!

Marketing Skills Gained at the Paper

Jody always challenged me to think outside the box to find creative ways for advertisers to pay for bundles of papers to be delivered to schools, so teachers wouldn't have to pay for them. As a former teacher, I appreciated that. The fewer the classroom expenses, the better. Companies partnering with schools helped reach a common goal for relationships to be built between the two—a win/win for both.

One such time was when the Super Bowl came to town in 1996, when the Cowboys defeated the Steelers, 27–17. A local bank wanted to sponsor a student and a parent to go to that game. They became the sponsor of an essay-writing contest to put $10,000 of scholarship money into schools. Essays came in from all over the valley. A winner was selected for an all-expenses-paid game day with VIP passes! What a thrill to be a part of the think tank for that project, which was so well received all over the valley. The best part—the winning student and his dad got to go to Super Bowl XXX to see their favorite team win!

Another time, we were asked to produce a tutorial video with advertisers on how the paper was made, from start to finish, for schools to review as a follow-up after their field trip to the paper. (Oh, to have had YouTube and TikTok back then!) It was a super-fun and challenging project, from helping to write the script, to producing, editing, and being the tour guide in the twenty-minute video. It highlighted interviews with directors and editors, explaining all aspects of the paper, from story creation to editing, to advertising, to printing on huge rolls of paper in four colors—cyan, magenta, yellow, and black—and delivery. The project was well received and was a helpful resource to classrooms across the valley.

It was hard to fathom that newspapers would become almost extinct someday, as was the prediction from some of those interviewed in that video, explaining that news would be generated in screen form in the future, and so it has become. The reality of newer and faster ways to generate news came into focus for me when I decided—when I was in the area years ago—to visit that big red-brick building on First Avenue. I wanted to see my workspace past the newsroom and all the ins and outs of that building I knew so well from all the many tours I had given over the years, as well as the picnic table area out back where we had company barbecues. You can imagine my surprise to find the paper was no more! The huge newspaper compound that once was had been repurposed as a state facility. It felt like a scene from *Back to the Future*, when something that *had been* was no longer. I walked into what used to be a very inviting and engaging front lobby, which now was filled with long lines and security at every checkpoint. It felt as if a piece of history was gone.

It was very telling how much our world has changed. News today is accessible any time, any way, by tapping, scrolling, touching, or clicking. Printed papers are definitely not in demand as they once were, but back then, they were all the buzz, and I'm so thrilled I got to work at one.

News that will never go extinct is God's *good news*, the timeless, never-changing news that brings hope, joy, healing, and everlasting peace. And just like the daily news, you can get God's Word any way you want, through Bible apps or turning the pages, which I still love to do, marked with years of God's truths, highlighted with stories and sermon notes written in the margins. The Word of God will withstand any news story *any* day. I always thought about that when I worked at the paper. Although the newspaper complex and producing the daily news on First Avenue was no more, God's Word lasts forever and will never die.

> The grass withers and the flowers fade, but the word of our God stands forever. (Isaiah 40:8 NLT)

Radio

Theresa, a friend from Single Vision, worked at a local country radio station and shared about a new position they were creating—Community Relations Director—and suggested I look into it. Marlene advised me once again and suggested this would be a wise career move for me. She knew the COO well and knew the position would be a good fit for me. She saw it as a tremendous opportunity to be effective in the community. She was and continues to be actively involved on the board of the Salvation Army and knew God opened those doors for her to be a blessing to people through her connections. From her advice, I sent in my résumé, and after a few weeks of interviewing with the station, I was offered the position and accepted the job. No one at the paper knew about my interviews, except my sweet friend Laurie, who was praying God's will over the situation. Squeezing in time for those interviews without compromising my job was a balancing act, but God made it work. Sometimes, it's unclear why God calls us to different things, but that's when we know we need to walk by faith to follow what He's put in front of us. God was truly up to something, and I had to trust His bigger plan.

To accept a position in radio, in which I had no experience, was a bit daunting. I remember questioning God, "What are You doing, Lord?" He may place you in uncomfortable situations without revealing why. As difficult as it may be, trust Him when He calls you to a job or situation for which you feel inadequate, and He will equip you. The feeling of leaving the paper felt similar to how I felt about leaving the classroom, especially saying goodbye to my newspaper family and my amazing boss, Jody. We cried together when I told her the news. She had poured so much into me and believed in me, sometimes more than I believed in myself. I felt like I was turning my back on her for all her loyalty of being my biggest cheerleader. Even though she was sad to hear my news, she was so happy for me and the opportunity that awaited me. To walk away from the paper, my coworkers, and my job would be hard, but I had to remind myself that my identity was (is) in Christ and not in my job. He would go with me wherever He sent me, and He'll go with you too.

> Now may the God of peace … equip you with everything good that you may do His will, working in us, that which is pleasing in His sight. (Hebrews 13:20–21a ESV)

God, in His goodness, put the right people in front of me at the station to teach me the ropes, from my kind and supportive boss, Michael, to department directors, especially Vicki, who helped me every step of the way, and our department secretary, Tina, a sweet Christian whose loving patience was so endearing.

I was in a new environment and had so much to learn, but it was exciting all the while! I think back to the gifted industry professionals who made the station so exceptional in the valley. It was a privilege to work alongside them. The station was a tight-knit family who embraced me with loving arms.

One of those colleagues was the station's private trainer who was a Christian. He later married a friend of mine from high school. Together, David and Holly started a prison-reform ministry called Cross Strength Ministries[2] where they share their life-changing stories to men and women in prisons, at churches, and with groups. I love how God connects the dots with other believers in the workplace.

The music director's office was right behind mine, and, on occasion, he would share new artists he was listening to and would ask my opinion. What a treat it was to weigh in on new songs and artists who would play on the airwaves. I only ever listened to Christian radio, but at work, my dial was on our station. Stepping into the country genre took some getting used to, as it was all very new to me to learn the artists and their music, but I quickly learned it was a world all its own, with diehard fans everywhere we went.

New on the scene then were greats like Faith Hill, with her song "This Kiss." Faith had recently married country artist Tim McGraw. They gave the country world their famous duet, "It's Your Love." Their love story continues to capture the hearts of audiences as they give credit to praying together daily and loving each other well. Tim has a Christian fish tattooed on his arm to share his faith.

Then there was the new voice that was compared to the legendary Patsy Cline when then-thirteen-year-old LeAnn Rimes came on the scene with her hit "Blue" and, on the heels of that, "You Light Up My Life" (originally recorded by Christian singer Debby Boone in the '70s); she would later give the Christian world her unforgettable song "I Need You." There's a lot of faith in the country music industry, with so many who grew up in church choirs or singing gospel music. A vocalist's faith reaches audiences, such as in Carrie Underwood's song "Jesus, Take the Wheel," or in the 2019 release of Dolly Parton's pairing with Christian artists For King & Country in their hit song "God Only Knows," and so many others who share their faith through music.[3]

Music moves people in powerful ways! It is so encouraging to see faith lived out in artists' lives and celebrities across the board who choose to walk with Jesus and showcase His love in the platforms He's given them. It is said that you may be the only Jesus people see. In whatever platform of influence the Lord has given you, never fear to let your light shine bright for Christ!

> Let your light so shine before men that they may
> see your good works and glorify your Father who
> is in heaven. (Matthew 5:16 MEV)

Since my position was community-driven and we were a well-known valley station, we partnered with a lot of nonprofits to better their causes through on-air support. The artists we reached out to embraced our causes and, without hesitation, joined our efforts to make an impact.

One artist who lived in the valley and attended the church I grew up in was Glen Campbell. He was at our station from time to time, joining in to support. What a dear man he was, now with Jesus. His beautiful faith legacy lives on.

One such cause was to come alongside a local children's hospital and build a youth cancer wing on the teen floor. Through a celebrity golf tournament, we were able to raise a large sum of money to sponsor the building of the cancer teen room, where teens could hang out, and artists could visit them when they were in town for concerts. The joy of seeing those kids' faces light up when artists visited them and serenaded them was priceless. They gave the kids hope, and some even said a prayer over them, which was incredible to witness.

It wasn't long afterward that the sales department caught wind of my enthusiasm for spending time with the kids at the hospital and offered me some side work to represent some of their clients. First, I was a penguin in a penguin suit, passing out Popsicles to people at live remotes during Frozen Food Month. (Who knew it was a thing?) Let's just say I gained a new appreciation for those who are mascots for their high schools and colleges, as those full-body fur costumes and huge headpieces are hot and heavy. (Oh, how I was thankful for the walk-in freezers at the stores that I could step into to cool off during those hot Arizona days!)

Then I became a character called Strawberry Swirl for an ice-cream client to represent their new flavor of the month—none other than Strawberry Swirl Cheesecake. In full costume made specifically for this created character, I'd join the station's radio personalities at trade shows, car shows, you-name-it shows, I was there. I passed out ice cream and sang a little jingle that the station wrote and aired. Oh, the silly things I did to make children smile and clients satisfied—funny memories! The Lord has a sense of humor, for sure!

It wasn't too far of a stretch from when my mom seriously suggested that after high school, I should attend the Ringling Bros. and Barnum & Bailey Clown College to become a clown for the circus, or the time I seriously considered moving to California to audition to be a singing princess at Disneyland. I highly considered it and am almost sad I didn't give it a try. Perhaps all of the work gigs were preparing me for an interest later in life to get involved in local community theater that spanned from my late thirties throughout my forties to sing, dance, and act in *Hairspray, Annie, Oliver!, The Music Man,* and *Bye Bye Birdie,* with the amazing director Ms. Molly, who loves all her casts like her own family and is a dear woman of faith. God always has a plan.

Oh, the fun God gives us when we take time to look around and spread our wings. I'd encourage you to do the same. Try something new you thought you'd never be good at or have a shot at, and trust Him in the process. Never underestimate God. If He wants you to be a part of something, He'll open the door. The best part is, you'll meet new people, make new friends, and make great memories along the way. Never let Satan rob you of the beautiful treasure God has placed in your heart.

GMA Week

One of the most incredible experiences in my life while working at the station was going to GMA Week (Gospel Music Association) and the Dove Awards, equivalent to the Grammys but for the Christian music industry. I was so thankful for the opportunity to go.

As a radio rep, I got to attend intimate concert settings at coffee shops and similar venues to hear Christian artists, up close and personal, talk about their music and inspirations. That year's theme (*as mentioned in the previous chapter*), "Bloom [or Grow] Where You Are Planted," resonated with me, as at the time, I was leading worship for Single Vision. What a great perspective and life lesson to gain—to be faithful right where God has "planted" you, to be used by God with the giftedness He's given you. Be thankful for where He has you, and don't be discontented but be fully present in the season He has you in, rather than plotting what-if or why-not thoughts.

For over three decades, God was so kind to allow me to be in choirs, on worship teams, and a vocalist in bands, singing in weddings and memorial services along the way. Those experiences weren't because of anything special I had to offer; it was all God's doing. He allows us to use the gifts He's given us to worship His name. I learned that God may take your dreams and reshape them over time, but He'll *always* keep a song in your heart, allowing you to use those gifts throughout your lifetime.

He's been my precious source of worship all this time, and I'm so thankful! That experience in Nashville shaped my heart toward worship that has stayed with me to this day. Worship is how we respond to God, our audience of One, in everything we do and in everywhere we go. It's lifting our lives up to Him in gratitude and thanksgiving in every breath we breathe.

> Delight yourself in the Lord, and He will give you the desires of your heart. (Psalm 37:4 ESV)

> You make known to me the path of life, in your presence there is fullness of joy; at your right hand are pleasures forevermore. (Psalm 16:11 ESV)

New Direction

After almost a year and a half at the station, there was a shift in department roles, and I was offered a position in sales. As much as it was such a terrific offer, I didn't feel called to sales, as my interests were in the community aspect of the job. I chose to take a leap of faith and left the station, trusting God for the next season ahead. In His goodness, He used all that I had learned to prepare me for the next opportunity. He was indeed working in miraculous ways.

Let me tell you that if you feel a nudge from the Holy Spirit to take a leap of faith away from your current employment, check in first with your employer to learn all your options, and make wise decisions accordingly. Your current employer potentially will write you a letter of recommendation, so leave in good standing. I was thankful that my boss wrote a very nice letter of reference for me. It carried me to the next open door. At the time, I had no idea where that was, but I was equipped with his reference when God chose to open the next door.

In Between Jobs

If you find yourself in between jobs and wondering what the next job will be, be diligent and put yourself out there by sending out your résumé and filling out online applications. Go back to school, if needed, or get more training in a specific area. Don't underestimate God's willingness to carry you through what might feel like lean times. Don't get discouraged, as the enemy wants you to be depressed, so be diligent to not succumb to his deceitful ways.

In moments of unknown employment, do what you need to do to secure "legal" employment (be wise and discerning, never compromising your faith with shady money or shady people). Find work that pays your bills and puts food on the table, even if that means a job for which you are overqualified. If God is providing provision for you, be humble and take it. He may very well place you in an in-between job for a season and/or for a reason.

To everything there is a season, and a time to every purpose under the heaven. (Ecclesiastes 3:1 KJV)

It's a great reminder that seasons of life will come and go, and as much as unknown seasons may feel like an eternity, they are not. This feeling of despair will surely pass in God's good timing. Just trust Him in the process.

If there's a job loss, a loss in a relationship, or a death of a loved one (and the list goes on), be encouraged that God is in the midst of your pain and suffering. He's there to carry you through. If you're suffering right now, be reminded that God loves you. He is there for you and cares deeply for you. Don't lose hope!

Retail

My in-between, go-to job was retail, as I had worked retail in college. I was hired on the spot, reminding me again that God is good all the time. God used that job to sustain me while He was paving the way for the next door to open. While at that job, I got to share Christ with a fellow employee who was going through some really tough stuff. I was humbled to be called to that assignment for that hurting soul, to be there as my coworker weathered the storm. Looking back, I realized that if God was closing the door on the once-fancy title I had at the radio station to be there for a new friend in need, then He was directing that path for a reason.

It was scary to leave a secure job with insurance and benefits, going from being a name on a business card to a no-name and no business card, but it was evident my identity was wrapped up in what I did and who I was. God used that situation to draw me to His truth that I am a child of God, first and foremost, a banner I need to wear proudly!

> Where does my help come from? My help comes from the Lord ... Maker of heaven and earth! (Psalm 121:1b–2 NIV)

Precious Lord, You were there to help me. Thank you!

> Why am I discouraged? Why is my heart so sad? I will put my hope in God! I will praise him again-my Savior. (Psalm 42:5 NLT)

Trusting God in Unknown Seasons

It was hard to see God's plan at the front end of that season, but He sustained me, working out every detail. He showed me His love through that time of uncertainty. He was my rock and my redeemer.

> May the words of my mouth and the meditation
> of my heart be pleasing to you, O LORD, my rock
> and my redeemer. (Psalm 19:14 NLT)

We never need to question God. Keep trusting Him in the unknown seasons. Know He has a plan for you. Even if looking for a job becomes a full-time job, be diligent in doing so, and continue trusting that the right door will open in His perfect timing. Don't lose hope!

> Be strong and courageous. Do not be afraid; do not
> be discouraged, for the Lord your God will be with
> you wherever you go. (Joshua 1:9 NIV)

While You're Waiting

There's a song I love by John Waller called "While I'm Waiting."[4] The lyrics are perfect in moments like these when we are waiting on the Lord. It's a given; you will wait a lot in your lifetime. You will wait for answers, directions, clarification, confirmation, and understanding about things you are going through. In those in-between moments when you don't know what God is doing, and you feel discouraged and defeated, be encouraged. He is calling you to trust Him in the waiting.

> Be still and know that I am God.
> (Psalm 46:10a NIV)

He wants you to trust Him like never before. "While I'm Waiting" was the feature song in the movie *Fireproof*.[5] (It's an awesome faith movie worth checking out on your movie streaming devices; as well, pull up this song and let the lyrics flood over your weary soul as you take a deep breath in your season of waiting.) God doesn't want you to miss out on what He is doing in your season of waiting. Be proactive and responsive in this period of waiting He has you in. Whatever your season of waiting may be—a job, a relationship, health concerns, a loss, any of it—it's painful, and He wants you to know He is there. Even while you're waiting, be encouraged.

> Wait for the Lord, be strong and take heart and
> wait for the Lord. (Psalm 27:14 NIV)

Here are some of the lyrics to "While I'm Waiting."

> I'm waiting
> I'm waiting on you Lord
> And I am hopeful
> Though it is painful
> But patiently, I will wait
> I'll be running the race
> Even while I wait

Reality-TV Pilot

As I was busy working full time at the retail store, I was also busy keeping my contacts alive and looking for the next opportunity God had for me. Sure enough, through phone conversations with different contacts, God led me to the creator and producer of a new teen reality-TV show, the first of its kind, to air on a local TV station. I'd join their team to serve as their community relations director to help promote the show in their opening season, which led me to embark upon the beginnings of freelance work and the flexibility it afforded me. It'd be a new challenge—and an exciting one at that!

The show's producer, Louisa, had a great passion to make a difference in teens' lives by creating a reality show with a select group of teens from different backgrounds and ethnicities from high schools across the state, who would talk openly and honestly about issues they faced. They traveled in an RV, touring the nation, while footage of their unscripted talk of the hardships teens experienced was filmed. They interviewed people who had gone through similar hardships and shared their stories of growth and personal victory. Whatever you can think of that is pressing today were the same issues that were discussed on the show, minus social media, as smartphones weren't a thing yet. If a show of this nature were produced today, social media would no doubt have dominated the conversation.

It was a powerful project that was well received by sponsors who were interested in the teen market. Most notably was the Phoenix Suns, thanks to Louisa's dad, who had been a scout for the team and connected her with the former team owner, Jerry Colangelo, a powerful Christian figure in the state, to partner with the show. It was so awesome to see God work through all these connections.

As the show's teens quickly became local celebrities, we joined efforts to market and create a platform for them to make public appearances in the community to get their message out about teens talking to teens, being open to the issues they faced, and finding the support they needed. One of the venues was a red-carpet event at the state fair. They were met with fanfare and long lines of star-struck teens who wanted their autographs and a chance to meet and take a picture with their favorite teen from the show.

Freelancing and Volkswagen

Taking notice was a nearby vendor, Volkswagen, whose VW director was fascinated by the enthusiasm of our project and the crowds we drew. He was interested in my work for the show, which led to a meeting with him. He offered me a freelance contract to oversee an intense six-month media marketing campaign for the debut of their iconic refurbished Bug coming to the valley. God's timing couldn't have been more perfect, as my work to promote the show would be coming to an end, and it was essential that I find a new project to embark upon.

Once again, God, in His provision, landed another amazing opportunity in my lap! I was excited about this new challenge. I learned there are die-hard vintage Volkswagen lovers who would travel from city to city for VW events. This darling new traveling VW Bug, including its signature flower vase and a fresh-cut daisy, was a hit, as people would come from all over just to see it and sit in it.

I always wondered why God opened this amazing door for me with Volkswagen, but after I was hit in a hit-and-run car accident while freelancing for them, it all made sense. Not only did I need to land employment at the end of my time with the show's opening run, but I also needed a reliable car after mine was totaled. It was a very scary, traumatic moment on impact. When the airbags deployed, I said, "Are you OK, Jesus?"

The first officer on the scene asked who I was talking to, assuming someone else was in the car. When I told him I was talking to the Lord, he was understanding and smiled with a sigh of relief. I walked away with bloody scrapes, multiple bruises, and whiplash but was amazingly OK, thanks to the Lord!

Although I was quite rattled to get behind the wheel of a car after the accident, God, in His goodness, was there to walk that path with me. My connections allowed me to get into a used VW Jetta for a screaming deal. It *really* is true; God is in all the details of our lives and is always looking out for us. Not only did He provide employment for me but a car as well!

Moving, Leaving Single Vision, and Pet-Sitting

Freelance work allowed me to join my then-roommate, Angela, from Single Vision. I moved farther north with her to another city in the valley, where she was in her dental residency program in that area. She'd eventually go on to open her own dental practice. I was so proud of her! It was a joy to see her living out her dream of becoming a dentist, getting married, and having a family of her own.

Moving across town with Angela also meant leaving Single Vision where I had been involved for nine years—many of those years leading worship, as well as being part of the discipleship ministry—wait, can we pause a moment, nine years, people, nine years! I think I was the longest-running participant in a singles ministry *ever*. It was hard to leave something I loved, especially being a part of the worship band, but I was thankful for the beautiful season God had blessed me with.

Also in this season, I landed additional side work with a pet-sitting company that serviced the area where we lived. I mostly pet-sat for domestic dogs and cats, but sometimes, a client had an exotic bird or a scaly reptile. I would meet the owner(s) and their four-legged fur fam or feathered or scaly pet and provide whatever services the client wanted. Some preferred that I stay overnight, and some requested that I swim with their dogs or take them on walks. I loved animals, so it was a great fit. I would tell friends of my pet-sitting stories and thought that if I ever wrote a book, it would have to be about all the funny animal stories I collected along the way. I guess God had other plans regarding a book, but nevertheless, pets are the best!

Side note: If you ever struggle with loneliness—I know I did— consider getting a pet. I always had a cat in my single adult life, as cats are the easiest for apartment living and tend to be pretty independent. If you're a dog person, you know they are loyal and will cuddle and give tail wags and kisses. Cat or dog, fish or hamster, or other, get a pet that fits you best. They are the best and will bring the best out of you! Pets are a gift from God. They are loving, forgiving, and truly a best friend. I couldn't imagine a day without a pet. But if a pet isn't doable in your life, get a stuffed animal in its place—or a plant is always a good joy-filler too!

A.C. Green Foundation

When the TV show ended for Louisa, her connections led her to work with GinaMarie, the director of the A.C. Green Foundation. It was the same foundation our newspaper partnered with a few years earlier to help make the "Stay in School" commercial for Phoenix Suns' player A.C. Green[6] whose programs help teens and teen athletes reach their potential through camps and classroom curriculum.

Louisa would oversee his program in junior high and high schools and needed to hire an Arizona-certified teacher to teach his curriculum. She reached out to me and offered me the job! I was *so* in awe to see God bring everything full circle, connecting all the dots—His provision once again, writing His story! From being a teacher, to having coordinated kids to be in his commercial—who got to spend their entire afternoon with him during the shoot, all enjoying how personable he was and how he encouraged each student to stay in school and make wise choices—to now getting to work for his foundation, I was so thankful and excited for this new opportunity!

A.C. Green, a dynamic Christian and role model who is so humble and kind to everyone he meets, was nicknamed "Iron Man" for playing more consecutive games than any other player in the NBA—1,192 games, spanning sixteen seasons. Truly incredible! He positively impacted the NBA and people all over the globe with his gifts, on and off the court that embodied everything he is about—integrity, focus, and living a disciplined life. His inspirational book *Victory*, about his career from high school to the NBA, shares his personal commitment to his spiritual life and offers principles for championship living. His other book, *A.C. Green*, depicts his character and courage while standing for sexual purity, never wavering amid the ever-pressing peer pressure while in the NBA. When challenged about his own purity in the throngs of all the pressure, his heartfelt response was, "You need to have self-respect, values, and virtue in your life." Even to those who were sexually active, A.C.'s message would encourage them—"It's never too late to start practicing abstinence." A.C. lived a life of purity that never wavered! At age thirty-eight he married his beautiful bride and together they inspire others. (Google "A.C. Green: Iron Virgin" for an eight-minute video of his purity story in the NBA. So powerful! As well, search YouTube for his name for interviews he's in. And for great resources, see acgreen.com.)

School districts gladly welcomed A.C.'s message and his presence in their schools. His curriculum, "I've Got the Power," and study guide "Game Plan"[7] instilled values of abstinence and helped students make better choices to stay in school, make better friend choices, avoid drugs and alcohol, and choose sexual purity over the pressures to engage in sexual activity. His name A.C. nicely fits his message of being Abstinence Committed.

GinaMarie and Louisa continued hiring staff—from Katie, who ran the front office and whose smile brightened all our days; to Kenneth, who oversaw the high school classrooms and would later move to California to pastor his own church; and Kim, another teacher I'd co-teach with in the program. (Kim went on to get her law degree to serve adoptive families and would play a very significant role later on in my life.) It was an exceptional team that God put together, with A.C. at the helm, and God at the center of all we did at the foundation. We started each staff meeting in prayer, with one of us leading a devotion. The message we were promoting in the schools would sometimes come with great resistance, so we knew we needed to be covered in prayer for the spiritual warfare that awaited us.

A.C.'s passion and his presence on campuses resonated in powerful ways. We saw God working every day on our behalf in schools and in the community. At the end of our two-week classroom sessions, before moving on to the next school, students would fill out commitment cards, which they'd take to heart, pledging to make wise and better choices in their lives. We weren't alone in our efforts in the schools; we had great support everywhere we went, most notably from the hospital, St. Joe's (where, coincidentally, I was born). We collaborated with hospital staff—Sister Judith Lynn, caseworkers, and others—to address teens' drug and alcohol use and to brainstorm effective ways to promote abstinence in the schools.

The hospital's program had statistics of students who were sexually active in the schools we served. Our team would be available to come alongside a struggling student, usually a girl, who had lost her virginity when a boy told her she was pretty and that he'd be her boyfriend. We loved them in that space and helped them make better choices. I knew God had given me this job because it put me in direct contact with students who were falling into similar traps that I had experienced. I knew exactly how they felt.

For me, personally, God used A.C.'s message to encourage my own heart to redeem all that was broken in me from my past, to live in newness with Him, being on the path of "abstinence again"— pure, forgiven, and restored! I owe A.C. a lifetime of gratitude for all he taught me about God's forgiveness and moving on. It was an amazing job and a huge privilege and honor to work for a man with such *incredible* integrity and vision. I was so thankful to be a part of it all. It thrills me to see all that A.C. and his foundation have accomplished and continue to accomplish, for the good of youth around the nation and beyond, with the message of abstinence, self-respect, integrity, and love for Jesus.

Little Green A.C. Bears

A fond foundation memory was going to the newly opened Staples Center Arena in L.A. on Christmas Day for a sold-out game to watch the Lakers play, the team A.C. was playing for at the time. We had flown out a few days before to meet with his L.A. staff to un-package twenty thousand little green bears from boxes that went on forever! Our staff helped facilitate a crew of volunteers stationed at every exit to give away these 8-inch little green A.C. Green bears to every person who left the stadium that day. And to think A.C. gifted every single participant was remarkable, as these cute little bears were in such high demand, that we could barely keep them on our foundation shelves.

On game day, wearing Santa hats and A.C.'s "I've Got the Power" t-shirts, our team prayed over the mission at hand. And indeed, it was mission accomplished, as we got to tell every attendee, "Merry Christmas!" while handing them a little green bear with a tag that was a little Bible with a cross on the cover and a verse inside. On the bear's back was embroidered, "I've Got the Power!" It was amazing to see God at work, spreading the love of Jesus through the simple gesture of a little bear people couldn't resist. It was "God-perfect" in every way!

(To see these darling little bears and all his other resources, visit acgreen.com. His message, "I've Got the Power" still rings true today that through Christ, you do have the power against all obstacles. Amen!)

God Paved the Way

Looking back over all these working years since college, I know that God was paving the way and not wasting anything from my past. The relationships made, the connections gained, and the common themes interwoven with new skill sets gained along the way would open new doors to the next opportunity that God had for me, all to be used for His plan and purpose. Whenever you ask, "What is God doing?" step back and remind yourself that He is the same God who created the heavens and earth and set the stars in motion, and He indeed has a plan for your life. He never gets weary or tired, as we do, but is there to encourage you to take the next step. Be willing to follow His lead. He has things for you to do if you pay attention to His calling in your life.

> "For I know the plans I have for you," declares the Lord, "plans to prosper you and not to harm you, plans to give you hope and a future." (Jeremiah 29:11 NIV)

What I Learned as a Working Young Adult

I look back on God's kindness to me during those working years and am thankful for faith mentors who helped me stay focused to better understand God's bigger picture in the workplace. Marlene gave me sound advice that helped me see Jesus in the midst of a media career that could've been difficult to navigate—faith under pressure. My young-adult pastor, Jeff, encouraged me to not let my work be my idol. A.C. Green's integrity and focus inspired me to stay the course. Tom's teaching at Priority Living and at church impacted my life to stay true to God's Word. When the uncertainties of life are intimidating, God's loving guidance and encouragement can help you stay the course. He did that for me through kind and loving people, and I know He'll do so for you too. He loves you and is there for you! Be intentional, get to know God, and grow your faith.

The Gray Zone of Life

Kahdeem, a young adult in our group, coined a phrase that summed up the young-adult years perfectly. He said, "This season we're in right now is the gray zone of our lives." (Meaning things aren't necessarily clear and precise for a young adult in this season but instead are foggy and vague.) It is true! It's the unknown season, when all the big decisions are being made. It's a good reminder to find a faith community who will stand in the gap with you, walk the line with you, pray with you, and encourage you as they help you stay accountable while making big life decisions. They will be your support at every turn.

If you're past your young-adult years, I'd urge you to find a young adult you can mentor, guy to guy and gal to gal. They need a firmly planted adult, ideally other than their parent(s), they can meet with to open up to about the things they're going through, who will help them navigate the decisions that are in front of them. You, as that adult, can pour into them and encourage and pray for them. It will make *all* the difference in their world.

Young adult, know you're loved by God. God stood by me in my young-adult years and never left my side. He will do the same for you! You have worth and purpose in God's eyes. You are God's child, resembling His goodness and kindness in your life. There is nothing you need to do or can do to gain His love! You are complete through His Son, Jesus. His presence and love are all around you. Embrace Him.

Closing Thoughts—Faith in the Workplace

In the workplace, you have an amazing opportunity to be an influence for good when you keep in mind your purpose and your mission. When staying focused on the bigger picture, you will be more diligent in your work by making good use of your time, and your integrity will stay intact. These two sections are timeless principles that God taught me about faith and balancing faith in the workplace, which inevitably show up through your actions and attitude. What you say and do matters as you reflect Christ in all your ways.

- ✦ Remember, first and foremost, you are an ambassador for Christ at your job. "We are therefore Christ's ambassadors, as though God were making His appeal through us" (2 Corinthians 5:20a NIV). Let all your actions resemble that ambassador banner in the way you conduct yourself. Be trustworthy, hardworking, accountable, punctual, and fully present with all aspects of your job, and never gossip.
- ✦ If you have an issue with someone or something, go to that person directly, and work it out quietly. If you need the

support of your boss or your company's human resources (HR), do so privately. You don't need to drag others into anything that is meant for just you and that other person. Be above reproach; be blameless.

+ Don't look for opportunities to be on your phone or do personal work or assignments of any kind other than the work that is yours to be done in the workplace. You were hired and are paid for a job. Do it, and do it well!

+ Receive criticism without complaining. Never argue. Ask permission to speak and give ideas about the situation. A boss wants you to always think about the company and how you can help better it with your ideas and innovations. That's why he or she hired you in the first place—he or she believes in you and wants to see what you have to offer. Constantly think in those terms.

+ Don't ever send mixed messages to others when interacting with them that might come across as your being interested in them in a relationship way. Always be a person of integrity and above reproach in your interactions with them. Respect boundaries. Never drive or travel alone with another person of the opposite sex on work-related outings. Either travel separately to a meeting spot or have another coworker in the vehicle and at the appointment. It will display integrity on your part.

+ The same is true for appointments or lunch and dinner meetings. As innocent as it may seem, it is dangerous and sends a wrong message to a significant other or a spouse at home. It doesn't bode well for you to be exclusive with someone's spouse. You can do your work the next day in a group meeting. Don't play with fire! It's dangerous. Too many marriages break up from casual workplace relationships, a lot of times with the single person in the office. Don't be that person. Marriage is sacred. If you struggle in this area, get the help you need. You have a job to do, and it's not to be the office flirt.

+ Remember, you are there for a purpose. Do your job well! God is your ultimate boss, and you report to Him. Do a job you are proud of so when you go home at the end of your work day or the end of your shift, you can gladly rejoice that God gave you energy and grace for the day, and allowed you to be a blessing to Him and to others.

+ Sleep, eat, exercise, and be mentally prepared for your job, but don't let it overtake your life. If it does, reevaluate how you spend your time at work to use your time wisely. Don't take your job home with you, and if you work from home, walk away from your workspace when the day is done. You need personal time away from your job. If you don't get a handle on this now, it will affect a future marriage. You may be good at your job but pay little attention to your marriage. Some people, sadly, lean more into their jobs and leave their marriages to ruin. I've seen it several times in my life—people who were so consumed with their jobs and their identities in their jobs that it took over everything, even their rational thinking. Watch for those blind spots, and think of better ways to manage your workload.

+ If you need help, check in with your boss about ways to scale back, or check with your Human Resources Department about ways to share your workload. You can also gain support from your church. There may be someone who is older and has walked in your shoes, who can help you balance all that you have in front of you. Embrace the community you're a part of by letting people encourage you, pray for you, and guide you.

- As much as your company may feel like family, make sure it doesn't replace your relationships with people outside of work and your relationship with God. If that describes you, step back and take inventory—you may have turned your job into your idol. Have a healthy balance of your priorities.
- If you find yourself thinking more about work than you do about the Lord or your family, get off that treadmill. If you don't, it will overrun you. You can get sick, anxious, and sleep-deprived by trying to do too much.

And He said, "My presence shall go with you, and I will give you rest." (Exodus 33:14 NASB)

My soul, find rest in God; my hope comes from Him. Truly He is my rock and my salvation; He is my fortress, I will not be shaken. (Psalm 62:5–6 NIV)

Balancing Faith in the Workplace

Faith in the workplace doesn't mean you bombard people by evangelizing at every turn. Instead, let who you are in Christ be displayed in how you treat people. If you're on social media, people will know who you are and what you are about by what you post. Choose to be a person who is approachable, whose love for Christ shines through in loving and caring ways. If you are perceived as being dominant in conversation by being pushy or argumentative, that behavior reflects poorly on the heart of God in the workplace and could ultimately cost you your job. Instead, be vigilant and ever present to see where God is at work, and establish relationships so when people are ready to talk and open up, you are there for them with a loving and kind ear to listen.

+ If you're to speak into the situation, He will prompt you. Otherwise, listen and show authentic compassion. God is at work. It's His doing, not yours. Sometimes your role is simply to be present, listen, and care for that person.

+ If God opens a door for you to share your faith with a coworker, always ask that person if you can share with them how you experienced hardships or if you can pray for them. If you've become a trusted person, that person will seek you out.

+ Walk the halls of your place of employment and pray quietly without drawing attention to yourself. Pray for your coworkers, their work, and their stress load, and ask God how you can come alongside them to encourage them.

+ Look for opportunities to engage in conversation with coworkers in free windows of space during the day, never forgetting that your first priority at work is to work; pay attention to not cross that line, as it could reflect poorly on you as an employee. It's a fine line to walk, so walk with intentional care and precision, following God's lead.

+ Most importantly, have a good attitude! Don't be the person who drags people down. Go to work, ready for the day. Be joyful and ask God to give you His eyes to see a person or situation where you can be His vessel. Do your job well and love others well in the process.

Do everything without grumbling or arguing, so that you may become blameless and pure, 'children of God without fault in a warped and crooked generation.' Then you will shine among them like stars in the sky as you hold firmly to the word of life. (Philippians 2:14–16a NIV)

In This World, but Not of It

Lastly, as a believer, never forget that you are *in* this world but not *of* this world. Daily, you step into the battlefield of the world you live in, and you can't go it alone. If you're not prayed up or standing vertical in step with God, you will be attacked when you least expect it. Read all of James 4, which is subtitled in the ESV translation as "Warning against Worldliness."

> Submit yourselves therefore to God. Resist the devil, and he will flee from you. Draw near to God, and he will draw near to you. (James 4:7–8a ESV)

You *cannot* function without God's strength, nor should you try. Be prepared for the spiritual battle that will attempt to confront you on a daily basis. Pressures will heighten at your job if your ideals and identity are challenged. It can move you into comparison, depression, anxiety, anger, and worry. Take heed to God's Word when He encourages you to be draped in His righteous love.

> There is no fear in love, but perfect love casts out fear. For fear has to do with punishment, and whoever fears has not been perfected in love. (1 John 4:18 ESV)

> Wondrously show your steadfast love, O Savior of those who seek refuge from their adversaries at your right hand. (Psalm 17:7 ESV)

As a child of God, you have a target on your back. (I've met the sweetest sister in Christ through Instagram from the UK who has a radical testimony of coming out of the New Age movement as a blood witch to being an on-fire Jesus girl. Jesus saved her from the devil who was out for her soul. Give her a follow @undone_ by_grace, Naela Rose, linktr.ee/naelarose). It is true, the enemy wants to trip you up, interrupt your day, and get you off track by distracting you in your busyness. Therefore, as you go out into your day, be dressed in the Lord by being prayed up, dressed up, loved up, and ready to go, for the battle is real.

> Finally, be strong in the Lord and in the strength of His might. Put on the whole armor of God that you may be able to stand against the schemes of the devil. For we do not wrestle against flesh and blood, but against the rulers, against the authorities, against the cosmic powers over this present darkness, against the spiritual forces of evil in the heavenly places. Therefore, take up the whole armor of God that you may be able to withstand in the evil day, and having done all, to stand firm. Stand therefore, having fastened on the belt of truth, and having put on the breastplate of righteousness, and, as shoes for your feet, having put on the readiness given by the gospel of peace. In all circumstances take up the shield of faith, with which you can extinguish all the flaming darts of the evil one; and take the helmet of salvation; and the sword of the Spirit, which is the word of God, praying at all times in the Spirit, with all prayer and supplication. To that end, keep alert with all perseverance. (Ephesians 6:10–18a ESV)

CHAPTER 18

So What Happened Next?

ngela and I found a new church home that offered great Bible teaching and promoted a healthy community. We both appreciated having each other to go to church with, as it allowed us to support one another's faith journey and, most importantly, helped us stay accountable to each other in all areas of our lives. We quickly got plugged into our new church and loved it.

It wasn't long after that my previous roommate—Amy, from Single Vision, still a part of the ministry—contacted me to ask if I'd go on their next ski trip, as it'd be her first time skiing. Amy knew how much I loved to ski and figured I could teach her some beginner moves on the slopes. I was excited about the idea of going, as I hadn't been skiing in a while. The ski meeting would be after their Thursday night Bible study, where I'd meet up with Amy and see old friends. I was excited to attend!

The room was dark upon my arrival, as a video had just started, so I grabbed a seat. The title flashed on the screen: *Meeting Your Future Spouse*. I about died—I absolutely cringed at the topic! Was this really what I'd be stuck watching for the next hour? I had run from this topic in my life for so long. I was at a healthy place, thriving in my singleness with Jesus, and I certainly didn't want to be confronted again with a topic that seemed so foreign to me. After the very awkward film, my then-previous pastor said a closing prayer and then announced the ski meeting. Amy introduced me to her friend, whom she'd brought from work— another ski enthusiast who was also going on the trip. I'd sensed he was looking my way before we were introduced. Now, everything felt incredibly awkward.

I privately told my pastor I couldn't go on this trip, as it was apparent Amy's friend was looking at me, and I felt paralyzed. My pastor knew my whole story and knew what an awkward situation this was for me. I told Amy I couldn't go after all because I had a work event. (I did have an event but had already told my team I wouldn't be there because of this trip; now, I'd change my plans and go to the work event after all.) I sensed she liked him, and I felt it wouldn't be right for me to go. I would never put a guy in the middle of a friendship, but with his immediate interest in me, it seemed like the right thing to do to politely excuse myself from the commitment and not go.

My pastor, however, encouraged me to go, saying how great it'd be to have our group back together again. He assured me privately this wouldn't be a problem, and Amy really hoped I'd go, so I bargained with God in that moment, telling Him, "I'll avoid this guy at all costs." I would not let this feeling that had overcome me get in the way of Amy's friendship with or interest in him. I entrusted some of my guy friends from the group to help me keep a distance from her friend on the slopes and during group gatherings on the trip.

Ski Trip, Day Two

The trip went as planned. On day two, Amy was faring well on the bunny slopes, so I decided I'd get in a blue run before lunch. I was in the chairlift line, tracking to get on a chairlift with a buddy from the group who was helping me with my situation, but it missed him somehow. The next in line to shuffle on and fill the available seat was from the snowboard line. And can you guess who was shuffled on? Amy's friend! *Oh, my goodness,* I thought, *this did not just happen!* I was now on a ski chairlift alone with him. *Oh, no! What just happened, Lord?* I had tried this entire trip to avoid him, and now I was face-to-face with him—well, side to side with him—slowly clicking up the hill in the chairlift. *Click, click, click!*

Our conversation was a lot about skiing and how his first attempt at snowboarding was going, as he was accustomed to skis. He was very shy, but he shifted the conversation with a sense of persistence to ask me questions about myself. Then, out of nowhere, he asked me, "Are you dating anyone?"

OK, that was just awkward! I had been around church guys for so many years now in our group; they just didn't talk like that, being so forward and all. Amy had said he was new in his faith and hungry to learn—based on a lot of his questions and the conversations they had at work—so it didn't surprise me he'd be so blunt and unchurched as to ask me this question. It also told me, in that moment, that Amy might be thinking their connection was a little different than he thought of their friendship. To that point, he explained he was certainly drawn to her knowledge of the Bible and that he admired her Christian faith, so he appreciated her friendship.

My response to his question was, "I'm dating God!"

His response: "Wow, that's a tall order!"

I proceeded to share that I was at a new place in my life, now at age thirty-two and a half, deepening my relationship exclusively with God, and I was complete. Since I stood my ground in expressing who I was, I decided to ski the run with him. Being new on a snowboard, he kept falling all the time, and I was charmed by his big smile, as I figured those falls hurt, but they didn't seem to faze him at all. He just kept smiling.

The rest of the weekend trip went as if there was a strong interest from him to me, and, with every ounce of preserving my friendship over a guy, I too felt a strong nudge toward him. By the end of the trip, we had exchanged business cards.

Once home, I was immediately on the phone with my dear friend Amy, sharing that I would never want anything to come between her and me because of a number exchange with her friend. I asked for her wisdom and heartfelt thoughts on the situation. She made amends with her friend—if there was ever a thought that she was leading him on with their visits over the Bible, she knew it hadn't been her intention. And likewise, he apologized that if his actions ever led her on in this manner, he was very sorry. She gave him her blessing to call me, and so he did.

Amy later met a wonderful man and married shortly thereafter. She has a beautiful life and family.

Long-Distance Relationship

Since we lived on opposite ends of town, an hour-and-a-half drive between us, we spent several months getting to know each other over emails and occasional phone calls when our schedules permitted. Rob was an electrical engineer for a large tech company with a busy work life, and I was busy with freelance work as well, so it made for a healthy balance, getting to know each other when work was still intact. We'd send messages to each other on our flip phones or his pager, such as "Hi" with the number combo of 44, or "thinking of you," which was number 869. As a new believer, his desire to know God better and to pursue Him fully was refreshing, bringing me back to when I first met Jesus. He respected my walk with the Lord and the boundaries God had placed before me. If this was moving into a dating relationship, it would surely look a lot different than any in my past. Since my 3:33 a.m. encounter two and a half years prior, I was thinking through relationships in a whole new light. God had sanctified me, and there was no turning back on my vow to God, nor did Rob want to break his vow with God in this area of his life, which was such a blessing.

We officially became a long-distance dating couple months later. Angela planned to move to a new town to start her dental practice, so I moved back to the East Valley, where Rob and I were now just thirty minutes apart. Rob's parents owned a condo that was sitting empty, as they were winter visitors from Michigan, so I moved in as their temporary tenant until they returned the following winter. Upon their return, I would move into an apartment with my friend Andrea from Single Vision, who was now attending a new church she loved that was pastored by Tom Shrader.

Since we wanted to find a church together to grow our faith as a dating couple, we visited Tom's church, as I had always loved his teaching at Priority Living in all my years attending. After just one visit, we knew we had found a wonderful church home and couldn't wait to dive into everything they had to offer. I joined the chorale worship team that Andrea was a part of and made lifelong faith friends there. It was such a joy to be a part of such talented and gifted voices and musicians, led by Music Director Gary Bloomquist, who faithfully prepared our hearts to worship the Lord every Sunday. It was a beautiful and blessed season indeed!

As a dating couple, we started attending the Singles Career Group they offered. There, we were immediately encircled by new friends who were on the same life journey we were on, either dating or recently married. God placed those newfound friends in our lives for accountability and for life-on-life living to help us grow deeper in our faith together. I loved and cherished all the memories we had in those early years together with couples Scott and Lisa, John and Beth, Jon and Bethany, Ignacio and Brooke, and Peter and Mary. God used those marriages as vibrant examples of what healthy and faithful marriages looked like. All these years later, it is so special to look at the beautiful lives they've built in the Lord. Even with the passing of one of those friends, it's that assurance that heaven is real, and we'll see our friend again.

God never failed to show up with people loving on me, standing with me, and pointing me to the cross. And here I was again, not alone, nor was Rob. Godly men stepped into his life to mature his newfound faith that was growing by leaps and bounds. Together, we were bathed in solid teaching and immersed in a strong community that didn't only embrace us individually but as a couple as well.

New Year's Eve 1999

It was the night of December 31, 1999. We were invited to the Dekkers' home, friends from church. Jan was an incredible host who planned a fancy dinner party with friends from our life group to ring in the New Year 2000, a new millennium, Y2K. It was a significant calendar change, with predictions of potential computer glitches and systems crashing that became the hype of news stories the world over. But for us, it was an unforgettable sunset with bright orange and red hues of colorful clouds dancing all around us.

Rob invited me over to his house before we'd head out for the party. I was greeted with puppy kisses from his sweet springer spaniel, Lolly. Although I was in a long, flowing black dress, and Rob was in a suit, he escorted me to his flat rooftop by climbing up a ladder to see the sunset before we left. I chose to take off my heels, which made it easier to climb. As we sat on a part of his roofline, admiring God's handiwork in the sky, he pulled out his Bible to read Proverbs 31:10–31, saying, "This is who you are to me, a Proverbs 31 woman."

I felt unworthy of the comparison, though his sentiment was so very kind. He then proceeded to get down on one knee and ask for my hand in marriage. Oh, my goodness! It was happening! A moment I knew was eventually coming but wasn't sure when, but in a flash, I thought, *This is that moment—the moment a girl dreams about!* I certainly wasn't a girl anymore, not even a young adult, but a thirty-four-year-old woman (Rob was thirty-five). Though no matter our ages, it was God's perfect timing for us. A man who loved me and wanted to commit his life to me was proposing to me. It was all so surreal!

Of course, I said yes! I cried tears of joy. Rob prayed for us, and then we hugged with delight, taking in the moment, just Rob, me, and God! It was perfect. We danced a little to the sound of our beating hearts of happiness, and I remember stubbing my toe on the rooftop—yes, the barefooted goof girl that I was in the moment. I put on my heels once we got off the roof as we headed to the party. Comically, but painfully, my toe swelled, so I'd spend the rest of the evening barefoot, wrapping my toe in ice.

We arrived at the party, and my girlfriends greeted us at the door in their fancy party dresses, excited for the fun evening awaiting all of us. When I showed them my left hand, they just lost it with excitement! They were over-the-moon excited for me, for us, for all of us as a group, and ready to celebrate. What ended up being a planned Y2K New Millennium Party was well on its way to being an impromptu engagement party all in one. How special it was! Our engagement was indeed an adventure, with a throbbing toe and all; it was truly an unforgettable night.

Wedding Day

We set the date for October 14, 2000, saying it would certainly make it easy to remember which year we'd be celebrating future anniversaries. I started collecting pictures from magazines and putting them in a scrapbook, filling the pages with things I thought were special. Plus, having been a bridesmaid over the years and having sung in several weddings, I had tucked away little ideas of things I thought would be special to include if I ever got married someday. To see all those ideas come to life was amazing! I'll never forget a sweet friend from Single Vision, Lanette, stopping by the night before the wedding to check in on me to see if I needed anything. She had been married a short while before and felt led to come over and help. How did she know? God bless her! She and so many others offered such loving hands that made it all so very special and unforgettable. I was so thankful!

After almost ten months of planning, our wedding day finally arrived, a perfect seventy-eight-degree sunny Arizona day. We were so thankful the sun had come out, as just two days prior, it had rained really hard, with lingering scattered showers the next day. We considered a plan B if we needed a last-minute location change for our reception—one of our groomsmen's dairy barns. God chose to clear the skies, but I was so thankful for our friends' willingness to support us if we would've had to make the last-minute change. God is in all the details. How good He *always* is.

We had a church wedding that included all the special details that made it personal and had lots of beautiful music sung by my amazing talented friends. My dad walked me down the aisle, lifting my veil, which was very special! My mom and stepdad, Allen, gave me away, praying around us with Rob's folks in a prayer circle. The prayer was led by Pastor Jeff from Single Vision, who had said back at the ski meeting that it would be OK, as if he'd known. Our pastor who oversaw the ministry we were a part of, Pastor Jim Harper, officiated our ceremony. We had gone through marriage counseling by a dear couple from church, John and Diana Mercier. Diana was also our wedding coordinator. She knew how much I wanted to communicate Jesus' love in our union, and she helped me follow through with every detail the Lord had laid on my heart. She was a dream-maker that day, as were so many others who helped make our day so special.

What I prayed for and hoped would shine through the most was Jesus' fingerprints all over our ceremony. The verse on our wedding program read, "I am the vine; you are the branches. If you remain in me and I in you, you will bear much fruit; apart from me, you can do nothing" (John 15:5 NIV). It was the verse that would set the tone for how we wanted our married life to look—to serve others in whatever opportunities God would give us.

During the ceremony, Rob served me Communion, which was very special. We also gave a little A.C. Green bear with a cross necklace to my then-eight-year-old niece Sarah and five-year-old nephew Greyson, as a promise and a pledge over them to honor the Lord with their lives. To this day, they are kind and caring adults whom we adore. Sarah's a film director, living in England with her husband, Malcolm "Bubba" McCarthy (google him—a real talent), and recently welcomed their first child, a little boy! We're SO happy for them; they are a beautiful couple in the Lord. Greyson's a film colorist and producer in Los Angeles. My younger niece Sarah was our flower girl (now married and a mom of three beautiful girls), and my Cousin Mark's son Noah was our ring bearer. They were adorable that day! Fun to see them all grown up. So proud of them all!

I gave away a dozen individual long-stemmed ribbon-laced white roses with a note attached to all the women who were significant in my life—my mom, my sisters, Grandma Mary, my aunts, my godmother Paula, Rob's mom and sister, Sister Judith Lynn who helped with the A.C. school program, as well as to sweet Marlene, who helped me in so many ways. After being announced husband and wife, we walked down the aisle as choir friends led our guests in worship songs. What a joy it was to end with worship!

The reception was in my Aunt Bonnie and Uncle Gary's beautiful backyard, decorated with twinkly lights everywhere. I changed out of my wedding dress and put on a long evening gown, perfect for the outdoor setting. Rob had built a small platform where we sat for dinner that had a beautiful arch draped in flowers and lights.

Our dear friend Jan, who hosted the New Year's Party, was a florist who made all the floral arrangements for the day and created a stunning floating arrangement that bobbled in the pool. Jan was eight and a half months pregnant. I will never forget her incredible act of kindness in doing all that work for us when she was beyond uncomfortable. I preserved the beautiful bouquet she made me and kept it in a hutch for almost twenty years.

Before dinner started, we were so touched by A.C.'s kindness in saying a prayer of blessing over us, and what a joy to have all the foundation friends there supporting us. The toast, the dinner, the first dance, a dance with my dad, cutting the cake (which turned out so beautiful, with a cascade of sugared fruits draped along its side), the celebration with family and friends—all of it was so *very* special and memorable.

Never Replacing My First Love

That day, when I was then age thirty-five, I became Mrs. Robert H. Brown III. I was no longer a *Miss*, but a *Mrs*. My dream of getting married and being committed to another person till death do us part—all of it happened! I was no longer single; I was no longer by myself. I was what I always envisioned for myself—married. But deep down inside, as wonderful as all of this was, I knew *nothing* could ever replace my first love. I had thought my first love was the boy I lost back when I was twenty-three years old when driving on that lonely road to Amarillo, questioning and crying out to God, "Why?" But no, my first love was *and will always be* Jesus!

God was using all these experiences in my life to point me to Him. I can't help but think that when things happen to us that we cannot control, God works it out for our good and for His glory. He orchestrates every outcome, even when we get in the way. He was, is, and will *always* be my first love! It was *all* about Jesus the entire time. I just didn't know it yet. He had so much to teach me. I was complete in Him exclusively before marriage, and now, afterward. Jesus was thirty-three and single for a purpose. He was there for me then, and even now, and will be, even on the day when He calls me home.

God used all these years—many that were wandering years in the wilderness—to bring me to Him. Aside from Him, I could (can) do nothing. Marriage was *not* the end-all; *Jesus* is! A person cannot complete you, only God can. Whatever you think might be your end-all, it is not—only Jesus is! He wants all of you.

CHAPTER 19

A Whole New Chapter

t all made sense now. Being married did not make me more or less complete in the work Christ did for me at Calvary. He loved me just the same, married *or* single. I previously had put all my worth in that "other" person, always making that person my idol. This time was different. God was my treasure! He loved me just the way I was. God is the author of my story, which is *His* story of His work and good plan in and through my life.

Now that I'm married, our stories have merged as one story, one flesh, made in the image of God's design of a man and woman leaving their father and mother to become one in Him. Our stories were different from our tainted pasts, but God did a beautiful work in refining us and sanctifying us individually so when He brought us together collectively, we were able to say it was Christ's love that brought us together, and it is Christ's love that will keep us together. We are His, bought with a price, committed to Christ, and each other. His love became the cornerstone of our marriage and is still to this day. All praise and glory to His holy name.

It bears repeating that marriage is not the end-all; Jesus is! The same is true for whatever you may be putting energy into—a career, finding that special someone, owning your own home, the list goes on. Whatever "it" is, none of it is the end-all; only Jesus is. That other "thing" that has your affection, directly or indirectly, even if it's a good thing, becomes an idol if not kept in check. From earlier, this statement—"All of life is all for Jesus"—now makes sense and is worth living out.

It's a hefty statement to ponder, questioning one's own affections for Jesus. You may feel it is unattainable, but He calls us to not hold back but to surrender all of our lives to Him. Like the jar analogy, put Him front and center.

Maybe you've heard the saying, "Let go, and let God!" It parallels with Proverbs 16:9, which says, "In their hearts humans plan their course, but the Lord establishes their steps." It is true. When you let go of your will and let His will take hold of your life, He is the only true path, the only one who can help you! A lyric from an old hymn we sang every Sunday at church when I was growing up encourages our souls to do that very thing—to let go of our pasts and our current idols and surrender all to the Lord. "I surrender all. I surrender all. All to Jesus, I surrender. I surrender all."[1] Make that your anthem cry, and then, proudly and boldly, without hesitation, say of your life, "All of Life *is all* for Jesus." Amen and amen.

God Forgives; Therefore, We Must Forgive

Any person's redemptive story has to begin with forgiveness. Jesus forgave us. Therefore, we *must* forgive others. Forgiving is a healing balm to the soul. Before I give some closing points on what the Lord has taught me throughout my journey, my story would not be complete without telling you how healing stepped in on all sides.

It was important for me to realize that when things hurt the most, God forgave me. In that forgiveness, I needed to forgive myself, as well as the boy who had hurt me, regardless of if I'd get to tell him this side of heaven. If you don't forgive completely, that memory of hurt will eat you alive. Through the act of forgiveness, you can live freely in Christ. It is worth *everything* to be freed from that pain.

God gave me the opportunity to see forgiveness played out full circle when I was working at the newspaper, as well as another time, years later. One of our clients at the paper was the sister of that boyfriend. After a meeting with her once, she shared with me how God saved her, her mother, and others in her family through her brother's changed life. Wow! That was huge! Praise the Lord! He had married that girl from the surf shop, a wonderful Christian woman, and was living a life for Christ, raising their kids in the faith. I couldn't have been more thrilled. She shared that even though she knew things didn't turn out the way I had hoped they would, God had worked it out in a beautiful way—and, indeed, He had.

Many years later, I ran into that man, who was now a brother in the Lord, for the first time in decades at a graduation we both attended. He saw me from across the auditorium after the graduation and made his way over to say hello to me and to share with me how thankful he was that God had gotten a hold of his heart. He then said if he would've had any of the faith training he and his wife were pouring into their kids, none of his past behaviors would have happened. He said how very sorry he was for hurting me in any way.

I was encouraged and thankful to hear those words. I had forgiven him in my heart a long time ago, but to receive his apology and to tell him I had forgiven him completely was a healing moment on all sides. God had done a good work in his life and in mine as well. Closure through forgiveness had come full circle.

Me and My Dad

After my encounter with God on the road to Amarillo, I desired a deeper relationship with my dad, which really blossomed in my young adult years shortly after that trip. His service in the army in Vietnam and his work and travels abroad kept him away while my sister and I were growing up, so we saw very little of him, but he helped provide for things along the way, which I learned years later, such as paying for my braces, and when things got tight in college, he'd send me money to help me out. I never held any grudges against him for not being around.

As the years passed, I was able to get to know him better and start a relationship with him. We've remained close all these years. I'm thankful he is someone I can always call on and get sound advice on things. One of the greatest joys in my life was to see him come to Christ after many years of praying for him. He and Rob get along well and have similar interests in engineer-minded things. I've heard it said a girl will marry someone like her dad. I guess that's kind of how things ended up. God always knows.

He Will Never Leave Us, nor Forsake Us!

What a journey! Just like the Israelites finding God at the end of their forty-year journey that He had them on, I too can look back and see how God used forty years in my own life that started at age thirteen and went to age fifty-three, with thirty-three wrapped right in the middle, to see all He had done. God's relentless love won't let us go. He taught me—a silly girl, searching for love—that what my heart *really* longed for all those years was to know and be affirmed that my first love was there all along, and His name is Jesus, who was thirty-three and single, waiting for me. His love would be there every step of the way and has continued to be there every day since and will be there in those days yet to come. He will *never* leave us nor forsake us. We can trust Him completely.

As it is, I've become quite fond of the number thirty-three. It makes me think of Jesus. When it appears on the clock, 3:33 (a.m. or p.m.), I pause a moment to thank Jesus and tell Him I love Him. Every time I learn someone is turning thirty or thirty-three, I'll tell them the story of Christ at their age and what He did for them—that their Lord and Savior identifies with them; He's been in their shoes, and I wish them the best birthday ever.

While I've been writing this book, I'll glance down at the clock on the computer, and I seem to always catch it at thirty-three minutes past a given hour, as if the Spirit is encouraging me, "Keep going! Don't stop now! Look at all the Lord has done!"

+ When I was *thirteen*, Mom married stepdad Allen— my first impression of a godly union, as they built their foundation on the Lord as the center of their relationship. I'm thankful for the godly parents they've been. Looking back, a lot of my escaping emotionally as a teen was my gravitating toward what I thought I lacked or needed.

+ When I was *twenty-three*, the dream of being with the love of my life ended. I surmised that my life would end. I was crushed beyond words and remained that way for a very long time, functioning out of grief and hurt, and I was silently angry. When forgiveness entered in, healing could begin.

+ At age *thirty-three*, I was thankful for all God had taught me that night when I turned thirty. Here I was, the same age Christ was when His stripes set me free. I'm forever grateful for His sacrifice for me. God had healed my heart from all my past brokenness. I'd been in a healthy dating relationship for six months now with my future husband and was committed to God to stay pure and keep my relationship with Him accountable to others. We were growing individually and as a couple, moving toward marriage two years later.

♦ At age *forty-three*, I was in a whole new season of life—married and a mommy of three. It was what I had hoped for twenty years earlier, but God's timing is always best, and His blessings are ever so sweet. I made the decision to stay home to raise our family. Plus, with the hour-and-a-half commute to the office every day, it made sense for our season of life. It was hard to say goodbye to the foundation staff I loved dearly, but they were very supportive of my decision. We lost our first baby to a miscarriage. That was a lot to grasp, but God, in His goodness, carried me (and us) through that difficult season of loss. Because of the miscarriage and my age, I was considered high risk, so when I became pregnant a second time, it was advised we go through genetic testing. We chose against that recommendation and left the results in God's hands. At age thirty-six and a half, I delivered a healthy baby girl, who came three weeks early. We named her Elizabeth, after Grandma Mary Elizabeth. (We'd call her Libby, after my sweet sorority sister Libby, whose jubilant joy for Jesus I loved. She was exactly like our Libby today!) Our second baby, Tatum, came two years later. She was named after a street near where I grew up, and I'd always loved the name. To this day, she'll tell people that her mom named her after a street, but she's grown to love it. Her middle name, Grace, was fitting for all the grace God showered upon my life. A second unofficial middle name, Ryan, came about because the day before Tatum was born, our sweet friend Jan, our wedding florist, lost her sixteen-year-old son Ryan to a motorcycle accident. It was heartbreaking and tragic news! Rob decided that when

Tatum was born, we'd include Ryan's name to honor his mom's important role in our early engagement and married lives. Jan's journey through his passing taught me a lot about a mother's love. Every year on Tatum's birthday, I think of my sweet friend and her loss that day. Her faith has sustained her as she carries on, knowing Ryan is with Jesus.

＊ When the girls were eleven and nine, Rob retired from his company after a twenty-four-plus–year career as an electrical engineer to buy some properties to manage and rent. One of the properties the Lord led us to buy was a nonprofit Christian retreat in the mountains. It's been such a delight to see God use it for His kingdom's good through church retreats, young-adult leadership camps, and family gatherings. Rob's leaving the demands of corporate life and travel to be closer to home allowed him to be more available for the girls' childhood years—helping with homework, coaching their soccer teams, assisting at FCA (Fellowship of Christian Athletes) camps, and taking them on mission trips to Mexico with 1Mission for house-building projects. He's a wonderful husband and dad, and our girls are amazing young ladies, who are now both in college, living their young-adult lives. They are a gift from God, as is my marriage to Rob. God knew what I needed all along.

＊ For eight years during this window of time when the girls were young, I volunteered at a local boys' ranch, singing with a worship band and counseling teen boys who needed help making better life choices. Within the ranch property, one of the homes was designated as a group home for younger boys, ages eight through eleven, who were there until they were reunified with their families or were adopted, or they aged out of the system at age eighteen, which was the case for many. My heart grew tender toward these boys and all they had been through. That journey of God tugging on my heartstrings would continue for many years.

+ You can imagine the look on my extended family's face when, on my fiftieth birthday, we announced we had met a seven-year-old boy we were planning to adopt. They were beyond shocked but elated just the same. During a three-month interim, we spent time getting to know him through the state system and were prayerfully moving toward the decision to adopt him. We adopted that sweet little boy shortly after his eighth birthday. Two days later was Mother's Day 2016. It was also Libby's fourteenth birthday and Dedication Sunday at church (a time of prayer over your child before friends and family), so we dedicated our new son, Dylan, that day.

+ My sweet friend Kim, from our teaching days together at A.C.'s foundation, served as our attorney for Dylan's adoption. She graciously walked us through that process. What a joy to have her be a part of that special time in our lives. Dylan was born when I was forty-three years old, right about the time God was pressing on my heart to start praying for a little boy—I never knew who he was, but God did. God would prove faithful to heal him from his painful past, stepping into his journey to give him hope and security. A sweet neighboring church we love, Calvary Chapel (watch the 2023 movie *Jesus Revolution* to learn more about them; a super-good movie!), invited Dylan to their Vacation Bible School when he was eleven. He came home excited to share that he prayed with Pastor Al and had invited Jesus into his heart. What a joy to know God met Dylan and showed him that Jesus can always be trusted and will *always* love him!

✦ Dylan's now a teenager, taller than me, and will move on with his life in all the seasons yet to come. One day, he hopes to reconnect with his biological siblings and mom. We are completely supportive of that for him, and pray, should it happen, that their time together will be a beautiful reunion his heart desires, as God is always in the business of restoration, healing, forgiveness, and second chances.

✦ Looking back, I always longed to have three children, and by God's kindness and provision, He graciously gave us three children. We are so thankful for each of their amazing lives! They bring us great joy, even when the road of parenting can be a crazy ride. We always say, as older parents, that they keep us on our toes and keep us young at heart. He is steadfast with new mercies every morning. Amen.

✦ Then, at age *fifty-three*, after serving our young-adult ministry for over five years at church and having shared my story with young adults over the decades, God impressed on my heart it was time to write my story, *Thirty-Three and Single*. After navigating young-adult journeys with parents over the years, it had come full circle to now raising my own young adults and seeing life from a mom's perspective— oh, the irony. I pray I can pass on to my daughters and son all these things that proved faithful and helpful to me in my journey and that hopefully will be helpful to them in their pursuit of following after Him. Most importantly, I will always lift them up to the Lord in prayer that they follow Jesus in all His ways and trust Him, as He knows what's best for their lives. I will pray the same for you, too!

(And a quick pause—I must share with you the coincidence of having celebrated my 40ᵗʰ high school class reunion in 2023, at age 58—again, oh the irony! It was great fun sharing memories with

cherished friends! Had I not allowed God to heal my heart all those years ago, it might've been taxing emotionally to attend. I'm so glad God is in the business of mending broken pieces and restoring lives.)

I started writing shortly after that last lunch mentioned at the beginning of my story and have been writing, researching, meeting with people, and editing ever since, with every spare moment I've had. Life, however, and life demands take precedence, so it has been shelved many times over the years, returning to it whenever time permits. Anyone who knows I've been writing has encouraged me to stay the course, to not give up, to not get discouraged, and to trust God's timing that it will finish when it's meant to finish. Because you're holding this book in your hands right now, and you're reading these words, know you're an answer to prayer and are a part of God's plan for its completion. Thank you for reading.

God in All the Details

God is indeed in all of life's details, loving us every step of the way, never leaving us or forsaking us (Hebrews 13:5). I sadly spent many years questioning God's purpose in my life, which in turn had me asking Him why He allowed me to hurt so much. He was there all along, allowing me the freedom to make the choices I did, which always brought me right back to Him. His ways are always better than our own (Isaiah 55:8–9), and like the prodigal son, our Father always welcomes us home (Luke 15:11–32). His father never left; his son left. And sadly, we do the same sometimes. We choose our own destructive paths by our wayward thinking. We follow the crowd. We follow our deceptive hearts (Jeremiah 17:9). We do as we choose because we think we know better than God. We go so far as to run into a brick wall. We get to the end of ourselves, crying, "Abba Father, where are you?" Oh, how He loves to hold us in our brokenness, as a father holds his child. "I'm right here child. I'm right here. I've never left. I've been here all along!"

> Come to me, all who are weary and burdened, and I will give you rest. (Matthew 11:28 NIV)

The Greatest Love Story Ever Written

God took my once-broken heart and repaired it through His Son, Jesus. God is writing His love story in your life, too, through His Word, with the centerpiece being Jesus. He allows you to be a part of the story He is writing because He is good. Your story will always showcase His good and glorious plan throughout your life. No matter the good or the bad, He is there and will carry you through.

His Word is "Good News" for all to hear! The good news is the Bible, God's love story of creation, the world, and all that's within it. The fall of sin entered in at the garden from God's very own creation of humanity, from which point all are born sinners; no one is righteous before God. God redeems His people to Himself through the ransom of His Son, Jesus, to pay the penalty for our sins so that we may know Him personally by His redeeming blood at Calvary, saving us from ourselves, and giving us new life in Him. Through His Resurrection from the grave three days later, we can go to Him, seeking forgiveness, surrendering our old selves to God, and asking Jesus into our lives to change us and make us new.

New life in Christ sets us free from our old nature and brings us into a saving-grace knowledge that He is ours, and we are His. We live in obedience, not out of obligation but because of His free gift. We desire to serve Him completely with our whole being. Jesus came to serve with the ultimate gift of serving us by giving His all, His very life at Calvary. He chose His public ministry from age thirty to thirty-three as a single man to change the world. He chose to identify with me. He chose me as His own, an adopted child. He loved me and pursued me, and He is pursuing you too. It is the greatest love story *ever* written!

Upcoming ABC Bible Verses

To capture the essence of God's faithfulness throughout my life's journey up until now, it seems fitting to display God in all His glory from beginning to end, A to Z. If He grabbed my heart when I doubted and lacked trust in Him through a digital clock flashing 3:33 a.m., He will do whatever He needs to do to get your attention as well. Here's how these verses came to light.

Tatum's prekindergarten teacher, Mrs. Chapman, an amazing woman of faith, taught her students their ABCs while memorizing verses. I was so intrigued that children so young could learn scripture by learning their ABCs and vice versa. I was fascinated by how their little brains were sponges to memorize twenty-six verses.

In the next section, you will find those verses that give an overview of how God was present in every fabric of my story. He truly is the beginning and the end, the Alpha and the Omega (Revelation 1:8), and will continue to write my story until He calls me home—and the same for you too. He is so faithful! It's important, when you come to the end of a chapter or season in your life, that you take note of all God has done. Never doubt, even when you ask, "What good will come of this situation?" Good *will* always come forth!

God used those years to draw me closer to Him, and for that, I am forever grateful. Jesus understands the heartbeat of a single. He understands better than anyone the mindset of a single because He Himself was single. He chose to mark His life through loving and serving others while He was single. Being married or never marrying isn't relevant, nor is it the point. He wants to meet you where you are now, in this season of life. Time and resources are uniquely afforded to singles during this life stage that shouldn't be wasted. Like Christ, love and serve. Once God got hold of my heart in that very profound way, it woke me up.

I was single—and this was not a curse. This was a gift! I could serve in my church without restrictions. I could serve in my community. I could serve my extended family. I could serve my friends. I was joyful, knowing He had me right where I needed to be. I was loved by God, the greatest love *ever*. He fulfilled that desire of wanting to be in a relationship by giving me a relationship with Him. The burden I carried of thinking I needed a significant other to complete me was now His to take. I was thankful His grace forgave me for trying to do things my way. When I surrendered completely to Him, I was set free.

Yes, it is true: "All of life *is* all for Jesus." I pray you desire this to be your heart's message as well—no holding back! The following ABC "Promise Verses" are to encourage you to see God's Word applied to your life. They hit all the hot topics so don't overlook this section. They cover everything from addictions to self-worth, pride to suicide. It's all there to unpack. After each verse and its teaching point, there are self-reflection questions, designed for you to dig deeper. Be sure to open your Bible to these verses and read the full passage where they're found. God has so much for you in His Word and invites you to join Him. He desires a relationship with you. How cool is that?

After these verses, you'll find a few lyrics to the song "Reckless Love" by Cory Asbury. This song captures the heart of this message of thirty-three and single, of Christ's love pursuing you, to give you hope and a purpose so even when single and experiencing the gray areas of life, your life is complete. Another person won't complete you; only Jesus will! He is who you long for. It is Jesus who is pursuing you.

The song "Fear Is a Liar" by Zach Williams is another powerful song to remind you of where your hope comes from. It is important to understand that fear will lie to you. Don't listen to those voices. Run to Jesus!

A Few Last Things

After the songs, you'll find a poem called "Becoming a Fully Devoted Follower of Jesus Christ." This was given to me when I was in Single Vision, so it's a very old poem I've held on to for all these years. I don't know who the author is, but I always thought it was a powerful poem to describe what it looks like to be a follower of Christ; it challenged me to live boldly for Jesus. I hope it encourages you as well.

After the poem, you'll find the testimony of my sweet friend Michelle, who I had the privilege of mentoring. We'd meet at Starbucks every Wednesday evening after work, which was always such a sweet time of fellowship, digging into God's Word together, and praying toward matters that were pressing on her heart. She relishes the goodness of Jesus, knowing, too, that instead of wishing when, she can rest in the completeness of His fullness in her life and not measure her life by the merit of her personal life status. I know you'll be encouraged by her story.

After that, you'll find shout-out thanks to all those folks who walked with me when we were overseeing the young-adult ministry. Their gracious love and kindness extended to me will stay with me always.

And last, there's a note of thanks for your taking the time to read *Thirty-Three and Single*. My prayer is that it blesses your life, challenges you, and carries you forward in your pursuit to know and love Jesus with all your heart.

ABC Verses—God's Promises to You

A—<u>A</u> friend loves at all times (Proverbs 17:17 NIV).

Yes, it's true. I have a friend in Jesus, and He loves me all the time. Even when things were confusing, God never gave up on me. God gave me wonderful friends along my life's journey and still does today, as new seasons are always on the horizon. God is love, and He loves you *all* the time. Amen.

How are you experiencing God's love? Who are friends you're thankful for who show you God's love?

_____

_____

_____

B—<u>Be</u> kind to one another (Ephesians 4:32 ESV).

The Golden Rule: Treat others as you would want to be treated. It is a simple, but profound verse. Had I allowed others to speak into my life back when I was in my twenties and had not been so quick to shut them down in my thinking, I believe God would have saved me from a lot of heartaches. But I couldn't hear from God specifically in this area because I was doing what I wanted to do. I wasn't allowing His kindness through others to step in. Instead, I listened to the lies and lived by my own standards. If someone of faith is pouring into you, be kind to receive it. It will make all the difference in your world, and then go be kind to the next person.

What is God teaching you about being kind to others? What are ways you can let others speak into your life? How does the mindset of "others first" help you in this area? Who benefits in your life when you put them first?

_____

_____

_____

C—<u>Call</u> to Me and I will answer you (Jeremiah 33:3 NIV).

Well, look at that! God being God—33:3. Oh, you of little faith, sweet girl! My cries were for my own desires. I wanted this, not that! I was strong-willed to the core, and God had a work to do in me. "Oh Lord, hear my cry!" And He did. All those years, He was there, faithful and just. I needed that *just* quality of God. I needed the discipline from my loving heavenly Father. He knew me better than I knew (or know) myself, and I would never need to question or doubt Him again. Thank you, Jesus, for Your faithfulness!

What do you need to call out to God for right now? What are you holding back from God?

_____

_____

_____

D—<u>Do</u> all things without complaining (Philippians 2:14 NKJV).

Oh my, conviction! I did a lot of complaining to God. "Why are you doing this, Lord? This isn't what I wanted!" Drip, drip, drip—on and on I'd go. God gives good gifts and teaches us contentment. He teaches us what is lovely and pure, kind, and gentle. A complaining spirit brings forth strife, not only upon ourselves but to all those around us. When we have hearts of gratitude and think of others first, our outlook on life changes. God knew the desires of my heart and wanted me to trust Him in the process without complaining. His timing is not our timing.

If, for example, you bring a complaining spirit and biting tongue into your marriage, it will be very damaging and destructive. Work that out with the Lord before you attempt a relationship with another person. Neither of you will benefit or flourish in your relationship with God or with each other if that negative attitude is not resolved. Confess your sin to God and operate in a new mindset that is laced with kindness through your words and actions. Start practicing that now. You will be glad you did.

What is an area of complaint you are holding on to that is causing you so much strife? What do you need to turn over to God for Him to start healing your complaining tongue?

_____

_____

_____

E—Every good and perfect gift is from above (James 1:17 NIV).

It is true! When you're walking with God, His gifts are for you and not against you. Even though you don't understand God's blueprint for your life, He is taking you from point A to point B and so on. Our fleshly nature is to take shortcuts and navigate our own paths, but He teaches us to rest in His better plan. He is the good shepherd going after his lost and lonely sheep (Matthew 18:12–14). The end of the song "Reckless Love" includes this theme from this passage. He leaves His flock of ninety-nine for one lost sheep. We are that lost sheep. He pursues us to give us His perfect gifts. For example, if you pray for patience, He'll give you something difficult in your life to teach you how to be patient. It's His nature to mold and shape you into Christ's likeness. It's not always easy to be molded and shaped like clay in the potter's hands, but it is *always* for our best.

What are good gifts God has given you to help mold and shape your heart to be more Christlike? How is God pursuing you like the lost sheep?

_____

_____

_____

F—<u>For</u> God so loved the world that He gave His only Son, that whoever believes in Him should not perish (die) but have eternal life (John 3:16 ESV).

When individuals grasp God's love for them, the good news of the gospel starts to make sense. God's love was such that He gave His very best gift, His only Son, to die on a cruel cross for me, for you. This verse gives such great hope! When you think there is no love out there for you, pause a moment and ask yourself, "What greater love is there than God giving His only Son to die for me and give me new life in Him when I believe?" The question asked throughout these pages—and I'll ask again—is, "Have you received God's free gift of love through His Son, Jesus?" If not, the gift is yours to receive. Take it! Jesus is enough (#jesusisenough). Here's a simple prayer suggestion:

"Lord, I want to change the way I'm living. I'm broken and have sinned against You. Save me from myself, and change me. Forgive me for the things I've done. I invite You, Jesus, into my heart to make me new. I believe in You and surrender my life to You and You alone! Thank you for Your sacrifice. Help me to follow You all the days of my life. Amen."

If your heart was sincere in what you just prayed, you just received Jesus! Welcome to the family of God. You were once dead in your sins, and now you're alive in Christ! No longer do you live for yourself. Those days are behind you. Now God has the reins of your life. Trust Him. He will mold you into the image of His Son. Get involved with a Bible-believing church where you can be fed God's Word and grow in your newfound faith.

When did God move in your heart to accept His free gift? Was it just now or another time? If this prayer doesn't resonate with you, what are some things you'd like to learn more about Jesus?

_____

_____

_____

G—God is with you wherever you go (Joshua 1:9 NLT).

Amen. It is true. God is with you always! There is nowhere you can go where God is not with you. When you feel you are at the bottom of your pit, God is there. If you are sensing God is absent from you, pause and look around. He is the creator of heaven and earth. He created you! You are loved! You have a purpose! Don't let Satan rob you of this great promise, leading you to think you are alone. It was something God had to continue to remind me in my journey—"Child, I am right here." How comforting that promise was and is. I was never alone. God is and will always be with me and with you. Just trust Him.

Do you believe God is always with you and for you? What are some ways God has walked with you in your journey so far?

_____

_____

_____

H—He will save His people from their sins (Matthew 1:21 NIV).

I think one of the hardest things I felt was the grief I carried from the mistakes I made. I was walking with Jesus but was walking in guilt and shame, wondering who would ever love me when I had a hard time loving myself, so I'd push people away in my actions. God's love at Calvary covered all my sins, those I had committed and those I will commit even today before the day is done. The beauty of the gospel is that God is in the business of forgiveness and reconciling Himself daily to us in the grace and love of His spilled blood on the cross. He sees Christ's righteousness wrapped around us in our new lives with Him. There is nothing I can do to save myself or to save me from my sin. Jesus paid it all, and I needed to turn daily to His forgiveness and His love poured out for me. Once I grasped that I was free from all the past hurt that had caused me to live in shame and doubt, the bondage of past sins was gone. I am a new creation in Christ. "Thank you, Lord, for saving me! I was a sinner saved by Your redeeming blood. I am free, free indeed in Christ Jesus. Amen."

What sin(s) are you chained to and need to release to God? How are you allowing Jesus to step into your mess and change you from the inside out?

_____

_____

_____

I—I can do all things through Christ who strengthens me (Philippians 4:13 NKJV).

What a wonderful verse to claim! Knowing Christ is for me, I can do those things that I thought were too hard to do when it came to trusting God. When I invited Jesus into my life, He gave me a helper, the Holy Spirit (John 14). God's Spirit resides in me. Thinking back on my story, there were many times I chose my ways over God's ways by not following His lead or trusting His path. When I finally surrendered my life to Christ completely, His strength lived out in me. My eyes shifted off drowning in self-pity and onto Him. Because He is my helper, I gain His strength when I feel I have no strength of my own to carry on.

In which areas of your life is God teaching you that through His strength, you can do that which you previously thought you could not do? How has His Spirit helped you in areas where you are weak?

_____

_____

_____

J—Jesus said ... all things are possible with God (Mark 10:27 NASB).

Once I grasped this truth, it was apparent God really did have my best interest at heart. At first, I didn't understand why He was making things so hard, or so I thought, though I was looking at life from a skewed perspective. I wasn't trusting God in all His might and power. I was placing myself above God with my limited thinking, allowing me to be the god of my own making. Once the Holy Spirit moved into my heart, God became dominant in my life. I was set aside, and His goodness moved swiftly through the brokenness of my own doing. He's the master builder that a broken soul craves. Only He can rebuild.

Others may fail you, but God *never* will. When you start to understand that *very* important faith principle, you won't get so out of whack when something doesn't go your way or doesn't go the way you think it should go. That's wrong thinking! From the old hymn mentioned earlier, embrace its meaning for your life.

He is the Potter, I am the clay,
Mold me and Make me,
This, Lord, I pray.

What is the Lord teaching you about His power and might? How is God shaping and molding you and giving you hope?

K—<u>Keep</u> watching and praying ... [that you may not fall into temptation ...] (Matthew 26:41 NASB).

Yes, prayer is essential! Prayer is my lifeline to God every day. I may not be able to make sense of everything that happens, but God always will be at work until the day He calls me home. It is true that Satan wants to trip you up in the lures of temptation. Instead, be in step with God's movement in your life. He is ever present and calling you into a right relationship with Him. That relationship grows by talking to Him and being with Him in His Word. Continue to always watch and pray. He hears you. He loves you!

How is God showing up for you in your prayer life? What temptation(s) trips you up that you need to give to the Lord in prayer? How does He assure you of His love?

L—<u>Love</u> is patient (1 Corinthians 13:4 NIV).

This passage was read in its entirety at our wedding—always a favorite. And with an adopted son, the picture of God's love is more real than ever. God adopted me, is patient with me, and loves me in my mess. I am that little child, crying out, "Abba, Father." He knows our hurts and loves us in our tantrums. I've had many tantrums before God. He's our loving Father who sees us through our stuff. Love is patient; love is kind and never boastful. Love never fails. Understanding this kind of love has helped me through many chapters in my life. I can't thank God enough for His patience that He's bestowed upon me.

God is the author of love. God calls us to love all people. Don't get caught up in injustices unless God positions you to voice concerns in their proper format—God will guide you in your words and actions so He is represented well through you. Most often, it's not your battle to fight. God will meet people in His timing and in His way, laced always in righteous love for His creation and humanity. He is a just God who will not be mocked. We are called to be Christlike and to love. Jesus taught compassion, peace, mercy, and unconditional love. Every person is created in God's image. Respect all people and treat them with kindness. The 2019 movie *A Beautiful Day in the Neighborhood*[1] told the story of the life of the beloved Mister Rogers. Fred Rogers, once a minister, was a very kind man, and his children's program *Mister Rogers' Neighborhood* taught children how to love their neighbors and how to be kind to themselves. He'd share his favorite number, 143, telling his viewers he loved them when explaining that "I" has one letter in it, the word "love" has four letters, and the word "you" has three letters, spelling "I love you." His tender ways reminded me of how Jesus treated others, always thoughtful and caring, engaging, and kind. God is patient with you! Be patient and loving toward others, as well as to yourself. "Put on a new self" (Ephesians 4:24 ESV). Be an image-bearer of Christ in all your ways.

Who are you being called to love? How are you showing patience toward loving them? Overall, how can you be more patient and loving toward others and toward yourself as an image-bearer of Christ?

_____

_____

_____

M—<u>My</u> help comes from the Lord (Psalm 121:2 NIV).

Amen and amen. It is true! Once I learned of His help for me through the Holy Spirit and embraced Him as my own, things really started to change for me. Things I used to get anxious about or lose sleep over were things I needed to completely surrender to God. "Lord, I can't do this. It's too big for me. Please take this from me. Help me, I pray." His help rushes in at every turn. His help may be displayed through the hands and feet of others or the prayers of a friend to lift you out of your pain. Even though we are weak emotionally, mentally, and physically, He is strong! God comes alongside and carries that burden for us.

Any night when I can't sleep, with something difficult pressing in, I tell God, "All of this [whatever the burden is], I'm laying at Your feet. Take it from me, Lord. It's Yours to have. I trust You with it completely." Without fail, God allows me to go back to sleep. In the morning, when I'm rested, He regroups with me on whatever that thing was when I'm in His Word or quietly praying. He then directs me to what the next right move is to do, or to do nothing at all.

Sometimes, we're too quick to try to fix something that God doesn't want us touching. "Your will, Lord, not my own." We get in there and make a mess of things. Wait! Be patient! He is working out that situation or that circumstance for your good and for His glory. Trust Him.

What areas do you need to surrender to God, relying on His ever-present help in your life? How can you start today by leaning into that help from the Lord?

_____

_____

_____

N—Nothing is too hard for You [God] (Jeremiah 32:17 NIV).

Even as a broken young adult, driving cross-country by myself, wondering how God could ever heal me, He calmly answered my cry through that mighty storm. "Nothing, child, nothing is too hard for Me! Completely let all that hurt go." So, I ask you the same. Are you willing to release everything to God? *Everything?* Complete abandonment of your old self and turn complete control over to Him? He's the God of the universe and can certainly handle your mess. Trust Him! Remember, *nothing is too hard for God!*

What do you need to turn over to God so He can start healing you? Have you made God too small and yourself too big? How can you start to hear better from God when you're feeling defeated?

_____

_____

_____

O—Oh, give thanks to the Lord, for He is good! (Psalm 107:1 NKJV).

Yes! Yes! And yes! He is *so, so* good! I recently heard a sermon that said, "It isn't easy to follow Jesus, but how can you not? He is so, so good!" Amen! That's worth celebrating. He is for you, not against you. Give thanks! Have a heart of gratitude. Once our eyes shift off ourselves, He allows us to see things from His perspective. The needs are *so* great out there. Join Him where He is at work. That is the entire premise of *Thirty-Three and Single.* In those three years of Jesus' public ministry, He was single and spent His time serving others by loving and healing them and by stepping into their lives, their mess, when no one else would. He embraced them with kindness and love. Be Christlike and show everyone you meet that

He *is* good! Be the loving, caring hands and feet of Jesus, and serve. Give Him praise always because He is good. Amen.

What are ways you give thanks to God for all the good He has done in your life? Who is God laying on your heart right now to serve, and in what ways? (Thanks for your servant's heart. God will surely lead you!)

_____

_____

_____

P—Praise the Lord your God (Nehemiah 9:5 NIV).

Even when things fall apart, such as the relationship you had hoped for that didn't work out, the job you wanted that didn't pan out, your housing situation that fell through, or whatever the case may be, still praise the Lord through the storm because His mercies are new every morning. What might look and feel despairing one day may completely turn around the next. No matter the outcome, when your hope is in Jesus, He is good and is working *all* things out in His perfect timing. A precious friend from church, Linda Noble, when battling breast cancer, encouraged all who knew her that though her struggle was real, she continued to have a steadfast joy and devotion of praise to the Lord, even in her difficult and painful circumstance. After her valiant effort to never give up but to have joy in her journey, no matter the outcome, God called her home, and she is now free of pain and with Jesus. The following poem was on her memorial program, and it spoke volumes of her faith in hard times. "God didn't promise you days without pain, laughter without sorrow, nor sun without rain. But He did promise strength for the day, comfort for the tears, and light for the way!"

What can you praise the Lord for that He has turned around or is turning around in your life, even when at first it didn't seem that way? How has God worked through your hardship, or storm, and how can you praise Him through it?

_____

_____

_____

Q—Be quick to listen (James 1:19 NIV).

Listening is an important life skill to master. It takes intentionality and practice to focus on the person speaking to you so you're not quick to respond but are, instead, truly listening. And like the end of this verse says, "be slow to speak and slow to become angry."

When someone entrusts you with their story, rid yourself of any distractions (your thoughts, your schedule, your phone), and be present with that person, looking at them and listening to them with great interest. If you find yourself dismissing a person because you've already summed them up of what you think about them, get rid of that thinking immediately. Confess your sin to God and refocus on that person. It is *critical* that you respect people by listening to them and not judge them. As the saying goes, "Don't judge a book by its cover." Instead of giving advice or trying to fix their problem, listen with compassion and tenderness, allowing God's love to speak to their hearts through the way you care about them by listening.

The same is true when praying. Quiet yourself so you can hear from God. When you're so busy all the time, you shut God out with your busyness and never give Him the time of day. If He's your all, then treat Him as such. Pause, listen, and know the heartbeat of your heavenly Father. Hearing from God sets the tone for your day and gives you the right attitude and outlook on life. Listen as He speaks through His Word, through worship music, and through prayer. God is there; meet and listen as He speaks.

Who is God prompting you to be there for? How can you be a better listener to them? How can you be a better listener to God?

_____

_____

_____

R—<u>Rejoice</u> always (1 Thessalonians 5:16 NIV).

In truth, this isn't always easy to do. Finding joy and rejoicing, especially when you're hurting, is a tall order, no matter how mature your faith is. Life is hard. The verse goes on to say, "Give thanks in all circumstances." When you're in physical or emotional pain, or both, a good cry can be good medicine for the soul because the only *real* way to get through hardship is through God's strength. He is there! He will comfort your deepest pain. When our daughter Libby was a senior in high school and captain of her cheer and dance line and her varsity soccer team, she broke her fibula in January from a soccer accident. She used a wheelchair when returning to school. The next month, her cheer and dance line competed in California after spending the semester preparing for that competition. She sat courtside to watch them perform and place in their division. Afterward, her teammates took turns wheeling her around Disneyland. She was sad to miss out on the rides and was in a lot of pain, but her team was so sweet to include her—though, hands down, the entire experience was exhausting, both mentally and physically. One month later, COVID-19 hit, and online school became a reality. For any graduate across the globe, the class of 2020 had a dismal outcome. For high school seniors, it meant no prom or graduation or a reduced version at best. Her last semester of high school wasn't what she expected.

After her surgery, she was in the worst pain of her life. My heart broke for her! I wrote her the following letter, never knowing how much more emotional pain was around the corner for her senior year. I hope this encourages you in whatever you're facing, especially when all feels hopeless, remember, God is there!

My precious daughter,

I am so sorry you're going through all of this! I wish I could take away all your pain! I know everything feels so unfair after all the hard work you've put into your high school sports career. I am so, so sorry this happened, but I am so very proud of you! I know it's hard to understand and grasp in this moment, but God wants you to see things from His perspective. Even in this moment of affliction when all seems hopeless, God is at work for your good, and you can trust His plan! He loves you so much and understands what you're going through, and He desires you to turn your heart to Him for His strength. Even when things are feeling close to impossible, breathe through all that difficult pain, and He will rescue you. Each passing day, you will get stronger! Wake up each new day to see what the Lord has done for you! Don't listen to the lies Satan is telling you that you can't make it past this moment. You can! You can! You can!! Remind yourself, "I can do all things through Christ who strengthens me." Rejoice and celebrate in all He has done for you and all He will continue to do in your life! You've got this, sweet girl! God won't let you go!

I love you so much, Mom

When life hurts really bad and it feels impossible to "Rejoice in the Lord always, and again I say, Rejoice" (Philippians 4:4 KJV), be sure to bathe yourself in worship music during times of hardship and adversity. Every song you hear will minister to you and pour over you like living water. The late songwriter and incredible vocalist Christian artist, Mandisa, a gift to countless, gone too soon at age 47 on April 18, 2024, gave us greats like "Overcomer,"[1] for example, that encourages you that God will see you through, no matter what you're going through, and you can rejoice against all odds! Remember, tune in to Christian stations[2] like Air1, KLove, Family Life Radio, *Intentional Living* with Randy Carlson, *Focus on the Family* with Jim Daly, *The Boundless Show*, specifically for single young adults, with Lisa Anderson, and all the awesome pastors, podcasts, and bands the world over on your streaming device. All will fuel your soul as you walk closer to God, planting yourself on a firm foundation. Plug into a Bible-teaching church to be fed and be in community. "All who listen to my instructions and follow them are wise, like a man who builds his house on solid rock" (Matthew 7:24 TLB).

What is one thing right now you can stop, pause, and rejoice in? How has God delivered you in the past, or how is He currently shepherding your heart through a painful situation as you trust Him in the process and rejoice?

_____

_____

_____

S—Serve [the Lord, your] God with all your heart (Deuteronomy 10:12 NIV).

Jesus is on display in your life when you set aside your own agenda and serve others with love. Even if you are wallowing in the waiting and asking, "What's next, Lord?" recognize that in this season, God will use you in beautiful ways. Don't be the young adult who is so self-consumed that you miss those around you. Be present with people, and engage with others. Start by turning off your phone!

When you serve others, God is glorified. Even if you're going through a difficult season, He shines brightest. When God is shaping, molding, and sanctifying you, choose to serve. When you always see yourself as a servant, it will *completely* change the way you live your life. Whether you're at school, home, with a roommate, in a relationship, in a community, or at work, ask God to show you who you can serve. Say a prayer such as this: "Lord, open my eyes to see the needs of others around me, and help me serve them with my whole heart. Use me, Lord. Amen." Without fail, your prayer will be answered because needs are endless and are everywhere. Serving another human being by simply being kind to them can turn a person's day around. We serve a big God. Go *big*! Don't be so busy that you miss what God is doing. God is at work *all* around you and is inviting you to join Him. Be available. The needs are many.

Remember the story of the Good Samaritan (Luke 10:25–37)? Two others passed by a man, but when the Samaritan came along, he saw a man who needed help. He lifted the burden of another human being by being helpful, loving, and kind. Can you be that person? Let Christ move through you in such a way that it is Christ they see living in you because of how you treat others. When relationships are built between people, trust is established, and the door may just open for the good news to be shared. God may be setting up a situation in your life right now to use you to draw someone to Christ. Isn't that awesome?

Some ideas to serve could be to buy lunch for a stranger (and if the Lord prompts you, pull up a chair and join that person), hold babies in the nursery, help a neighbor in need, give a listening ear to a friend, or go on a short-term mission. We joined 1Mission[1] in Mexico as a family for years when the girls were younger. They impact the community in *beautiful* ways! There are lots of short-term mission trips to explore. Look into one with your school, church, college, or young-adult group. You'll be a changed person for the better from your experience—guaranteed!

How is God calling you to serve? What giftedness has He given you that would be a blessing to others? Who does He want you to serve right now in this season of your life?

_____

_____

_____

T—Train up a child in the way they should go (Proverbs 22:6 KJV).

Just as children need a parent to lovingly guide them, point them in the right direction, help them when they hurt, and discipline them when necessary, so too do children of God need training, to yield to a firm yet loving hand.

What I admired most about our recent young-adult group was their dedication to making God a priority. Independent of their being raised in a Christian home or not, they made the decision to attend church and be a part of a faith community with other believers. Watching God prepare the next generation in all aspects of worship and involvement completely amazed me, motivated me, and inspired me. Once an individual embraces Jesus, no matter their age, God does a beautiful work in their life, producing a changed heart. It was such a privilege to meet so many.

Dr. Randy Carlson[1] from Intentional Living (theintentiallife.com) gives great points if you get stuck on the part of the verse that says, "In the way you should go." (His stuff is great! Check him out sometime and tune in.)

+ "If you lack clarity in your life, redirect your purpose. Life without purpose keeps a person busy, but not purposeful. Find what you're good at ... and move in that direction. Make your life count!"

+ "If you lack resolving problems in your life, focus on how to resolve the problem by getting the help you need and set goals."

(My story input about this point.) I believed the lie that I needed stuff to make it in corporate America—the clothes, the car, the travel. None of those things were bad in and of themselves, but when they became my idols to keep up my image, I had credit card debt. It was time for me to reevaluate my finances from God's perspective. Lesson learned; don't be enslaved to your own debt.

In premarital counseling, we addressed my debt and got my cards paid off. It's an important reminder to never keep secrets from your future spouse, be it about money or any other thing that can tarnish a relationship. The divorce rate of couples disparaging over finances, for example, stems from not being honest with each other in the first place. Decide together how to handle your joint money and finances by coming up with a plan that works best for your future marriage. As mentioned earlier, take a financial class.

God wants to help you move on from your addictions and sin patterns that you've kept in the dark, from drinking, drugs, and gambling to gossip, cheating, and stealing—the list goes on. God is the God of second chances who will heal you from your past and give you a fresh, new start; so lean in and learn from Him, who loves you so much!

+ "If you lack following through … get the help you need to do what needs to be done. Set goals, and know God will rescue you. Trust Him."

+ Life, in general, is hard and messy for any of us, but God is there to lean on. If you struggle in following through, get the help you need—professional or medical help, counseling, or a life coach to come alongside you to help you with your schedule to become successful with intentional life-skill habits. Put a good team around you. There is no shame in needing help. God calls us to help one another, and if you need help, it's a phone call away. "If you lack accountability, know you can't do it alone and need others to keep you accountable."

This is *so* true! As mentioned above, you can't go it alone! As much as you think you can, you can't! First and foremost, ask the Holy Spirit for help where you struggle. Get involved in a small group where you can share openly about your life. Also, seek help from an older believer who will mentor you when you're struggling with a situation. A mentor will point out roadblocks you don't see, especially in the area you struggle in, and will gently guide you in the right direction by pointing you to Jesus. God will use a mentor to correct you, to help shape your thinking, and to encourage you in your pursuit of godly living. Consider that counsel as God's gift to you!

How is God shaping your heart and training you in ways you should go, even when things are difficult? Who do you call on or reach out to when stakes are high, and you need help? Who do you turn to? (If you don't have a person like that, pray that God will bring someone along in your life to walk this journey with you.)

_____

_____

_____

U—Unto Thee O God ... we give thanks (Psalm 75:1 KJV).

The psalms provide great inspiration and reflection through songs of praise and lament, pointing us to the Lord to give thanks and praise, even in the hard times.

Friend Ellen Marrs (mentioned earlier),[1] shared with our young adults her personal story of abandonment and later being adopted by extended family. That experience opened her heart for the foster system. She and her husband adopted four siblings, adding to their three bio kids—such a beautiful story! She wrote the book *Lessons from the Finish Line* after completing a marathon every month for a year. Wow! Incredible! She then ran the Boston Marathon two years in a row to raise awareness and funds for underprivileged children. When sharing her story, she'd always include her heartfelt gratitude in all circumstances. She'd then challenge her audience to share their stories, as someone might need to hear it.

Ellen's words encouraged me to overcome my fear of writing my story and sharing it—thanks, Ellen! In doing so, I give thanks to God for the opportunity to tell you how great He is. Even when we don't understand where God is and wonder if He's even working at all, we can be assured that He is working all the time. Trust Him completely with your whole life, and be thankful always.

How is God working in your life? What calling has He placed on your heart? How can you have a heart of gratitude and thanks in your situation while trusting His plan?

V—Very truly I tell you, the one who believes has eternal life (John 6:47 NIV).

The older I get, the more people I know in heaven, making me long for my heavenly home even more. In the waiting, I must always remember that life is a gift. God used Billy Graham to reach Mom's heart about the love of Jesus. Dr. Graham passed away on February 21, 2018, at age ninety-nine. Coincidentally, that's my mom's birthday. We thought it was a special way to remember him. True of his life, when all is said and done, all that matters is our relationship with God and with others. Accolades, degrees, worldly possessions, and contributions to society, though noteworthy as they may be, are all secondary to a relationship with God and others. When speaking of Dr. Graham's legacy and a desire to live out that truth, Kathie Lee Gifford, a Christian TV personality, said, "As long as I have a pulse, I have a purpose." How true that is! Let your legacy point others to Christ by living every day with purpose and letting your faith be the cornerstone of your life.

When we lost Keli and Justin from our group a few years apart from car accidents, our group was heartbroken and devastated to the core. Keli was an amazing singer/songwriter who had just placed first in Alice Cooper's Arizona Vocal Competition. After several hours of visitors streaming through her hospital room, I was the last person the hospital staff allowed into her room to sit with her grandmother while her parents were on their way from their trip out of town. Her grandmother, a mighty woman of faith, was singing "Amazing Grace" over Keli and was praying for a miracle. The hospital chapel was packed with people praying that same miracle for Keli. Her folks later made their way to the chapel to share that Keli had gone home to be with Jesus and thanked everyone for coming and praying. Oh, the tears we all shared that night as the worship team she was a part of led worship.

Justin loved everyone so deeply and served others in incredible ways by positively impacting every person he met. His mom called me the morning after his accident; it was a Sunday. She was calm and tender as she spoke through her tears. She asked that I let our group know of his accident and his passing. Her strength emboldened me to be strong in that moment. We met that day as a group to be together to remember Justin through our tears and hugs. It was hard to make sense of it all.

Both lived out their purposes so intentionally. Their charisma and magnetic personalities lit up a room. They were filled with incredible faith and passion as life-changers for Jesus—*big time!* We found ourselves asking, "Why, God? Why were they taken so soon?"

To watch these two families cling to hope in their deepest sadness and grief was incredibly raw and inspiring. God made beauty from ashes in their most difficult and painful losses, which they'll feel for a lifetime. Even in their brokenness, they've kept their eyes on Jesus, pointing others to Him as they moved forward from their devastating losses. Keli's mom and dad, Cynthia and Warren, created the Keli May Foundation in her honor, which provides hygiene kits to underprivileged teens in the foster care system. They're keeping Keli's memory alive by giving out scholarships for other young aspiring artists, and they share her songwriting, music, and singing on Instagram @kelimayfoundation.[1] *(Enjoy clips there of her singing. You'll be an instant fan. She was amazing!)*

Justin's mom, Missy (@missy_linkletter_)[2], is an incredible writer and blogger who has shared her raw emotions of God's sustaining love to see her and her family through their tragic loss. Missy's the women's director at their church, sharing with women in grief-recovery classes. Justin's younger sister, Sarah, carries on in God's strength. Even though her pain in losing her best friend is devastating, her faith still stands, as God continues to use her story to encourage others.

Keli and Justin are both with Jesus now because they put their faith in Him. It is in that hope and assurance that we embrace God's promise of being with Him in heaven someday. Because of His resurrected life, we will meet Jesus face-to-face and will live with Him in eternity.

As Justin's Instagram bio read, "I'm an Ambassador for Christ." Be that ambassador for Jesus. *As long as you have a pulse, you have a purpose.* Justin and Keli lived that out every day. If you're not sure what happens when you die, turn your life over to Jesus. You will *never* regret following Him.

Do you see yourself as an ambassador for Christ? How so? What legacy are you building right now that will reach the next generation—your future children, grandchildren, and great-grandchildren?

_____

_____

_____

W—<u>We</u> love because He first loved us (1 John 4:19 ESV).

This is *very* important to understand. There is nothing good inside any of us to draw us to God. We are sinners who deserve death. We've done *nothing* to deserve His grace. We cannot work for our salvation. By God's grace—and grace alone—He chose us unto Himself. God plucked us out and drew us in, saving us from ourselves.

Because of His great love for you, He gives you the capacity to love others. Some lyrics from "You Love Me Anyway"[1] by Sidewalk Prophets say it well:

I am the thorn in Your crown, *but You love me anyway*
I am the sweat from Your brow, *but You love me anyway*
I am the nails in Your wrist, *but You love me anyway*

Why? Because *He first loved us!* When you ask Jesus for His free gift of forgiveness and salvation, He becomes yours, and He *never* lets you go.

He is the great shepherd going after His lost sheep. We are that lost sheep heading toward the cliff, which ends with us blindly jumping off. The saving grace of the shepherd's staff is that it grabs the lost, wandering sheep and pulls it gently to Him, saving the sheep from the brink of death. "I am the good shepherd. The good shepherd lays down His life for the sheep" (John 10:11 NIV). Sometimes the shepherd will carry that sheep around his neck, carrying him close so he knows the love of his shepherd to watch over him, remembering his complete reliance upon the shepherd so the sheep will never wander off again. That's what God does with us. He pulls us in, holds us tight, and saves us from ourselves, lovingly caring for us and taking us on the ride of our lives. We are no longer our own; we are completely His. Our lives now showcase His goodness, which points others to Him. (As in the song "Reckless Love,"[2] God's love "fights till I'm found, leaves the ninety-nine." Amen!)

I love the analogy of a tandem bike. God is in the front seat, using His leg power to propel me forward. From my view, all I see is Jesus in front of me. He blocks the wind blowing on my face, the sun glaring in my eyes, and even the bugs smashing into me. He is my protector. I can't control the direction of where we're going; only Jesus can maneuver the direction we travel. He is in control, I'm just along for the ride. As you explore all the wonderful things He will show you, just trust Him. You might encounter some rough patches that require hard pedaling, as well as smooth roads to coast downhill where you take your feet off the pedals and just glide. Because He loved me first, He gives me the ability to love Him and love others completely. Don't be ashamed to follow Jesus. Embrace Him, and He will guide you *all* the days of your life. That's truth you can believe in.

How do you know God's love is sufficient for you? How do you experience God's grace in your life? How does God's love in your life encourage you to love others?

_____

_____

_____

X—Exalt the Lord our God (Psalm 99:9 NIV).

When life is going well and all is moving forward in a positive direction, it is easy to forget about God. We set Him on the shelf as we function just fine on our own, making ourselves invincible. In that, we exalt our own worth and accomplishments, not even pausing a moment to give God praise. If a person has a thought toward God, it's when something goes wrong, or the person needs something from Him. Like a genie in a bottle, God becomes small, and we become big as we sit on the throne of our own making. We put others' opinions above God's and live for their approval, minimizing God's opinion about us.

I was a people-pleaser. I remember how important people's opinions were to me. I'd be the chameleon, appeasing whatever group I was a part of. During those years of self-discovery, what my peers thought of me was more important than what God thought of me.

Why do we do that? Why can't we simply rest in Christ and not worry about what others think? When we truly grasp that Jesus is all we need, our assurance is then secure, and His approval is all that matters. It is then that God's light shines through us and is seen by others when we're, for example, in a friend group, a work group, a friendship, or in a relationship. Don't succumb to the opinions of others that overshadow what God thinks of you; instead, be true to the person He created you to be. Live out His good and glorious plan in your life, and *exalt* the Lord, your God, and worship Him, for He is holy!

Do you allow social media to dictate the opinion you have of yourself? If so, what do you need to turn over to God so you're not conformed to the opinions of others? How can you step into the person God created you to be? How do you exalt God in your life and show adoration for Him?

_____

_____

_____

Y—<u>You</u> are from God, little children ... (1 John 4:4 NASB).

The rest of this verse says, *"and have overcome them; because greater is He who is in you than he who is in the world."* Satan loves to prey on hearts with doubt, loneliness, affliction, and confusion. When you feel you have nowhere to turn, know, first and foremost, *you are not alone!* Taking care of your mental health is important. Never feel ashamed or embarrassed to care for yourself. If needed, take time away to mentally rest and regroup. Life is hard, and sometimes we just need time alone; that is healthy *and* OK.

If you feel like running to your vices to numb your pain to escape painful emotions or experiences; succumb to an eating disorder thinking your body image isn't what you think it should be; self-medicate by turning to drugs, alcohol, or pornography; self-inflict pain by cutting yourself or others, or consider suicide, be mindful that addictions of any kind, self-hurt, or thoughts of suicide are all meant to harm you and not help you. If you're in a place of desperation, *please* reach out for help! Call a trusted friend, a professional, a church or school counselor, or dial **9-8-8** from any phone. Caring people are there for you and want to help! (988-Suicide and Crisis Lifeline).[1]

The music video of Zach Williams's song "Fear Is a Liar"[2] has scenes of people going through difficult situations. As the song turns to hope, it puts those lies dead in their tracks with the line, "Cast your fear in the fire." It is true! Satan is the author of lies and will haunt you with fear. Tell him he's not welcome anymore and to get out of your life, and in the name of Jesus, flee!

> Submit yourselves, then to God. Resist the devil, and he will flee from you. Come near to God, and He will come near to you. (James 4:7–8a NIV)

Pray for a hedge of protection around yourself. Your life has *immense* value. You're loved and cherished by God! You're a treasure. God will love you through your pain. You're God's child and *no* one, not even you (yes, you) or Satan, messes with that. Your family loves you and needs to know that you're OK. Call them. Let them in. People are ready to stand in the gap with you.

As with childlike faith, believe! God created you. You are His handiwork. He created you before the beginning of time.

When I had a miscarriage, I was deeply depressed and longed to understand why we'd lost our first child. This verse comforted my weary soul: "Before I formed you in the womb, I knew you, before you were born, I set you apart" (Jeremiah 1:5a NIV). Though I was sad for a very long time, grieving the loss of our first child, God assured me of His faithfulness that He loved that child deeply, knitting that little life together with His unfailing love. That loss drew me ever so close to Jesus. To experience that brevity of life gave me a deeper appreciation to never take life for granted and to truly grasp that every breath is indeed in His hands.

> There is a time for everything, and a season for every activity under the heavens: a time to be born and a time to die. (Ecclesiastes 3:1–2a NIV)

When I think back on my past and how God chose to spare me from ever experiencing an unplanned pregnancy, I empathize with women in these situations, as the emotions and pain they go through are so high. A few dear women in my life have been there—alone and feeling unequipped to care for a child—and they chose what they felt was their only option—abortion. God walked with them through their pain and loss, graciously healing them from their guilt and remorse, which they carried with them for a very long time. They would undoubtedly be the first to tell you that you have options.

If you're ever in a situation where you feel you have no one to turn to with a decision too weighty for you to carry, be assured there are people who are there to help you. That baby of yours is loved and was created by God. The organization Voice for the Voiceless[3] was started by young-adult friends of ours (and has grown into a sizeable staff, all available to you) to reach young adults with their message: "Twenty-two percent of our generation was aborted. We are the 78 percent." You can find them at <u>www.voicesforthevoiceless.org</u> or on Instagram @_vftv. Or visit a crisis pregnancy center in your area to walk you through options. God created life. Life is a gift. Our son Dylan is a gift. If it weren't for Dylan's birth mom choosing life, we wouldn't have him today.

How do you tune out the lies of the enemy and run to God when you're hurting? How does recognizing you're a child of God change your perspective on life? Who are trusted people you can call on if you need help?

_____

_____

_____

Z—There was a man named <u>Zacchaeus</u> (Luke 19:2 KJV).

We're at the end of the alphabet and are landing on the story of Zacchaeus. Maybe you can hear the little nursery song in your head right now.

Zacchaeus was a wee little man, a wee little man was he.
He climbed up in a sycamore tree to see what he could see.
Then Jesus said, "Zacchaeus, come down from that tree,
for I'm going to your house today."

Isn't that just like Jesus? He calls us to Him. He wants a relationship with us, to dine with us, sit with us, and commune with us. He's there; are you? When God is shut out by the constant drone of noise on every side, it's a constant drip of distraction. Best-selling author John Eldredge, in his book *Get Your Life Back: Everyday Practices for a World Gone Mad*,[1] focuses on the twenty-four/seven onslaught of today's never-ending screen life that demands our attention with its continual feed of social media, global tragedies, and pressure on all sides, leaving one to feel ragged, wrung out, and emptied, with no margin to breathe. Learn to unplug and disconnect during the day to be still and quiet with God; go outside and take a walk. When God is shut out, we can't hear Him, but He *is* there! He will refresh you every time.

Aren't we all a little like Zacchaeus—curious about this Jesus? We might not be able to see Him, so we search high and low. He's right where He's always been. We just need eyes to see Him!

Distractions that replace our affection toward God become our idols if not kept in check. When we give more attention to something other than our relationship to God, even if they're good things, those things push God away. Reevaluate your priorities and put God first so everything in your life falls into place. He never changes from wanting our attention and focus to be on things that matter to Him and His purpose.

Let God's Word challenge and change you as you grow in your faith and walk with Jesus. Be involved in a church community, such as a young-adult ministry, a Bible study, or wherever the Lord leads you to grow, and be equipped to be a disciple of Jesus Christ, sharing His love with whomever He puts in your path. Be like Zacchaeus. Seek Christ. Jesus is better than anything this world will *ever* offer you—ever! Amen.

In what ways are you pursuing Jesus as Zacchaeus did? How are you putting margins in your life to rest and be still before God? What do you need to reprioritize in your life to put Jesus first, to make Him your treasure and Lord of your life?

_____

_____

_____

These A–Z verses are all simple truths and promises that you can hold on to. They are helpful references you can tuck away, always being reminded of how loved and cherished you are by the Lord Almighty, the Alpha and the Omega.

For fun, try memorizing all twenty-six verses, like Mrs. Chapman's pre-K kids did. Young minds are like sponges, and so is a soul hungry for more of Jesus. Be that sponge. Soak up God's Word, and treasure it in your heart today. Draw near to Him, and He will draw near to you.

Here are the alphabet verses in summary.

A-Z Verses

+ A "A friend loves at all times" (Proverbs 17:17 NIV).
+ B "Be kind to one another" (Ephesians 4:32 ESV).
+ C "Call to Me and I will answer you" (Jeremiah 33:3 NIV).
+ D "Do all things without complaining" (Philippians 2:14 NKJV).
+ E "Every good and perfect gift is from above" (James 1:17 NIV).
+ F "For God so loved the world" (John 3:16 ESV).
+ G "God is with you wherever you go" (Joshua 1:9 NLT).
+ H "He will save His people from their sins" (Matthew 1:21 NIV).
+ I "I can do all things through Christ who strengthens me" (Phil 4:13)
+ J "Jesus said, all things are possible with God" (Mark 10:27 NASB).
+ K "Keep watching and praying" (Matthew 26:41 NASB).
+ L "Love is patient" (1 Corinthians 13:4 NIV).
+ M "My help comes for the Lord" (Psalm 121:2 NIV).
+ N "Nothing is too hard for You [God]" (Jeremiah 32:17 NIV).
+ O "Oh, give thanks to the Lord, for He is good" (Psalm 107:1 NKJV).
+ P "Praise the Lord your God" (Nehemiah 9:5 NIV).
+ Q "Be quick to listen" (James 1:19 NIV).
+ R "Rejoice always" (1 Thessalonians 5:16 NIV).
+ S "Serve God with all your heart" (Deuteronomy 10:12 NIV).
+ T "Train up a child in the way they should go" (Proverbs 22:6 KJV).
+ U "Unto thee O God" (Psalm 75:1 KJV).
+ V "Very truly I tell you...who believes has eternal life" (John 6:47 NIV).
+ W "We love because He first loved us" (1 John 4:19 ESV).
+ X "Exalt the Lord our God" (Psalm 99:9 NIV).
+ Y "You are from God, little children" (1 John 4:4 NASB).
+ Z "There was a man named Zacchaeus" (Luke 19:2 KJV).

He Had Purpose, Thirty-Three and Single, Because of You

In closing, here are partial lyrics of the two songs mentioned earlier, "Reckless Love" by Cory Asbury, speaking of God's amazing love for you, and "Fear Is a Liar" by Zach Williams, that God is bigger than your enemy. Following after is the poem that I had from when I was a young adult, of what it looks like to be a follower of Christ. It's a good one! Are you in? Then you'll find friend Michelle's story. She weathered deep pain and through it all found true solace and peace in Jesus. May God encourage you through these final pieces.

Reckless Love

When I was Your foe, still Your love fought for me
You have been so, so good to me
When I felt no worth, You paid it all for me
Oh, the overwhelming, never-ending, reckless love
of God ...
It chases me down, fights 'til I'm found, leaves the
ninety-nine

Fear Is a Liar

When he told you you're not good enough ...
Not right ... not worthy ... not loved
When he told you you're not beautiful,
That you'll never be enough
Fear, he is a liar
He will rob your rest and steal your happiness

Becoming a Fully Devoted Follower of Christ Jesus

Describing the Commitment of a Disciple

I am a part of the "Fellowship of the Unashamed." I have the Holy Spirit's power. The die has been cast. I've stepped over the line. The decision has been made. I am a disciple of His.

I won't look back, let up, slow down, back away, or be still. My past is redeemed, my present makes sense, and my future is secure. I am finished and done with low living, sight walking, small planning, smooth knees, colorless dreams, tame visions, mundane talking, chintzy giving, and dwarfed goals!

I no longer need preeminence, prosperity, position, promotions, plaudits, or popularity. I don't have to be right, first, on top, recognized, praised, regarded, or rewarded. I now live in His presence, learn by faith, love by patience, live by prayer, and labor in His power.

My face is set, my gait is fast, my goal is heaven, my road is narrow, my way is rough, my companions are few, my Guide is reliable, and my mission is clear. I cannot be bought, compromised, detoured, lured away, turned back, diluted, or delayed. I will not flinch in the face of sacrifice, hesitate in the presence of adversity, negotiate at the table of the enemy, ponder at the pool of popularity, or meander in the maze of mediocrity.

I won't give up, shut up, let go, or slow up until I'm prayed up, preached up, paid up, stored up, and stayed up for the cause of Jesus Christ.

I am a disciple of Jesus. I must go till He comes, give till I drop, preach till all know, and work till He stops.

And when He comes down to get His own, my colors are clear. He's washed me clean, for I am a part of the Fellowship of the Unashamed!

—anonymous

Michelle's God Story

Growing up, there was never an example of a healthy, respectable relationship. Dysfunctional and toxic relationships were the norm, and I set my relationship standard to that "love bar."

After high school, I fell fast and hard for a nonbeliever. I threw my morals and Christian beliefs out the window and began a downward spiral. I put my trust, faith, and dreams into a person instead of Christ. We are all sinners, and putting your time and undivided attention into a person will always disappoint you and let you down.

At age twenty-three, the relationship ended, and I did everything to numb the pain and forget the mess I had made of my life. I wanted to forget all the worries, all the hurt, and all the pain. I was ashamed of my decisions and embarrassed by the things I had done.

After two years of this cycle, I joined a young-adults group led by Tina and found comfort in the love of God that they showed me—true convictions that Jesus is my treasure because He loves me even when I don't love myself. He promises me I am not alone, and He has a plan for me. No matter what hurt this world brings, Jesus knows your pain and never forsakes you.

Looking forward and hopeful for the future, this is a verse I focus on—Romans 8:18, which says, "For I consider that the sufferings of this present time are not worth comparing with the glory that is to be revealed to us" (ESV). Whatever life phase you are in, be encouraged that God is bigger than you can ever imagine.

Do not be ashamed of your past! God has a story He is writing, and it is beautiful.

Now, at age thirty-three and looking back, I am stronger in Christ than ever before. Hold true that God causes or allows things in our lives because it is a blessing when God takes something out of our lives, even if it hurts in the midst of it. I still fall and pick myself back up, but I stand firm, knowing God is by my side for each step.

To conclude, here's a powerful chorus from the song "Brokenness Aside" by All Sons & Daughters.[1]

"'Cause I am a sinner. If it's not one thing it's another. Caught up in words. Tangled in lies. But you are a Savior. And you take brokenness aside ... And make it beautiful!"

Special thanks to these guys and gals for support of the young-adult ministry and this book:

Teaching pastors Luke Simmons and Seth Troutt at Ironwood Church and Josh Watt at Redemption North Mountain, who oversaw the ministry. Thanks, guys, for great teaching you feed my soul weekly. (*When approaching Luke about starting a young-adult ministry, he was very supportive of the idea. Seeing it grow since then has been incredible. Our daughter attends now as a young adult! So awesome when churches pour into young adults!*)

Trey Van Camp is an author and pastor of Passion Creek. Trey was a great support to our ministry, visiting and speaking to our group. He is a vlogger making faith videos for this generation, inspired by his life: DocumenTrey.com, @treyvancamp. His tagline says it all: "I wake up every day to inspire and inform others that Jesus is better!"

A group of go-to brothers in the Lord helped shoulder the ministry by teaching, counseling, hosting events, and being there for young adults. Thank you, Eloy Garza, Anthony Indie, Anthony Colello, Tom Rowley, Brandon Campton, Cody Lingelbach, Rick Fisher, Joe Leavell, Bob Barrett, Arnold and Josh Ruiz, Brett Berger, and Jon Benzinger. (Jon pastored our ministry for a while and is now lead pastor at Redeemer Bible in Gilbert, Arizona.) I'm thankful to these men for their help and support along the way.

Kelsey and Kahdeem, then young adults and leaders in the ministry, shepherded the group in the transition, helping young adults in their "gray zones." Both are now married and enjoy doing ministry life with their spouses.

Gals at a women's Bible study (table 7)—Cali, Carolyn, Moe, Ginny, Rebekah, Charity, Theta, and Brittany. We read through the book *Adorned* by Nancy DeMoss Wolgemuth from Titus. Her book affirmed that older women need to come alongside younger women (and the same is true for men to mentor younger men). These women prayed for me while I went through this ministry transition and encouraged me all along the way in writing my first draft of this book. They were my rock!

The women at church who supported me in ministry, and in the writing of this book—thank you, Channon Balkan, Nikki Reeves, Missy Linkletter, Dawn Kelch, Deb Bongiorno, Tammy Lewis, Rebekah Leavell, Lisa Lew, Bonnie Jolly, Etelka Hendrickson, Tabatha Petella, Carolyn Simmons, and Rochelle Billeter.

A special thanks to Dani Indie, Sara Colello, and Keri Garza, who helped shoulder the ministry, and from staff, Cristina Adams and Robbin Howey. Valerie Shinpaugh and Laurie Lus always said yes to help me with our son during young-adult events. Also, a special thanks to Holly Cline, a lifelong sister in Christ and dearest friend and neighbor who was always there to help with our kids and ministry life, and to Kim Turner, dear friend and attorney for our adoption and support to read through this manuscript. Lastly, my mom and sisters, Stephanie and Michelle, who always have my back. These women are all amazing!

Michelle Carella, whose story you just read—I'm so thankful for her willingness to share and for being candid. I'm so excited to see the ministry God has put in her life to serve young adults in counseling and walking life with them.

Chelsea Leonard, who lived with us when she was in college, now married, with two sons—Chelsea was a great encouragement to me when I was transitioning out of ministry, saying, "God must want you to start writing that book now. Your story touched me deeply. Let others be encouraged by it too." Thanks, Chelsea!

Thanks to my daughters Libby and Tatum who helped with the footnotes. And to Tatum who encouraged me in the final push of edits and finding the right color for the cross. Thanks sis!

To Editor Emily Heaton, so thankful for all her help! What a blessing she's been. And to WestBow Press and the great team who helped get this project over the finish line, especially Deena and Kelly, thank you SO much ladies! You have been my lifeline!

And lastly, to the brother in Christ in my story, who allowed this book to be shared—thank you for your trust in God's finished work!

Dear reader,

From the bottom of my heart, thank you so much for reading my story! My hope is that something you read between these pages has spurred you on in your faith and has pointed you to the only true source of freedom and joy, and that source is Jesus—and Him alone!

It is my constant prayer that whoever reads this book will find it to be a source of encouragement. If you found it encouraging, please consider passing it on to someone else. God prompted my heart to write this book decades ago. And though I am not a writer, He has led me through each and every page to be a source of hope to you, the reader.

Keep these final thoughts in mind as you move toward being servant-minded. Being a servant isn't easy. At its core, it means putting others first, which means personal sacrifice. That's why Christ came, sacrificing His very life as a single man at age thirty-three for you! Serving looks a lot different from what the world would teach.

> Everyone loves the idea of being a servant until you're treated like one. (Tom Shrader)

That is so true. Rise above the tide, and remember Christ served you perfectly and set an example for you to follow. Love, be kind, and serve with purpose by looking beyond yourself, and care for those around you by pointing them to the hope you've found in Christ Jesus.

May Jesus, who was thirty-three and single, be your source of strength and courage as you carry on in His good name.

In closing, I'll ask one final time, "Do you know Jesus personally?" If you don't, ask Him now. He's there, waiting for you. Invite Him into your heart. "Everyone who calls on the name of the Lord will be saved" (Romans 10:13 NIV).

Thank you again for reading! God bless you and keep you always.
In Christ's precious and loving name,
Tina Brown

@tinabrown_az, tinabrown.az33@gmail.com (Please feel free to reach out if I can ever pray for you or if you'd like to share how Jesus invaded your heart, I'd love to hear it!)

Bible Translations Used in This Book

AKJV—American King James Version
AMP—Amplified Bible
CSB—Christian Standard Bible
ESV—English Standard Version
GNT—Good News Translation
GW—God's Word Translation
ICB—International Children's Bible
ISV—International Standard Version
KJV—King James Version
NKJV—New King James Version
MEV—Modern English Version
MSG—The Message
NASB—New American Standard Bible
NIV—New International Version
NLT—New Living Translation
NLV—New Life Version
TLB—The Living Bible
TPT—The Passion Translation

Notes

Introduction:

1. Miller, Paul E. *Love walked among us: Learning to love like Jesus.* (Colorado Springs, CO: NavPress, 2014).
2. Miller, Paul E. *J-curve: Dying and Rising with Jesus in Everyday Life.* (Wheaton, IL: Crossway, 2019).

Bible and References:

1. "Access Your Bible from Anywhere" BibleGateway.com: A searchable online Bible in over 150 versions and 50 languages. https://www.biblegateway.com/.
2. "Read the Bible Online. A Free Bible on Your Phone, Tablet, or Computer." YouVersion | The Bible App | Bible.com. https://www.bible.com/.

Chapter 4:

1. Lauren Daigle's online interview about her song, *You Say*, release date 7/13/18. billboard.com/music/pop/lauren-daigle.
2. Tenth Avenue North, active from 2000-2021, *By Your Side*, song from debut album Over and Underneath, (Contemporary Christian, Brentwood, TN, Reunion, Provident Label Group, August 2008), www.tenthavenuenorth.com.

Chapter 9:

1. Paris Archbishop, Aupetit, Michel, 2018-2021, quote in The Holy See after Notre - Dame Cathedral fire, 2019. www.vatican.va/documents/letter.
2. Graham, Billy, televised evangelist from late 40s till his passing in 2018. TV sermon. Quotes by Billy Graham. www.brainyquote.com.
3. Hesler, Jonathon David and Melissa, featuring with Bethel Music, *No Longer Slaves*, song reference, (Redding, CA Bethel Music, recorded and released 2015), www.jonathnanhelser.com, www.bethelmusic.com.
4. Simmons, Luke, Lead Pastor, Ironwood Church, Mesa, AZ Sermon notes. www.ironwoodchurch.org.

Chapter 10:

1. *Rules without Relationships Lead to Rebellion | Building Relationships. YouTube.* YouTube, 2010. https://www.youtube.com/watch?v=Tx1SOiawASw&t=134s.

2. Strobel, Lee, April 7, 2017, movie *The Case for Christ*, inspired by his 1998 book with the same title, directed by Jon Gunn, (USA, produced by Triple Horse Studios, released by Pure Flix Entertainment on April 7, 2017).

3. Fritz, Chery, Christian Blogger for Bible Reasons, "Religion vs Relationship with God: 4 Biblical Truths to Know." Bible Reasons & Bible Verses for Relative Topics, (Miami-Fort Lauderdale, FL) https://biblereasons.com/religion-vs-relationship-with-god/.

4. "Gospel-A users Guide" reference from Bible Boot Camp material by Chris Mueller adapted by Redemption Gateway Staff for in-house classes, Ironwood Church, (ironwoodchurch.org).

5. Miller, Paul E. *Love Walked Among Us: Learning to Love Like Jesus,* (Colorado Springs, CO NavPress, 2001) Sermon notes from series: He is the Good Shepherd, Jesus washed disciples' feet from John 13:1-17, by Arnold & Josh Ruiz, Brandon Campton, Redemption Gateway, Mesa AZ.

6. Wells, Tauren, partial lyrics to *God's Not Done with You,* song, album Hills & Valleys, (Franklin, TN, production by Bernie Herms, Label: Provident Label Grp, released April 5, 2019).

7. "What Does It Mean That the Church Is the Bride of Christ?" GotQuestions.org, January 29, 2007. https://www.gotquestions.org/bride-of-Christ.html.

8. Spiritualism – sermon notes, Luke Simmons, Pew Research Report, church attendance. https://www.pewresearch.org/short-reads/2017 spiritual/not religious/none.

9. #JesusisBetter, Trey VanCamp, Lead Pastor, Passion Creek, www.treyvancamp.com "Your Dream is Not About You" series, author *The Non-Anxious Pastor,* release Sept 1, 2022. http://www.amazon.co/Non-AnxiousPastor-Becoming a Person at Peace in a World at War.

10. "We Are" Colorado Community Church, Mission Statement, Denver, CO.

11. "Pink Spoon People" Ephesians Series, Luke Simmons, Lead Pastor, Ironwood Church, Mesa, AZ, www.ironwoodchurch.org.

12. Kauffman, Dr. Richard "Dick", Plant Pastor of Harbor Churches in San Diego, CA. My Faith Magazine, "The Gospel, Key to Conversation and Ongoing Change", http://www.cru.org/the-gospel-key-to-change.html Dr. Kauffman passed away Feb 18, 2023.

13. *Two ways to read the Bible,* Bible Boot Camp material by Chris Mueller, adapted by Redemption Gateway staff for teaching purposes, class set, Bible Boot Camp, 2014, (see ch 10 #4).
14. *Why so many versions/translations,* article: www.biblica.com. Sites to find verses: www.biblegateway.com and www.biblehub.com.
15. *Jesus, My Treasure,* poem by Luke Simmons, Lead Pastor, Ironwood Church, Mesa, AZ. www.ironwoodchurch.org.
16. *Christ has a grip on Me,* In His Grip/Our Daily Bread http://odb.org/2013/12/31/in-his-grip/.

Between chapters ten and eleven:

1. *Please Come In* Please Come In/Our Daily Bread, http://odb.org/2016/3/9/please-come-in/.

Chapter 11:

1. Ross, Herbert, Director, *Steel Magnolias,* movie reference, starring Sally Fields, Dolly Parton, Shirley MacLaine, Daryl Hannah, Olympia Dukakis, Julia Roberts, (United States: Tri-Star Pictures, 1989).

Chapter 13:

1. *Have faith God will walk with you,* Have faith God will walk with you/Our Daily Bread http://odb.og/2022/2/5/have-faith-God-will-walk-with-you.
2. Branagh, Kenneth, Director, *Cinderella,* movie, 2015. "Be Kind and Courageous", quote, performed by Lily James, (United States, Walt Disney Pictures, 2015).
3. Kanew, Jeff, Director, *Revenge of the Nerds,* movie reference, starring Robert Carradine, Anthony Edwards and Ted McGinley, (United States, 20th Century Fox, 1984).
4. Queen, Freddie Mercury, lead singer/writer, *We Are the Champions,* (USA, Elektra, 1977), song mention in *Revenge of the Nerds,* movie, 1984.
5. Curtis, Adeline. 1912. *Founded on a Rock* motto, sorority Gamma Phi Beta, Syracuse University, (Syracuse, New York, 1874).
6. Hughes, John, Director, *Sixteen Candles,* movie reference, starring Molly Ringwald, Michael Schoeffling, Anthony Michael Hall, (United States, Universal Pictures, 1984).
7. Lightner, Candy, Founder, 1980. *MADD: Mothers Against Drunk Driving,* referenced, started in Fair Oaks, CA, now nationwide with 320 chapters.

8. Robinson, Lawrence, and Melina Smith, M.A. 2023. *The Dangers of Underage Drinking*, HelpGuide.org

9. Supreme Court Justice's joint statement, *Treat each other with respect and dignity*, News Release, The Hill, newspaper, Washington, D.C., September, 2018.

10. Monteverde, Alejandro, Director, *Sounds of Freedom*, movie, starring Jim Caviezel, Mira Sorvino and Bill Camp, (produced by Eduardo Verastegui, Santa Fe Films, USA, distributed by Angel Studios, release date, July 4, 2023). (Budget $14.5m. Box office $246.7m).

11. McGraw, Dr. Phil, Psychologist and television personality, Interview of "Kendell" a sex trafficked victim, *Exposing elitist child sex trafficking and murder*, YouTube 2017. https://153news.net/watch video. php?v=9MWS6RBG83SD.

12. Simmons, Luke, Lead Pastor, Ironwood Church, *Prayer is bringing your helplessness to God* quote, Ephesians series, www.ironwoodchurch.org.

13. Fields, Ligonberry, *Mainline Church Spreading Christianity*, The Christian Post, https://christianpost.com/author/ligonberry-fields, 2016.

14. Lewis, Lee, *The Holy Spirit in Counseling: Our Great Advantage that is Often Overlooked*, Biblical Counseling Coalition, ttps://www. biblicalcounselingcoalition.org/2016.

15. Saldanha, Carlos, *Ferdinand*, movie, voiced by John Cena and Kate McKinnon, (USA: produced by Blue Sky Studios, distributed by 20th Century Fox, USA, December 15, 2017).

16. Peretti, Frank E., *This Present Darkness*, book referenced, (Wheaton, Illinois, Crossway Books, 1986) and sequel, *Piercing the Darkness*, (Des Moines, Iowa, Turtleback Books, 1989).

17. Blackaby, Henry T., *Experiencing God*, online quote from book series, (Nashville, TN, B&H Publishing Group, 1997. *Experiencing God, Revised Edition*, 2008).

18. Smallbone, Ben, Director, *Priceless*, movie, Lead actors, Joel Smallbone, Bianca A. Santos, Jim Parrack and David Koechner, (Production and distribution, Roadside Attractions, Albuquerque, NM 2016).

19. For King & Country, *Priceless*, song, on album: Run Wild. Life Free. Love Strong, Released: 2014. (Launch for movie *Priceless*, see footnote 18 with lead actor from King & Country two brother band, Joel Smallbone, 2016).

Chapter 14:

1. *"…you're a reflector of Christ … how you live your life privately and publicly"* Pink Spoon People – A taste of the real life, sermon notes continued and quote, Luke Simmons, see ch 10, #11.
2. Piper, John, *Desiring God*, (Colorado Springs, CO, Multnomah Publishers, Inc., 1986).
3. Kendrik, Alex, Director, *War Room*, movie, Lead actors Priscilla Shirer, T.C. Stallings, Karen Abercrombie, Alex Kendrick, Michael Jr. (Albany, GA, Kendrick Brothers Production, 2015).
4. "One Another's" (summarized piece from a handout by Revive the Hearts ministries), www.reviveourhearts.com.
5. Caldwell, Shannyn, Radio Personality, Family Life Radio, Christian station, *You've been given so much, give back … roar baby, roar* on-air quote, and Author of, *The Healing Season*, (United States, self-published, 2014).
6. Camp, Jeremy, *Give Me Jesus*, song, written by Eric Wise, produced by Steve Hindalong & Mark Byrd, (Lafayette, Indiana, track 12 on Beyond Measure, 2006).
7. Prayer, sermon notes, Seth Troutt, Teaching Pastor, Ironwood Church, www.ironwoodchurch.org.

Chapter 15:

1. Tebow, Tim. Christian, retired NFL Quarterback, Tim Tebow Foundation, helps underprivileged children around the world, *Sports Impact of the Year KLove 2022 Awards*.
2. Goheen, Michael Dr., *The Gospel and Globalization: Exploring the Religious Roots of Globalization*, (San Diego, CA, Regent College Publishing, 2009), referenced book in a sermon at church as a guest speaker, 2018.

Chapter 16:

1. Herek, Stephen, Director, *Mr. Holland's Opus*, movie, Produced by Ted Field, Robert Cort & Michael Nolin, Lead Actor, Richard Dreyfuss, (United States: American Film, 1995).
2. Boom, Corrie ten, with John & Elizabeth Sherrill, (1971) *The Hiding Place: The Triumphant True Story of Corrie Ten Boom*. (Ada, MI, Baker Books, Baker Publishing Group, 35th Anniversary Edition, 2005), book referenced.

3. Bloom, Jon, (@Bloom_Jon) article, *The Greatest Thing You Can do with Your Life*, section "God Has Called You" https://www.desiringgod.org/articles from Desiring God, 2018.

4. Piper, John, "Delight should fuel our doing" message excerpt from *Delight is our Duty* message, DesiringGod.org, January 15, 2018.

5. Chapman, Steven Curtis. *The Great Adventure*, song referenced, (Brentwood, TN, Producer Phil Naish, released June 19, 1992). Album and Song of the Year, 1993, 24th GMA Dove Awards.

6. Ruiz, Arnold, "Jesus is the Center and Purpose of all History" quote, email newsletter excerpt to parents, prior youth pastor, 2022, Redemption Gateway, Mesa, AZ.

7. Watt, Josh, "Jesus is the True Vine" sermon quote, Lead Pastor, Redemption North Mountain, (@redemptionnm, www.nm.redemptionaz.com, Phoenix, AZ.

8. Johnson, Tyler, "Why we need the local church," visiting pastor sermon notes, prior pastor of Redemption Arizona. Now with Surge Arizona. http://surgenetwork.com, Phoenix, AZ.

9. "God at work all the time" Excerpt from Experiencing God, notes from study in my 20s (see notes, ch 13, #16).

10. Stanley, Dr. Charles, *Getting ahead of God*, article, 7/21/18, In Touch Ministries, http://www.intouch.org.

11. Swindoll, Charles, (born 1934) pastor, author, educator, radio preacher, founder of *Insight for Living*. www.insight.org.

12. "God's call to obedience in work", "Obedient in your work" NIV study notes, (Grand Rapids, MI, Zondervan-Biblica, 1978, revision in 1984).

13. "Be obedient and work" Ephesians 6, sermon notes, Luke Simmons, Lead Pastor, Ironwood Church, www.ironwoodchurch.org, Mesa, AZ.

14. Blackaby, Henry, *Experiencing God Revised*, takeaway excerpts, (see notes ch 13, #16).

15. "Don't know how, but Who," Feeding 5,000. Quote online, Elevation Church, http://elevationchurch.org.

16. Work through Elijah that impacted a nation, *Experiencing God Revised*, (see notes ch 13, #16).

17. Kenrick, Alex, Director and Lead Actor, *Facing the Giants*, movie, "Prepare for Rain" movie reference, (Albany Georgia: Sherwood Pictures, 2006).

18. Mote, Edward, (first titled, "The Solid Rock"), *On Christ the Solid Rock I Stand*, written in 1834, lyric reference, (Horsham, Sussex, London: Brother Rees of Crown Street, Soho, hymn first featured in Hymns of Praise, A New Selection of Gospel Hymns, 1836).

19. Laurie, Greg, Senior Pastor, "Consume God's Word like social media," quote, Harvest Christian Fellowship, Riverside, CA @greglaurie (author of *Jesus Revolution* with Ellen Vaughn, Grand Rapids, MI: BakerBooks, 2018. Movie based on book edition, 2023. Directed by Jon Erwin, Lead actor, Joel Courtney, Jonathan Roumie, Kelsey Grammer, Kimberly Williams-Paisley, Anna Grace Barlow. USA: Lionsgate, February 15, 2023).

20. Ramsey, Dave, "Financial Peace University" Financial Expert, radio program, "The Ramsey Show" author, online classes at http://www.ramseysolutions.com.

21. Keller, Helen, "Blind without a vision" quote from *The Story of My Life*, autobiography, 1903. (Blind and deaf, author of 14 books, 100s of essays and speeches, and public speaker, named one of Time magazine's 100 Most Important People of the 20th Century.)

22. Washington, Denzel, American actor, producer and director, "A hearse pulling a U-Haul" "Can't take it with you" quotes, online interview for Boys & Girls Clubs of America, serving as national spokesperson since 1993, Bgca.org.

23. About pyramids – "Egyptian Pyramids" – Wikipedia, www.wikipedia.org.

24. Dayton, Howard, *Discovering God's Way of Handling Money* "Jesus talks money ..." quote, Howard Dayton Jr., Leadership, Vol 2, no. 2, Squarespace, Crown Financial Ministries, Course Workbook, 2001, https://www.crown.org.

25. Guthrie, Nancy, *Lessons from Job*, "When God is Silent" Gospel Coalition, 3/11/16, https://www.thegospelcoalition.org.

26. Study Bible – New International Translation, Paul in prison – footnotes from Philippians (Headquarters in Palmer Lake, CO, United States, Biblica, licensing rights to Zondervan, www.biblica.com, 1984).

27. Shrader, Tom, *Tom-isms by Tom Shrader*, "In Memory of Tom Shrader" "Tom Shrader Memorial" YouTube, Redemption Gilbert, February 5, 2019.

28. "What God Gave Gateway through Tom Shrader" Sermon, Luke Simmons, YouTube, Redemption Church Gateway, January 21, 2019.

29. Marrs, Ellen, *Lessons from the Finish Line*, "Faith over Fear" quote, author and friend, (Higley, AZ, Self-Published, 2015).

30. Merriam-Webster Dictionary, definition of ambassador "a representative" online dictionary, (Springfield, Massachusetts, U.S., original Merriam-Webster Dictionary, 1843. Revised and expanded to include Encyclopedia Britannica, 1964, online: www.merriam-webster.com).

31. Cain, the band, song, *The Commission*, partial lyric "Go tell the world about Me" (Franklin, TN, Provident Label Group, songwriters: Blake Neesmith, Carter Frodge, Logan Cain, Madison Cain, Taylor Cain, single release date, Dec 11, 2021, from album Rise Up).
32. "The Chosen" the movie series mentioned. Directed and co-written by Dallas Jenkins, (United States, Angel Studios, original release: Dec 24, 2017).
33. Simmons, Luke, "All of Life is all for Jesus" coined phrase for Redemption AZ campuses, (Pastor of Ironwood Church, formally Redemption Gateway), 2011.
34. Lemmel Haworth, Helen, hymn writer to: *The Heavenly Vision*, (first line) "Turn your eyes upon Jesus" lyric based on Isaiah 45:22, (England, 1918 first in a pamphlet, then in an American collection entitled Gospel Truth in Song, 1924).

Chapter 17:

1. Davies, Laurie, Online: Go Get Your Life, author of articles in Chicken Soup for the Soul & National Speaker at Women's Ministry Events, http://lauriedavies.life/.
2. Ashley, David and Holly, referenced, CEO and COO, Creators and Directors of Redemption Domestic Violence, (Mount Juliet, TN) https://crossstrengthministries.com.
3. Country Artists/songs mentioned Faith Hill and Tim McGraw, "I Need You" Leann Rimes & Debby Boon, "God Only Knows" Dolly Parton with King and Country, "Jesus Take the Wheel" Carrie Underwood, Glenn Campbell, (List of Country Artists & Christian Artists, country gospel, inspirational country, www.wikipedia.org.
4. Waller, John, Christian artist, partial lyrics from movie Fireproof, *While I'm Waiting*, (Nashville, TN, Beach Street Records under the Provident Label Group, Fireproof soundtrack release, July 14, 2009, johnwallerofficial. com, movie listing in, www.kendrickbrotherscatalogue.com).
5. Kendrick, Alex, Director of *Fireproof*, movie reference, co-produced by Stephen Kendrick, film stars Kirk Cameron, Erin Bethean and Ken Bevel. (USA, Production Co Sherwood Pictures, release date, September 26, 2008).
6. Green, A.C. NBA "Iron Man", 16 years abstinent during 16 NBA Seasons, YouTube, #celibacy (till marriage), April 20, 2022. *Victory & I've Got the Power*, books by A.C. Green (Portland, Oregon, Creation House, 1994).

7. Green, A.C., curriculum "Game Plan" study guide, www.acgreen.com (see ch 17 #6).

Chapter 19:

1. Van DeVenter, Judson W., (words written by), *I Surrender All*, lyric from hymn, (1855), Weeden, Winfield S., (music by). (New York, Sebring Publishing Co, 1ˢᵗ appeared in Gospel Songs of Grace and Glory, 1896).

ABC verses:
Letter L:

1. *A Beautiful Day in the Neighborhood*, movie reference, about Fred Rogers, (minister, creator, producer, children's advocate, passed away, February 27, 2003), *Mister Rogers' Neighborhood* TV series, based on "Can You Say… Hero?" episode, (United States, movie director, Marielle Heller, starring Tom Hanks as Mr. Rogers, Tri-Star Pictures, Sony Pictures Releasing, September 7, 2019).

Letter R: (Rejoice)

1. Hundley, Mandisa, *Overcomer* referenced song/lyric by Mandisa. Explaining song's meaning (Wikipedia Overcomer album), (Brentwood, TN, Sparrow Records, August 27, 2013).
2. Airwaves/online Christian radio and broadcasts mentioned, on all streaming devices: Air1(www.air1.com), KLove (www.klove.com), Family Life Radio (http://www.myflr.org), Focus on the Family broadcast with Jim Daily (https://www.focusonthefamily.com), Boundless Show (for young adult singles with Lisa Anderson on Focus broadcasts) (https://www.boundless.org and https://podcasts.focusonthefamily.com).

Letter S: (Serve)

1. Law, Jason, *A Story Bigger Than Any One of Us*, online article on 1Mission's website published on Feb, 26, 2018. 1Mission in Puerto Penasco, Mexico, house building mission trips mentioned, www.1mission.org.

Letter T: (Train)

1. Carlson, Randy Dr., founder of Intentional Living www.theintentionallife. com on Family Life Radio https://myflr.org, topics: intentional purpose, God's design in marriage, sin/vices turn away, get help, get accountability. Dr. Carlson, licensed marriage and family therapist and author of several books including: *Starved for Affection, Parent Talk* and *The Power of One Thing.*

Letter U: (Unto)

1. Marrs, Ellen, *Lessons from The Finish Line* book reference, author/friend, see ch 16 #28.

Letter V: (Verily)

1. Rutledge, Warren and Cynthia, Parents of Keli Rutledge and Directors of *The Keli May Foundation*, @kelimayfoundation, www.kelimayfoundation. org, based in Gilbert, AZ.
2. Linkletter, Missy, Mom to Justin Linkletter, Keeping My Promise Justin, @missy_linkletter_, Women's Director, writer, speaker at National Women's events.

Letter W (We):

1. Sidewalk Prophets, band, David Frey, Ben, McDonald, Mark, DeLavergne, songwriters, *You Love Me Anyway*, a few lyrics shared, (album: These Simple Truths, Nashville, TN, 2009, Label: Word/Curb, Producer: Ian Eskelin, Shaun Shankel. Song release: February 25, 2011).
2. Asbury, Cory, musician, worship pastor, *Reckless Love*, song, partial lyrics "leaves the 99", (Redding, CA, producer Jason Ingram & Paul Mabury, label, Bethel Music, released: October 27, 2017, www.coryasbury.com).

Letter Y: (You)

1. 988 Suicide & Crisis Lifeline (formally the National Suicide Prevention Lifeline (800) 273-TALK), now from any phone dial 9-8-8. The network of over two hundred crisis centers in the United States provide 24/7 service. It is available to anyone in suicidal crisis or emotional distress. (Wikipedia: Suicide Crisis Lifeline).

2. Williams, Zach, songwriter and Christian Artist, *Fear is a Liar*, song reference/partial lyrics (from album *Chain Breaker*, Franklin, TN, Essential Records, Producer, Jonathan Smith, release date: January 19, 2018), https://zachwilliamsmusic.com.

3. Voice for the Voiceless ministries for adoptions, pro-life, *22% of our generation is aborted, we are the 78%,* quote (Phoenix, AZ based nonprofit advocating dignity and worth of every human being, that life is valued and no one faces an unplanned pregnancy alone. @vftv, http://www.voiceforthevoiceless.org).

Letter Z: (Zacchaeus)

1. Eldredge, John, author, *Get your Life Back: Everyday Practices for a World Gone Mad*, referenced. (Nashville, TN, Thomas Nelson, December 11, 2019), counselor and president of Ransomed Heart, ministry started in 2000, devoted to helping people discover the heart of God.

Michelle's God Story:

1. All Sons & Daughters, (active years 2009-2018), worship duet acoustic and folk, Leslie Ann Jordan & David Leonard, *Broken Aside*, partial lyrics referenced, (Franklin, TN, Integrity Label, Producer Paul Mabury, All Sons & Daughters Season One album, released March 13, 2012).

Printed in the United States
by Baker & Taylor Publisher Services